ROLE OF JAPAN AND NEPAL IN ASIAN POLITICS

ROLE OF JAPAN AND NEPAL IN ASIAN POLITICS

Editor

Dr. M.D. Dharamdasani

GYAN

GYAN PUBLISHING HOUSE

NEW DELHI-110002

Role of Japan and Nepal in Asian Politics

Rs. 590

ISBN: 81-212-0871-8

Published in 2005 in India by
Gyan Publishing House
5, Ansari Road, Darya Ganj, New Delhi-110002
Phones : 23282060, 23261060
Fax : (011) 23285914
E-mail : gyanbook@vsnl.com

Laser Typesetting at : Master Computers, Delhi
Printed at : Salasar Imaging System, Delhi

Dedicated To
My Parents
Late Shri Tekchand and
Mrs. Dadan Bai

Contents

Preface

This volume is the outcome of an International Seminar on Nepal's Role in South Asia organised by the Centre for the Study of Nepal, Faculty of Social Sciences, Banaras Hindu University, Varanasi. The Seminar was a major effort to analyse Nepal's role and attitude towards South Asia with particular reference to its role in SAARC and relations with India.

At the outset, I must express my intense gratitude towards Shri Chakra Bastola, former Foreign Minister of Nepal, who delivered the Key Note Addresses. I am equally thankful to Prof. K.L. Sharma, Vice-Chancellor of University of Rajasthan for inaugurating the Seminar. I also wish to express my sincere thanks to Professor S.K. Srivastava, Former Director of the Centre and Dean, Faculty of Social Sciences for presiding over the function.

I am also deeply thankful to Prof. Jitendra Dhoj Khand from Kathmandu and Prof. G.S. Kushawaha, Fellow, Institute of Advance Study, Shimla for participating in the Seminar.

My thanks are also due to participants from J.N.U., New Delhi especially Shri Amresh Kumar Singh, Shri Deepak Prakash Bhatt and Shri Nabarun Roy.

I must express my sincere gratitude towards Prof. R. Sahu from Centre for Himalayan Studies, North Bengal University and Prof. V. Chandra Mouliswara Rao from Tirupati and Dr. Bhaskar Majumdar from Allahabad for their contribution to the Seminar. My thanks are also due to Dr. (Mrs.) Manju Kumar, Dr. S.B. Singh, Dr. Anoop Mishra, Dr. V.K.L.

Srivastava, Anil Srivastava, Dr. Shafiuzzaman, Dr. Bhupendra V. Singh, Dr. Nripendra P. Singh for their fruitful participation in the Seminar.

It is a great pleasure to express my thanks to the colleagues, staff and research scholars of the Centre who did everything possible to make this Seminar a grand success. My special thanks are due to Dr. S.N. Jha, Mr. Kalyan Chaudhary and Mr. Manish Sharma.

Finally, I would like to add a personal note of thanks to my wife Vimla, and to my sons Ashok and Dinesh for their moral support when I was engaged in organising of the Seminar.

Dr. M.D. DHARAMDASANI

Contributors

Chakra Prasad Bastola	Former Foreign Minister, Government of Nepal
R. Sahu	Professor, Centre for Himalayan Studies, North Bengal University, Darjeeling
Bhaskar Majumdar	Govind Ballabh Pant Social Science Institute, Jhusi, Allahabad, U.P. North Bengal University, Darjelling.
Bhupendra V. Singh	Reader in Economics, F.S.S., BHU
Nripendra P. Singh	Research Unit, Department of Economics, F.S.S., BHU.
Jitendra Dhoj Khand	Professor, Central Department of Political Science, Tribhuvan University, Kirtipur, Kathmandu.
V. Chandra Mouliswara Rao	Professor, Department of Political Science and Public Administration, Sri Venkateswara University, Tirupati.
Amresh Kumar Singh	Jawaharlal Nehru University, New Delhi.
Deepak Prakash Bhatt	Jawaharlal Nehru University, New Delhi.
Nabarun Roy	Jawaharlal Nehru University, New Delhi.
Anup K. Mishra	Research Unit, Department of Economics, F.S.S., BHU
G.S. Kushwaha	Fellow, I.I.A.S., Shimla.

Manju Kumar : Reader, Department of Political Science F.S.S., BHU.

V.K.L. Srivastava : Department of Commerce, D.A.V. Degree College, Varanasi

Anil Kr. Srivastava : Senior Lecturer, Department of Economics, D.A.V. P.G. College (Purvanchal University), Azamgarh, U.P.

Shafiuzzaman : Head, Department of Political Science Mangrawan Degree College, Mangrawan, Azamgarh, U.P.

S.B. Singh : D.A.V. Degree College, Varanasi.

Siddhi Laxmi Vaidya : Prof. of Political Science Tribhuwan University, Kathmandu.

Iqbal Khanam : Professor, Department of Political Science, Aligarh Muslim University, Aligarh.

Bishnu Hari Nepal : Former Royal Nepalese Ambassador to Japan

M.D. Dharamdasani : Professor in Political Science, Co-ordinator, Centre for the Study of Nepal and Japanese Studies Programme, F.S.S., B.H.U.

Nishchal Nath Pandey : Dy. Executive Director of the Institute of Foreign Affairs, Kathmandu

Mikio Oishi : Department of Political Science, University of Canterbury, Newzealand.

H.S. Prabhakar : Chairman and Associate Professor, Japanese Studies, Centre for East Asian Studies, School of International Studies, Jawahar Lal Nehru University, New Delhi.

Arun Chaturvedi : Head, Department of Political Science M.L. Sukhadia University, Udaipur (Rajasthan)

Vijay Kumar : Professor, Department of Political Science, Bhagalpur University.

J. Balakomaraiah : Senior Lecturer, Department of Economics, F.S.S., BHU.

1

Keynote Address

Chakra Prasad Bastola

Mr. Chairman, Distinguished Guests,

Thank you, Dr. Dharamdasani, for that generous introduction. It is a great pleasure and honor to be back at my Alma Mater-the Banaras Hindu University-a great institution of the time, when its creator Pandit Madan Mohan Malaviya, was in struggle for the independence of the country under the leadership of Mahatama Gandhi, with an intent to inculcate timeless values and norms in the process of struggle against the colonial rule. This institution has a special place of respect and honor in our hearts. It stands as a towering symbol of enduring links that bind our two countries Nepal and India together.

Banaras has immensely contributed to the making of modern Nepal. The settings of the University have had a direct bearing on the evolution of a democratic Nepal. This was the place where the idea of freeing Nepal from the clutches of the Rana rule sprung in the minds of many young Nepalis studying in the 1940s. The first ever elected Prime Minister of Nepal, the late Bisheshwar Prasad Koirala, studied at this university, to be followed by Krishna Prasad Bhattarai, among other prominent personalities of the Nepalese public life. In the establishment of the Center for the Study of Nepal, we see the continuation of that strong linkage. We appreciate the continued interests, as has been displayed with regular forums such as this being organised under the aegis of the Center with a focus on key questions that have bearing on peace, security stability in the region of South Asia, and with a focus on developments in Nepal, Nepal-India relations, and Nepal's role in the world.

I thanks its Director, for his kind invitation and providing me with this opportunity to share my thoughts with such a distinguished group of friends and well-wishers of Neal. I appreciate my friends... ***(a few acquaintances need to be recognised by names there from among the audience)*** for being here with us today. I appreciate your presence and continued interests on what we have been doing in Nepal for democracy and development in Nepal.

I thank the Center once again for inviting me to this International Seminar on 'Nepal's Role in South Asia.' As suggested, let me now present a brief overview of Nepal's relations with India, its role in the SAARC and beyond, current political climate, implications of the eight years of the Maoist insurgency on security, democracy, and development of Nepal.

Mr. Chairman,

India remains a natural focus in Nepal's foreign policy. The historical, geographical, economic, social, cultural and political foundations run deeper between Nepal and India, than is visible to an outsider. There is a long history of cooperation between us both bilaterally and on a wider international scale. Foreign relations, in case of Nepal and India, do not remain the sole concerns of the government sectors. People on either side constitute a dynamic element, crises-crossing the borders daily in search of knowledge and skills and also in a mixture of hope and despair. Together with the people, communities, trade unions, media, and educational institutions such as this Center transcend officials and diplomatic boundaries. Nepalis have fought for India's independence to set an example that liberty is indivisible. Hundreds of thousands Nepalis have given their lives for the protection and preservation of the independence and integrity of India. No other people can understand more deeply the nature of these relations than the Nepalis and Indians themselves. This has been amply demonstrated time and again in times of adversity and critical moments in the history of Nepal-India relations.

Despite the relations pervading many aspects of life, our positions and interests do not always converge, but they have never become a source of conflict and confrontation, though hawks on both sides try to play or blow them out of proportion for their own cause. There are so many centers of good will in each country outnumbering such hawkish elements. No one can underrate the importance of our relations for each other. The people of Nepal are aware that no other country has contributed more to the building of Nepal as a modern nation and its transformation than India has. And this goodwill and cooperation will be needed in the years to come for development and democracy, and to maintain stability in the country, neighborhood, and the beyond.

Nepal and India enjoy so many complementarities that bind our two countries in both prosperity and adversity. Their intensity has effected our economic, social and environmental interdependence. As technology and communications shrink the global distance, and more so between our two peoples in an unbelievable way, indispensability of peace, freedom and markets has emerged as a framework for conducting these relationships. Knowledge based economy is generating powerful spillover effects. Spreading like wildfire, it is triggering further innovations in all fields. These intensive linkages are a compelling reminder to us to broaden our visions and perspectives, and shed the legacy of the inherited framework of the relationship in the context of freedom, democracy and market.

Mr. Chairman,

At the dawn of the 21st century, we had every reason to be happy and hopeful. Tyrants were giving in to a more open and democratic system of governance around the world; legitimacy was to be derived from the governed, bringing more countries and people under the democratic umbrella. The spreads of globalisation and liberalisation were facilitating the circulation of products and services. The flow of capital was in greater volume than ever before, more freely and widely. And human ingenuity was also on the rise pursuing a new battle of ideas. However the process suffered a great setback, with an unexpected surge in the criminal activities of some terrorist groups and gangs in different parts of the world. These groups and gangs, irrespective of pretexts, displayed common characteristics of ruthlessness and treachery. They defied the rule of law and respect for human life and property, as was demonstrated in the attacks on September 11, 2001 on the twin towers of the World Trade Center, Pentagon and intended target of White House, that left as many Americans dead as all terrorist incidents of the previous three decades combined. The visual image of this criminal assault as well as tragic loss of so many innocent lives sent a forceful reminder of the serious danger and disruptive capacity of terrorists.

These attacks changed everything and renewed a sense of awareness of the pains and sufferings of terrorist attacks that had overshadowed daily lives in South Asia, which was listed in the annual report on Patterns of Terrorism issued by the United States Department of State as an international hub of terrorism. Counter terrorism came to top the agenda of the national, international governments and institutions. The United States of America came to the front to lead the fight against terrorism as the leader of the international coalition against terrorism. Countries all over the world-big and small, rich and poor-came to be united in the fight against terrorism.

The attacks on America exposed the whole world to the scourge of terrorism. Its message was that poverty and terrorism are a threat to peace and development everywhere and prosperity anywhere must be shared. This incident highlighted the necessity of common and global responsibility for the social and economic development, and not to let the fertile ground grow for discontent and deprivation. This is a job that cannot be done alone. There has to be a multi-pronged strategy on multidimensional fronts. It is my belief that sustained multilateral approach alone provides opportunities to nations to neutralise the interactive problems of terrorism and weapons of mass destruction with poverty and deprivation, and chart a course for security and development.

Mr. Chairman,

South Asia remains bound in a spiral of human deprivation and despair. Mahbubul Haq, while launching the Human Development Report in South Asia in 1997, said of South Asia 'as the poorest, the most illiterate, the most malnourished, the least gender sensitive-indeed the most deprived region in the world.' The situation is no different today. Despite several years of planned development, pervading poverty houses the South Asian region, making it vulnerable to every possible lure and design by undesirable elements. Recent reports such as Human Development Report 2003, World Development Report 2004 and other research findings indicate that out of 1.3 billion people living in absolute poverty, 515 million live in South Asia. They are 27 per cent of the developing world's population, 40 per cent of the developing world's absolute poor, 45 per cent adult illiterate women of the developing world and 49 per cent of the malnourished children. These reports also point out that the number of the illiterates here far exceeds the population of the United States, Japan and Canada combined. If we transplant these figures in Nepal, it is even more appalling and alarming, where over 38 per cent of the population lives below the poverty line.

Given the magnitude of the pressing problems of poverty and deprivation, our attention and efforts must be directed towards preventing what Mr. I.K. Gujral calls, and I quote, 'the unending waste and misutilisation of South Asia's vast human and physical resources' unquote, and channelizing these resources for the economic betterment of the people. SAARC process needs to be revitalised and reinvigorated in every possible manner, and harness these potentials for the benefits of powerless, voiceless and vulnerable people. The process has long been a victim in a spiral of doubts, and discords between two big member states India and Pakistan. Recent events have established that Indo-Pakistan relations have their undeniable bearings in making or breaking the process of regional economic cooperation. What can be more satisfying than the SAARC emerging as a ray of hope to the one fifth of world humanity, and providing the hostile nuclear-armed neighbors a forum to initiate the confidence building measures for advancing the normalisation process? We wish them all the best and success as they try to make a transition, what Prime Minister Vajpayee says and I quote, 'from mistrust to trust, from discord to concord and from tension to peace.' A South Asia free of poverty and terrorism is sure to emerge as a center of power in global politics, and India coming out of the Indo-Pakistan trap, and be at peace with neighbors will clear all hurdles for its prominent and vigorous role at the global level. And thus India will be able to guide the destiny of the democratic community as the largest democratic country in the world.

Recently held SAARC summit in Islamabad has emerged as an important milestone, reflecting its maturity as an institutional process. The lunching of SAFTA comes as the first step towards the evolution of a South Asian Economic Union with a single currency The leaders of Nepal and India, (Nepal happened to be under democratic dispensation under BP Koirala then) way back in 1960, had envisioned the goal of *Common Market,* in the Treaty of Trade and Transit concluded on September 11, 1960. We have learned that we cannot live alone and our well being is entwined with the well being of our neighbors, friends in the region and also other nations that are far away. We therefore feel proud to have contributed to this notion through the SAARC process. This is my belief that It will inject confidence to work for many other institutional arrangements at the regional level. As both Nepal and India are in the International Coalition Against Terrorism, and pursuing the goals of globalisation through several measures in economic sectors, regional and multilateral frameworks seem to be providing spaces and answers for resolving longstanding problems confronting the world. Nepal looks forward to connect itself to the benefits of the flourishing growth of our two great neighbors.

Mr. Chairman,

Let me briefly outline the situation that pertains to Nepal.

Nepal entered into to comity of democratic nations in 1990 following the People's Movement. Constitution promulgated with the widest possible participation of the Nepalese people on November 9, 1990, sought to consolidate the adult franchise, the parliamentary system of government, and multiparty democracy with constitutional monarchy, free press and independent judiciary. Over these 12 years, Nepal has had three parliamentary elections and two local elections with over 70 per cent of the people participating in the process. This created layers of over 4000 democratic institutions from national down to the block level across the country, and ensured liberty and fundamental freedoms to the people, and economic road map for the development within the democratic framework.

As democracy started to spread, people's hopes were raised and long suppressed socio-economic problems erupted. Elected government had to confront monumental problems all at a time. The multiple tasks included the framing of democratic legislation through sovereign parliament, build political institutions and culture and address people's socio-economic needs, and at the same time channelise the previously unheard and stifled voices of millions into the democratic political process. The work, as we all know, along this path has never been smooth. Nepal that glaringly lacked any institutional infrastructures for a democratic start remained vulnerable to all maneuvers and manipulations by forces that were opposed to democratic process.

Many in this room are fully aware of Nepal's traditions, which have been more patrimonial, hierarchical and feudalistic. The functioning of political parties and governance cannot be thought of to remain independent from these setting and circumstances. Despite constitutional and legal framework in their places, change in behavior and attitude appears to be very slow. The tasks of injecting democratic behavior like moderation; tolerance and reconciliation into the process and initiating socio-economic reforms in these circumstances are never easy and smooth.

Under such setting, when elected government was busying itself to set the democratic process in place to confront the problems that had inflicted people for long, Communist Party of Nepal (Maoist), whose share of parliamentary seats in its earlier incarnation in 1991 was only 4.39 per cent, preferred bullets to ballots, and launched its so called 'People's War' on February 13, 1996. Their road to violence has done extensive damage to the fabric of Nepalese society, inflicted most glaring sorrows, taking tolls of about 10,000 precious lives for no justifiable reasons. Nation appears to have lost confidence and direction. Vital economic sectors have suffered a big blow. Tourism-the main foreign exchange earner has hit the lowest ebb. Vital infrastructures are being destroyed. Innocent people are victimised.

Educational institutions have been on the target list. Schools are being turned to be grounds for training and shelters. Teachers opposed to Maoist' faith are abducted from classrooms, and are either drafted or murdered. Several thousand children have been orphaned, maimed or displaced. National Human Rights Commission reports indicate that majority of Maoist soldiers are underage. School going children are abducted, indoctrinated, and coerced into signing a false a document stating that they have willingly joined the Maoist movement. Even more alarming news report is that the Maoist party has set the target of drafting 50,000 children by April-May this year as militias. The Global Report on Child Soldiers 2001 said: about one third of the Maoists rebels are children-school, college students and even younger, who were used as messengers, sentries and spies. The recruitment and use of child soldiers have gone to such an extent that Nepal is listed in the report of the UN Secretary General on Children and Armed Conflict.

Mr. Chairman,

The Constitution is in suspended animation. Ever since the dissolution of the House of Representatives came prematurely in May 2002, the crisis has compounded. Nation is without any elected institutions. The permanent chamber of the House-National Assembly exists in name without a head. Its electoral college of people's representatives remains shattered. Prime Minister of the day called for elections on November 13, 2002, and unable to conduct them in time, recommended the king to postpone elections by 14 months, requesting him to invoke the special 127 Article of the Constitution to remove difficulties in the implementation of the constitution. This in fact was the demise of the democratic process achieved through the 1990 pro-democracy movements.

The King now says he would like to be a constructive monarch of the twenty first century. Ever since he declared on October 4, 2002, that he had assumed the executive powers of the country, no improvement in any aspects of national life appears forthcoming, let alone the resolution of the conflict and restoration of the democratic process. Rather the loss of the legitimacy of the government has put the vital state organs under severe stress and threat, harming the Nepali nationalism and national unity, and ultimately weakening the foundations of the Nepali state.

The King and mainstream political parties stand far apart, when the need is to act in unison. The gravity of the situation demands that they come together and make joint efforts to pull the country out of current crisis for democracy and development. This is extremely a challenging time for Nepal. The immediate urgency is to activate the constitutional process, and restore democratic process to put an end to the present stalemate.

Mr. Chairman, and Distinguished Guests,

The only alternative to democracy is more and better democracy and not its replacement. Democracy may appear as one of the most fragile systems in the short run, but is the most stable form of governance in the long run. Democracy is the strongest source for developing world peace, development and prosperity. There has been a lot of criticism of the democratic governance of the last 12 years in Nepal. The failure is only in failing to highlight achievements made in this period. Tremendous awareness among people about their rights remains so embedded in their daily life that they remain irreversible. Please bear with me for a few seconds, as I would like to cite some portions of the official statistics from the National Planning Commission documents. Nepal's achievements in social sectors have been remarkable during the twelve years of Nepali democracy. Nepal's economy grew by an average of 2.5 per cent per year over the last ten years. But during the three decades (1960-1990) when there was no violence in the country and the king ruled directly, the economy grew at only 0.5 per cent. The number of health workers delivering health services that remained at 28 thousand at the start of the decade of 1990s, more than tripled to 87 thousands. Child mortality declined by 4.2 per cent, and the maternal mortality rate went down to 400 per thousand in 2001 from its level of 750 in 1990. Similarly, the average life expectancy of Nepalis rose to 59 years during 1990-2002 as against only 42 years in the three decades preceding it.

The number of schools primary, lower secondary as well as student enrollment increased sharply. Only 48 per cent of the men and 14 per cent of the women could read and write in Nepal till 1990, whereas in last 12 years (1990-2002) the male literacy rate has reached 59 per cent and that of women 24 per cent.

Similarly the progress achieved in infrastructure development is noteworthy. The total length of roads stood at 6706 kilometers in 1990, which more than doubled to 15905 kilometers by 2001. The population benefiting from the added supply of piped drinking water stands at 71.5 per cent.

It is my belief that democracies help resolve conflict, rebuild society after conflict, quicken recovery and rehabilitation, develop good governance, rule of law, transparency and accountability, spur progress, strengthen collective efforts to deepen democracy where it exists and defend it where it is threatened, promote and protect human rights, build bridges and strengthen cooperation among nations.

Mr. Chairman,

Nepal is strategically placed two Asian giants. Its population of 24 million lives in the neighborhood of over two billion. A strong, stable and democratic and prosperous Nepal is in their interest. Nepal, which shares about 1700 kilometers of its borders with India and about 1000 kilometers with China, can be a very important link connecting their fast growth for the people of Nepal, India and China.

Nepal's strategic value is great. Managing stability in Nepal will contribute to the security of the region and beyond. The world we live in is more interdependent, interrelated and interconnected. No event in any corner of the world can be seen in isolation. The Independent Commission Report on Human Security 2003 states, and I quote, 'The security of one person, one community, one nation rests on the decision of many others-sometimes fortuitously, sometimes precariously.' Maoist insurgency in Nepal, therefore, cannot remain insignificant to the international community, particularly so to India. If one of the pillars of Nepal's stability, progress and peace-democracy-remains broken today, the other pillar constitutional monarchy is badly shaken. Unless these two pillars are enjoined together again anarchy and instability will follow and Nepal is sure to become a fertile nursery for breeding the hydra-headed monster of terrorism.

Nepal's vast potentials of natural and human resources can contribute to the growth of region. Our people remain poor because these resources either go wasted or remain unutilised, underutilised or misutilised. The people of South Asia deserve common benefits from these resources. Delayed and deferred actions breed wastage of resources and resentment in people. If we dare to make the process of the regional economic cooperation under SAARC umbrella walk on the fast track, it can create a revolutionising effect to the achieving the goal of quality improvement in the life of our people. This will be the right path to lift majority out of deprivation and isolation, and give them a control of circumstances that determine their living. This empowerment will give them voices and choices in decisions that shape their destiny. This is how we can overcome the problems of poverty, deprivation and terrorism that afflict the daily life in our region. This is how we can help create enabling environment to deliver services to the people at present and generate long-term benefits to generations to come. And this is how we as nations and region can contribute to the making of a safer and better world, and this is how, we can contribute to dignity of human being.

Mr. Chairman,

Before concluding, I would like to thank the Centre for the Study of Nepal and its Director for the kind invitation to me to come to the Center and speak about the problems confronting Nepal. I thank you, Mr. Chairman, and all those present in audience to day for their courtesy and patience.

And with these remarks, it is my pleasure to declare this international seminar open.

Thank you.

2

South Asia as a Geographical Region: Concepts and Interpretations

R. Sahu

The encyclopaedia Asiatica in its Vol. I geographically defines South Asia as follows. "Travelling from the E. of Bengal to Herat, we find S. Asia everywhere bounded on the N. by a chain of mountains which is covered with perpetual snow for almost the whole of that extent and from which all its great rivers appear to issue. This chain commences near the Brahmaputra and runs nearly N.W as far as Kashmir. During this part of its course it is called the Himalaya, from Hima, the Sanskrit for snow, and alaya, abode. From Kashmir its general direction is a little to the S.W as far the snowy peak of Hindukush nearly N. of Kabul."[1]

From the above extract, it is amply clear that South Asia as a geographical region lies only to the south of the great Himalayan range. On the contrary, South Asia has been interestingly and befittingly interpreted as "Asian Asia" which is characteristically so distinct from Asia's European Asia. Thus, according to the author what is really 'Asian Asia' could best be described as South Asia. As has been said, therefore, South Asia having its Geo-spatial identity as a great geographical region is different from areas lying in the fringe areas of Asian continent as European Asia or 'Non-Asian Asia' etc. In view of the cultural heterogeneity of Asia there can be, therefore, several Asia's which are distinguished in terms of cultural differences. The most significant difference is that Asian continent is paradoxically divided into two, i.e.,

Asia which is Asian and the Asia that is not. The term is a negative concept and can be defined as that part of Asia which is fundamentally different from European civilisation. The term is also a positive concept because it is that part of the Asian continent which rims the southern and eastern margin of the great continent. This is non European and highly populous. The entire length and breadth of this area which is otherwise termed as the Asiatic crescent however, contains the lasting civilisations and the modern nations that are significantly found in great river valleys, oases, deserts and mountains and so on. The cores of civilisation and the modern nations in Asian Asia are largely separated by extensive unoccupied areas marked by desertic conditions, long mountain ranges and plateaus, steppes, barren and forested lands. All these features alone or in association act as formidable barriers to communications.[3]

It has also been argued that "the great tongue shaped promontory that juts southward from the continent of Asia is known to the world as India."[4] However, this part of Asia constitutes of about half a dozen small and independent countries and colonies besides Pakistan. Therefore, these countries lying south of Soviet and Chinese boundaries also lying between Iran on the West and Burma (Myanmar) on the East may not be accurately reffered to as a proper designate to the world 'India'.

On the other hand, no specific word has been found in any languages of this geographical realm that properly designates 'South Asia'. The word 'India' has been found to be a corrupted form of Sindhu (that means 'river' in Sanskrit hence also Indus).

It was believed to have been transmitted to Europe through Iranian usage. Ancient Greek geographers also used this word. It is, thus, said that the term has been used in the sense of greater India that encompasses all the regions of South and South East Asia since the 15th century. But presently "the concept of India as a precise geographic and political entity dates from the 19th century during the period of British rule in South Asia."[5]

Keeping the above discourse in view, it could be said that the group of countries even including Afghanistan and the Himalayan countries of Bhutan and Nepal-together with Sri Lanka and the tiny Islands of Bay of Bengal and the Arabian sea, the coastal Portuguese territories-form collectively a significant geographic realm and best be described as South

Asia. And this whole region stands between the South Western and South Eastern realms of Asia. The realm thus incorporates the territory in the British Indian empire as on the date of the dissolution of the same on the 15th August, 1947 and the adjacent areas excluding Burma (Myanmar) which were under British rule.

It is, thus, prudent to note that South Asia, by and large, coincides to a greater degree with the classical geographic concept of India and is said to be more inclusive than India's present political entity.[6]

The western authours of regional geography while classifying world regions have interpreted this region in varied ways. What it seems, no where a clear South Asian concept with a special geographical treatment is perhaps visualised. On one hand, when it is described as lying south of the Himalayan range as India and its adjacent territories, on the other, it is also interpreted as part of the Orient[7] (East) that comes under a regional group of countries. But interestingly enough, the countries belonging to South East Asia have invariably been found in global regional interpretation under the heading 'South East Asia' unlike South which is geographically, socio-economically and culturally a more coherent and vibrant unit.

Jesse H. Wheeler et. all (1969)[8] have treated South Asian countries as a regional group under the Indian subcontinent and their classification is primarily based on factors such as, (a) proximity, (b) environmental, economic and cultural similarities, (c) political relationships and, (d) historical ties. According to their classification of four such groups of countries of the Orient, the countries of the Indian Subcontinent include India, Pakistan and the small Himalayan states of Nepal, Bhutan and Sikkim. Sri Lanka is often included with this group of countries but the said authors have put in Sri Lanka in South East Asia.

In terms of systematic regional geography of monsoon Asia where grouping into regions is apparently difficult in view of great size and long history of the area, three major realms have been distinguished . The realms include "Southern Asia lying south of the Tibet mass, Eastern Asia sprawling east of it and South East Asia which fans south ward from a narrow mountainous neck in eastern Tibet"[9]. Each of the above realms forms a part of Asia's continental fringe and adjoins the cold, high and bare plateau of Tibet.

The first realm, i.e., Southern Asia is a subcontinent and is distinguishable from its surroundings in a way that the arcuate type Indus-Ganges-Bramhaputra plains adjoins the high Himalayan ranges an their offshoots. There is, thus, a physical change that is evident between people of the subcontinent south of Tibet and the people from Tibet approaching the continent. The dividing line between these people is supposed to be a high mountainous watershed.

II

As a world region though South Asia has a prominent role to play in global economy and politics, nevertheless, the region is still to emerge forcefully as a dynamically coherent socio-economic and political unit. In this context, it will be worthwhile to shed further light on its extent, boundaries and the process of peopling of this great region in greater detail. The underdevelopment of South Asian region could be directly attributed to the pressure of population on resources while South Asian region could be directly attributed to the pressure of population on resources while South Asia covers only 3.5 per cent of the world's area, it has given shelter to as much as 20 per cent of the world's population. The region is deemed as one among world's poorest regions in view of the fact that it produces as little as only two per cent of the world's gross product. However, it exhibits income level in terms of percapita GNP, i.e., as much as US$ 400. Political reasons for such state of affairs appear to be more prominent that even economic. It is, therefore, to be emphasised that if the political climate in the South Asian countries doesn't improve to a desired degree, the tempo of economic growth cannot be achieved.[10]

III

In conclusion, one can say that South Asia in this era of globalisation stands apart as a prominent region in terms of resources and a future prospect of economic development. The SAARC as the mouth piece of the region if acts with proper co-ordination can discharge wonderful jobs in influencing world economy and politics. It is therefore, pertinent to argue that South Asia as a vibrant world region has all the potential-social, economic and scientific and so on and so forth-to compete with any other region of the globe.

References

1. Taken from Balfour, Edward., Encyclopaedia Asiatica: comprising Indian Subcontinent, Eastern and Southern Asia, Vol. I, New Delhi, 1976, p. 183.
2. Ginsburg, Norton. (ed.), The Pattern of Asia, London, 1958, p. 21.
3. *Ibid.* p. 21
4. Ginsburg, Norton (ed.), *op. cit.* p. 458
5. Taken from *Ibid.* p. 458.
6. *Ibid.* p. 458.
7. Jr. Wheeler, Jesse H. et. all, Regional Geography of the World, New York, 1969, p. 403.
8. *Ibid.* p. 403.
9. Taken from Dobby, E.H.G., A Systematic Regional Geography. Monsoon Asia, Vol.V, 1961, p. 89.
10. Bimal Prasad, South Asia: Towards Dynamism and Cooperation, Bombay, 1997, p. 101.

3

South Asia as a Region in the Global Space: Some Conceptual Issues

Bhaskar Majumdar

In a globalised world based on compartmentalisation of countries as developed and developing, or dominant and subordinate, or first world and third world, the location of countries in Asia, in particular South Asia is to be understood. The regional concern for South Asia is not only to be read as a concern for the people settled in this region, but also for people settled in other countries, including the other states that often work as .political determinants in the countries in South Asia. The reason lies not only in economic parameters, but also in political-diplomatic frontiers. The reason for concern for the states and people in the countries in South Asia lies not only in having command over available economic resources, but also to protect the resources from 'others' aggression'. The same could be told about other countries in the non-South Asian region, but here we are concerned with the significant of South Asia as a geo-political region in the global space.

One reason, among other reasons, for decolonisation of countries now understood as the Third World was to pursue the non-territorial expansion through transnationalisation by the dominant country lobbies in the first world. It is to be remembered that Nepal and Bhutan as countries in South Asia were never colonisation and subsequently to recolonisation in history depends on cost benefit matrix of the colonisers. The hilly terrain of Nepal and Bhutan perhaps were not so attractive to the colonisers to get them annexed to the highest crown, namely India, for the-then imperial power, UK. The point is when we talk about South Asia as a region we consider Nepal and Bhutan also while focusing on the major countries like India, Pakistan as economic-political nuclear power countries, plus Bangladesh as a potential market power (alongwith her size of population, natural resource base etc), Sri Lanka as a country with high development of manpower, Maldives as a small island country. Each country is regionally significant for different reasons like being natural resource reserviour, having a big size of population, quality human resource, and importance by geo-political location etc. The question that remains to be understood is the significance of the country as the unit of analysis for herself within herself, or the significance of the country as linked with other neighbouring/ remote countries by geographic distance, and significance of the country understood as member in a group like that of SAARC, and significance of the country as seen by the aggressors.

We will consider here the significance of the countries in South Asia as a whole that covers countries namely, India, Pakistan, Bangladesh, Sri Lanka, Nepal, Bhutan, and Maldives, which incidentally are the constituents of SAARC. This is at least for two reasons. One is that the club of countries may understand the potential power of the unity, measured by any economic-political indicators. The second one is the group representation in the world fora. The third one could be the attractiveness of South Asia as a region for the global power leader, which we will not discuss in this paper.

This paper has three sections. In Section I, we talk about the potential power of South Asia. In Section II, we talk about the representation of South Asian countries in global fora. Finally, in Section III, we see what can be done.

I. Potential Power of South Asia

Following post-Second World War decolonisation, political independence of countries by partition of the major south Asian region, these newly independent countries not only dreamt of new vision of development as distinct from the countries in First and Second World by pledging non-alignment, but also got involved in conflicts and wars. This includes internal conflicts and conflicts across geographic boundaries, and also occasional wars. Partition-dependent premature political independence might be one reason for these conflicts. War is not a new phenomenon for the countries, particularly in European countries. But these wars that were fought in European countries led to peace of Westphalia in 1668 and led to formation of states as protector of settled people in those countries protected by revealed state power, some of the countries in South Asia surrendered their stability by getting involved in conflicts and wars for the newly independent countries in South Asia this really undermined the peace and stability of these countries and also for the people settled in these countries. This is because these countries were used as proxy warriors for the dividers of the world under antagonistic ideologies. This was the cold war, scenario for a period ranging from 1945 to 1989. These countries thus even failed to realise their potential economic-political power.

The year was 1962 when India first had to be involved in conflict with neighbour China. In 1965 India got involved in war with Pakistan. In the first case India had to retreat and the second case was indecisive. Following these two, India stepped up its military expenditure, so that the military budget quadrupled within the decade (Desai, 1975, p. 11). The development consequence was an additional strain on resources, and non-fulfilment of primary objectives of a welfare state of the-then period. The consequence for Pakistan was much more serious. Pakistan had two regional compartments, West Pakistan on the west side of India, and East Pakistan on the east side of India. Administratively-militarily it was impossible from the very beginning to control/govern both the regions under one state power. Pakistan paid the penality of unwise partition when following the 1971 War between East Pakistan and West Pakistan, Bangladesh came to be born. The immediate implication was accommodation of post-1971 three politically sovereign countries, in place of post-1947 two such countries. The long-term consequence was slicing away 40.0 per cent of former Pakistan's home market (Nations, 1975, p. 287). It is to be kept in mind that while pre-1971 India and Pakistan were the major power countries in South Asia, post-1971 South Asia shows three countries as the major and potentially power countries, namely India, Pakistan-(with a reduced power following formation of Bangladesh), and Bangladesh.

Let us focus on selected economic indicators. For the 1990s, these seven countries in South Asia had more than one-fifth of world population. This may show the potential market size of the region as a whole. Of this population size, alone India had one-sixth of world population, or four-fifth of population in the seven south Asian countries. In other words, India has the lion's share in population in South Asian region. Each of Pakistan and Bangladesh has one-tenth of population in-South Asia, so that these countries taken together constitute two-fifth of population in

South Asia. Each of Sri Lanka and Nepal has one-third of one per cent of world population, or one-sixtieth of population in South Asia. The size of settled population in each of Bhutan and Maldives is insignificant. The implication is, in addition of population-differential based uneven potential economic power, the countries that do not draw much attention from the world 'power lobby' remain also in South Asia. While the countries in South Asia may show some kind of like-mindedness, or homogeneity, in the global operational domain there remains a wide a gap between India on the one hand, and other countries on the other. Also India, Pakistan and Bangladesh remains potential platform for the rest of the world's economic operations, while the rest are either dependent on first three, mainly India, or on the power lobby outside India. For example, Nepal is a land-locked country that needs economic links more with India relative to other countries not only in South Asia but also in the rest of the world.

For the 1990s the seven south Asian countries command around 1.5 per cent in world output. India alone accounts for around one per cent of this world output share, or two-third of South Asian total output. Each of Nepal, Bhutan, and Maldives command insignificant share in world output. Following-the same logic, the countries that enjoy lion's share of output in South Asia are India, Pakistan, and Bangladesh. Sri Lanka remains a median country. Thus, there exists output based power-differential within countries in South Asia.

In world exports, for the 1990s, these seven countries in South Asia controlled less than one per cent. India alone had more than half of exports from South Asia. In world exports, as well as in exports from South Asia, Bangladesh and Sri Lanka occupy similar position, while for Nepal, Bhutan and Maldives, it remains, insignificant (World Bank, World Development Report, 1990s). The extreme" economic power-differential may have a possibility of not only leader-led relation within South Asia in the political-economic context, but also may weaken the power balance between South Asia as a lobby and the rest of the dominant world.

II. Representation of South Asian Countries in Global Fora

These countries jumped from the frying pan to the fire in a unipolar world followed by the 1989 disintegration of the former USSR. In the 1990s all these countries accepted the strategy of open-door industrialisation (Majumder, 1992, p. 237). Sri Lanka was an exception that chose the strategy long back in 1977.

Most of these countries followed a path of final commodity substitution-led import substitution based on liberal import of technology (including capital goods) during early decades of post-decolonisation development. In other words initial development was state-led through development and 'commanding height' of public enterprises. Because of dependence on technology, aid, and military support, the kind of growth did not lead to a situation whereby economic-political emancipation of these countries could be established and carried forward. The dependence led to not only military intervention through indirect means in these countries but also led to political-economic 'balkanisation' within and across these countries. The power-potential of these countries, thus, could not materialise in the global domain. A shift from import substitution regime to export promotion regime and subsequently to open door regime thus could not establish the power of these countries in the global fora.

While the state in these South Asian countries took the role of benevolent during the early decades in the form of declaration of welfare states, these states took also the role of entrepreneurs or developers in the pre-1989 period that showed 'development state'. Post-1989 period shows the shift in the role of the state to being 'host states' by inviting capital on a free scale (GOI, 1991, pp. 4-5).

Let us talk about the participation of these countries in world institutions like the World Bank, the IMF, the WTO etc. In IMF, for example, these seven South Asian countries had a voting share of only 3.1 per cent, with India's share at 2.1 per cent in 1996. It means, the other six countries in South Asia had only 1.0 per cent of share in dollar vote in IMF in 1996. This may be contrasted with the share of seven most industrialised countries in the world (G-7) which stood at 4 5.0 per cent in the same year with the share of US alone at 18.0 per cent (Majumder, 1996, p. 126). The similar picture holds for World Bank. In the dispute settlement processes in the WTO for issues related to labour related trade, environment-related trade, subsidies in agriculture, dismantling of the PDS etc these countries in South Asia, alongwith other countries in the Third World, are disturbed too much. Some of these countries in South Asia could manage to have some berth in global policy institutions like G-20, formed in 1999 as the latest and strongest policy institution, for example, India but the power that India can exercise in the body is not clear till date. The exercise of power, as and when it occurs in the global policy domain cannot be a consolation for the exclusion of other South Asian countries from the decision-making processes in the global fora that effect every country.

III. What is to be Done?

The tasks are easier said than done. Still these are to be said in the expectation that these can be done by the appropriate authority and through proper institutions. The most urgent task is to ensure cooperative growth and development between these seven countries in South Asia. It is true that there is already SAARC. The point is that SAARC has to be operationally meaningful not only within itself but also get represented in global fora with power. Both India and Pakistan are supposedly nuclear power countries. Rather than threatening each other based on possession of this power, these countries can think about pre-partition power and act accordingly in unity in the global space.

For this both these countries need to develop soft diplomatic relations. We stress on India and Pakistan because once the apparent conflicts that get surfaced on the geographic platform of these countries, may have its origin elsewhere historically and politically, the whole of South Asia gets disturbed. The smaller countries like Bhutan, Nepal etc may have space for positive action in South Asia once India and Pakistan resolve their border conflicts.

This again may show how the large economies like India and Pakistan can offer the space for market expansion for the land locked countries like Nepal and Bhutan, and also for the island economies like Sri Lanka and Maldives. One way could be to form product-based cartels and other groups with joint optimisation goals so that the economic flows do not lead to zero-sum game.

There has to free movement and mobility of people (visa-free) across these countries. Already there is such movement for the economically weaker sections between Bangladesh and east of India, whether or not acknowledged by the respective Governments. A free movement of people alongwith free flows of commodities, knowledge technology, and investment will not disturb the regional balance. Rather it will enhance regional integration.

The catalyst for this has to be the state of each of these countries. The supporting institutions may be the polity institutions at both country-level and regional level (like SAARC). These institutions may also cover the areas like the academia, the art and culture as components of civil society. In fact, the civil society alongwith the state of the countries in South Asia have to show the path of moving forward towards ensuring regional integration and exercising power in the global space.

References

GOI, 1991, New Economic Policy.

Majumder, Bhaskar, 1992, 'From Import Substitution to Open Door Industrialisation: An Evolution', productivity.

Majumder, Bhaskar, 1996, Capitalist Extensive Globalisation: Options for SAARC South Asian Studies, Vol. 31 Nos. I & 2, Jan-Dec.

Nations, Richard, 1975, 'The Economic Structure of Pakistan and Bangladesh', in Blackburn, Robin (Ed), 'Expansion in a Subcontinent', Penguin, England.

World Bank, World Development, 1991-2003.

4

South Asia: The Diversity of Unity

Bhupendra V. Singh
Nripendra P. Singh

The South Asian countries differ in terms of resource base, industrial strength, man-power strength, forms of local organization, government and representative institutions, the extent and the form of the dependence on the out side world. Similarly, ethnicity, regionalism, linguistic and religion based social relationship have different degree of balance in the countries of the region. Despite the uneven pattern of economic development; varying from state to state, area to area, nature and scope of present territorial boundaries of the state, concentration of certain ethnic group in a region as a result of migration, conversion and conquest; the region represents a complete whole. It is a sparse unity that is diversified due to political division of territory and blow of time. The unity lies in the Indocentric character of the region. The present endeavor is to discover this unity in diversity and to work out a case for united South Asia.

The Geographical Unity

The South Asia is a distinct region. The seven countries form the largest geographical reality in the Indian Ocean; unlike South West or South East Asia that are highly fragmented. Except Sri Lanka and The Maldives, rest of the countries are neighbourers of one or the other. The South Asia is almost a continental Whole. It physically dominates the northern part of the Indian Ocean, which serves as vital link between the west and the east, connecting Europe through the Middle East, with South East and East Asia. This region is transverse by important sea-lanes of international trade and vital oil supplies from the Gulf. Its island territories of Andman and Nicobar Screen the Malcca Straits.

The Cultural Affinity

The states in the region belong to what Curzon conceived as the Indian Empire as it is geographically compact yet at different periods a number of ethno-cultural identities have cropped up in different part of the subcontinent and even developed into political communities. The pluralistic nature of the South Asia is the main characteristics. The striking feature of the ancient civilization in the sub continent was lack of orientation of statehood. Therefore, the discovery of the South Asia will find its way through what runs in the water of the rivers, what smells in the air and what disseminates over the mountains. It will find its way through the emotive and cognitive resources of the inhabitants. It will be reflected through social relationship, dance and music and through various means of intrinsic and aesthetic expression of human formation.

Bangladesh, India and Pakistan were part of British India and even after more than fifty years their politics runs in terms of one other. This is an affinity reflected by the other way round. They directly share history and culture. The distinctions of the three nations are self imposed, deliberate and purposive. Bangladesh and Pakistan resorted to Islamization just to isolate them form the Indian past and to retain power by different political parties.

Bangladeshi culture needs no separate mention, as it is an alter ego of Bengali culture and part and partial of same historical process.

Like any other South Asian country, Pakistan is also a pluralistic society. The cultural complexity was reduced in Pakistan after partition. Region wise, West Pakistan was more homogeneous than East Pakistan (Bangladesh). Never the less, Pakistan is composition of distinct languages, dialects, ethnic groups, religious sects, tribes and culture. The Pakistani people are conscious of their rich social culture. However, the pertinent question remains intact that Pakistan is new country with old culture or Pakistani culture is a new concept as the nation itself? Is it Pakistani culture or Indo-Muslim culture or Muslim Culture all together?

There are people who trace Pakistani culture from 5000 BC to Indus Valley Civilization and consider it a boon of Indus, as Egyptian culture is on Nile. The imprints of which are claimed to be found in village life of modern Pakistan. There are others who annex it to 711 AD, a period of Delhi Sultanate.

A new trend cropped up to associate the culture to Middle East and trace it way back to Indus Valley Civilization via trade links.

Separate Muslim Identity-Pakistan's endeavor to search for a separate Muslim Identity is a failure. They are not descendents of emperors of medieval period, as no one clan ruled India. There were Turks, Arabs, Mongols and they were few in numbers. The major population of Muslims is converted.

The two-nation theory that Hindu and Muslims formed two separate nations was questioned at the time it was mooted and still poses serious doubts. Punjabi, Sindhi and Baluchi represented separate nationalities, so to say. They differ in terms of language, culture, tradition and customs. Mohazirs have different such definition. Such diversities are threat to Pakistani unity itself.

Four of the languages; Urdu, Punjabi, Sindhi and Gujrati, spoken in Pakistan are of Indian origin. Only Baluchi are Pasto may claim different origin. The official Language, Urdu, belong to Indo-Aryan Family and developed in North India out of Western Hindu or 'Khari Boli'. As literary language it was given patronage in Delhi, Lucknow, Azimabad and Rampur; even though the Persian remained the court language till 1835 AD.

Therefore, as Pakistani nationhood is still unestablished its culture has found no genuine definition. One may conclude more similarities than dissimilarities of Muslim culture of India and Bangladesh.

Nepalese Identity-The geography of Nepal has not only influenced Indo-Nepalese economic relation but also their cultural and social relation. Social customs in Nepal resembles with those of India. It is inseparable from Indo-Gangetic plain. Although, the civilization of Tibet has some influence but Indian influence is predominant. The Terai region was inhabited by Indian settlers so it could not save herself from direct influence or it can be termed as simply extension of Indian Culture. On the contrary, the mountain region had inhabitants from Tibet-Burmese origin. During the reign of Lichchavies, who ruled Nepal from the 5th Century AD, the relation between the two countries was deepened. Nepal was unified due to the efforts of King Dravya Shah who defeated Malla king in the year 1769.

Indian sages and rishis found secret resorts in the mountains and pilgrims from Nepal invariably visited to Varanasi, Badrinath and Gaya. Sri Pashupatinath is considered part of Kedarnath. Other important places are Muktinath and Lumbini. King of Nepal enjoys special privillege. The harmonious religious relations is found only in Nepal.

The closer link, other than Hindu religion, is the Nepalese language, which belongs to Sanskrit family.

The open link, other than Hindu religion, is the Nepalese language, which belongs to Sanskrit family.

The open border between India and Nepal has allowed settlement of a substantial Indo-Gangetic population in Nepal Terai while more Nepalese have settled in Darjeeling, Sikkim and Bhutan. India and Nepal are inseparable.

Sri Lanka, like other South Asian countries, again is a pluralistic society. The Palk Strait that separates India from Sri Lanka is only twenty-five miles wide at its narrowest point. The open beaches on either shore have made crossing easier. Therefore, the greatest influence on Sri Lanka is that of India. For centuries, she has drawn immensely from religious and ideological movements that dominated the Indian sub continent. Indian social customs, style of dress and the Indian caste system, have left their marks on Sri Lankan society. So have left the literature and art. Buddhism and Sangh played major role in shaping the polity where as Hinduism in 7th century AD and later Muslims played similar role.

Almost 74 per cent of the population is Sinhale. Sri Lankan Tamils account for 13 per cent, Moors (Indian and Sri Lankan) accounts for 7 per cent, Indian Tamils accounts for 5.6 per cent, and Malays, Burghers and Europeans collectively accounts for 5 per cent. In terms of division of population on the basis of religion depicts that two third shinhalese are Budhdhist, 90 per cent Tamils are Hindu. All Moors are Muslims. Christians and Muslims are almost in equal number. The strict categorical division remains intact in terms of language. The strict categorical division remains intact in terms of language. The number of Sinhali speaking Tamil and a vice versa is very small.

Sinhalese and Tamils are considered descendents of Aryans and Dravidians, respectively. Sinhalese migrated from Indo-Gangetic plain of North India, perhaps from Bengal and Urissa at around 500 BC, which was followed by Dravidian migration from South India. The migration of Tamils to Sri Lanka started with foundation of strong Hindu kingdom in South India around 500 AD. The periodic invasion by Cholas caused influx of Tamils from Malabar, Coromendel Coast and Trivancore-Cochin. This influx was further intensified by migration of labourers from different part of India for plantation during the British period. The Moors trace their origin from India and Malaya.

Bhutan has settlers from Tibet and Nepal. Buddhism is the religion and that defines the culture. Similar, Muslim population, which is the major population of the Maldives, migrated from India.

The Colonial Legacy and Ethnic Conflicts

The colonial rule in India changed the agrarian structure of the region. It was mainly feudalistic in nature. After independence and the partition of the country, the three nations inherited same system but alterations were introduced in different countries with different nature and degree. The British rule has its impact on every walk of life. It also has definite impacts on Sri Lanka and Nepal.

The biggest scar is in the form of ethnic conflicts that disseminates over the whole region. These conflicts within the countries of South Asia generate internal pressure and pulls that affects interstate relations.

Ethnic distinctiveness into 'Two Nations' partly explains the partition in 1947. The emergence of Bangladesh in 1971 demonstrated the successful culmination of another ethnic movement. Bihari Muslim group in Pakistan and Tamil and Sinhali conflicts illustrates that in every South Asian country there exists ethnic conflicts. However, in Nepal and Bhutan despite multi ethnicity, inter ethnic cleavages remain latent and less violent.

This existence of ethnic conflicts in various forms is another argument in favor of similarities and linkages.

The Crux of the present attempt is to underline some of the issues that could establish the close affinity of nation of South Asian Region. The region is one geographical entity that was conceived as the Indian Empire by Lord Curzon. The region shares history and lack of statehood. The cultural affinity still prevails and cherishes same social relationships in one form or the other. This is reflected in the caste relationship that defines economic stats as well. Different castes also define language pattern. The nature and scope of ethnic conflicts also substantiate the latent affinity.

The reintegration of the region of potent case of probing. The SAARC has provided such a forum. In the midst of globalization vis a vis successful occurrence of certain other regional groupings such as EMU, Asian unity is the call of the hour.

References

Anand, R.D.; South Asia: In Search of Regional Identity, Banyan Pub. New Delhi, 1991.

Aris, Michael; Bhutan: The Early History of Himalyan kingdom, Vikas Publication Private Ltd., 1980.

Bhat, T.; Mile Stones at a Distance, Financial Express, June 18, 1995.

Bose, S. (Ed); South Asia and World Capitalism, Oxford University Press, New Delhi, 1990.

Das, D.K. (Ed); SAARC: Regional Cooperation and Development, Deep and Deep Publication, New Delhi, 1992.

Deep Pub. New Delhi, 1992.

De Silva, Chandra Richard, Sri Lanka: A History, Vikas Pub., New Delhi, 1987.

Heyerdahe, Thor; The Malediv Mystry, George Allen & Unvin, London, 1986.

Ramakant, S.N. Kausik, Shshi Updhyay (Ed); Contemporary Pakistan: Trends and Issues, Kaling Publication, New Delhi, 2001.

Sengupta, B South Asian Perspective: Seven Nations in Conflict and Cooperation, B.R. Publication, Comp. New Delhi, 1988.

Shaha, Risikesh; Ancient and Medieval Nepal, Manohar Publication, 1992.

5

Nepal's Political and Security Relations with India

Jitendra Dhoj Khand

Nepal-India relations have been established since the time of the Golden Age (Satya Yug), the Silver Age (Treta Yug), the Copper Age (Dwapar Yug), and the Iron Age (Kali Yug). During the Golden Age, Nepal had been a play ground of Shiva and Parvati and people of India were and are devotee of Pashupatinath. Maharishi Veda Byasa Guru of Damauli Tanau District, Nepal who was the divider, writer, and compiler of the Vedas, Upanishads, Puranas, Brahmanas Granth, Gita, and Mahabharat. The people of two countries have faith and follow all the literatures. Yoga Vashista Guru taught to Bhagawan Ram at Deughat of Chitaun District, Nepal before the marriage with Sita, daughter of King Janak during the Silver Age (Treta Yug). Pandavs were also secretly resided at Morang district of Nepal near the palace of Birat King of Nepal. In the Copper Age (Dwapar Yug) Bhagawan Krishna accompanied with his son Pradyumna and Gopala had come in Nepal. Pradyumna married two wives at a time, one with Pravawati, sister of Mahendra Daman Giant King of Chandana Giri (Mahendra Daman Rakshesh) and another with Chandrawati, daughter of Suryakctu King of Mrigrendra Shikhar to establish peace and security in Nepal.[1] Gopala resided at Thankot and Chitlang of Kathmandu. Later they became the Gopala Bansha. Prince Gautam Buddha was also born in Lumbini Zone of Nepal at the beginning of the Iron Age (Kali Yug) and spread in India and other Asian countries. During the Shah Dynasty, Kings of Nepal and India exchanged their daughters for marriage. Recently, Crown Prince Paras Shah also married with Ms. Himani Singh of India.

Nepal is landlocked and nuclear locked, situated between India and China. It occupies a significant position between the two countries. It has no natural barrier with India and three sides open borders (1760 kilometers). The most significant factor nurturing them through the Ages is geography. The area of Nepal is 147,181 square kilometers. Its population is about 24 million. India is about twenty-one times larger in size about 42 times more populous. Socio-cultural ties between the two are as old as the flow of people and ideas across the national boundaries. Politically, they are adopting the Multi-Party Democracy. Both are the members of South Asia, SAARC, NAM, and the United Nations. Both have been supporting the settlement of disputes through negotiation and opposing the colonialism, neocolonialism; racism, and intervention in the affairs of others Structurally the economy of Nepal as a whole was feudalistic. The Ranas did not introduce reforms for fear of being toppled. But the revolution of 1950 opened the doors for economic development with the economic help of friendly countries, particularly India. Now, it has progressed a lot in the field of privatisation, transportation, communication, and education. The Nepali soldiers participated in the First World War and the Second World War. In addition, the Nepali in Indian army fought the war of 1962, 1965, 1971, Kargil and other small wars. More than 40 thousands Royal Nepali Army have been participated in the UNPKF since the UN in Lebanon.[2] Internationally, the victory of the Allied Forces led by the United States of America in the Gulf War of 1991, the end of Cold War, the downfall of communism in Eastern Europe and the Soviet, and break down of the balance of power after the Soviet's disintegration, and emergence of unipolar world have introduced the neo-realism.[3] Against this back ground an attempt has been made to analyze the Nepal's political and security relations with India.

I

Modern Nepal has a short political history. It dates from the later half of the 18th century when the rulers of Gorkha, who formed Nepal out of small principalities. One of these rulers, Prithvi Narayan Shah, conquered the Kathmandu valley in 1769. He established the rule of the Shah dynasty which exists even to this day. Present King of Nepal, Gyanendra Bir Bikram Shah Dev, being his lineal descendant.[4]

The relations of British India with Nepal date back to the 18th century, but the formal relations could not be established until 1885. The founder of Nepal, Prithvi Narayan Shah did not want the British influence to this country and he tried his best to prevent it. Later, Prime Minister Bhimsen

Thapa started a turning point in the political history of Nepal British India relations owing to the war from 1814 to 1816. But a new period opened with Jung Bahadur's rise in September 1846. Consequently, the era of misunderstanding, misconception, mistrust, jealousy, and enmity ended and that of good faith, understanding, and cordiality for mutual benefit began.[5]

Nepal had long standing relations with British, but owing to British withdrawal from the Indian sub-continent in 1947, some adjustments were necessary between Nepal, the British, and independent India. Hence they concluded a tripartite treaty on 9th November 1947. Nepal and India also signed the treaty of peace and friendship and treaty of trade and commerce on 31st July 1950.[6]

Despite efforts made for ensuring its survival, the chapter of the century-old Rana regime came to close when the Royal family took asylum in the Indian Embassy in Kathmandu on 6th November 1950. Earlier, King Tribhuvan had been in contact with the Nepali Congress and other anti-Rana elements for several years. Having failed to secure the King's return from the Indian Embassy, Mohan Shumshere Rana summoned the Council of Nobles on 7th November 1950. As a result, he dethroned the King and crowned Prince Gyanendra as the King of Nepal. Present King became the King of Nepal before his elder brother Birendra and father Mahendra. By the time, neither the British nor the American was prepared to break ties with India on that question. Negotiations between the Nepali Congress and the Ranas began in New Delhi in early February 1951 under the auspices of India. Consequently, the King and the Nepali Congress returned to Kathmandu on 15th February 1951. After three days, the King appointed a ten-member cabinet. In fact, India played a great role to solve the problem of Nepal.[7]

At the end of the Tribhuvan era in 1955, Nepal was in the process of introducing important innovations in its own politics and security. King Mahendra ascended to the throne on 13th March, 1955. He attempted to give an independent personality to Nepal.

Thus, he tried to erase the impression that Nepal had only a dependency status vis-a-vis India. In fact, the King's attitude towards India became quite clear when he appointed pro-China Tanka Prasad Acharya as his first Prime Minister. K.I. Singh succeeded Acharya after 18th months as the Prime Minister of Nepal in 1957. But, after the landslide victory of the Nepali Congress in the First General Election of 1959, more balanced relations between Nepal and India were maintained.

Politics in Nepal took a dramatic turn when on 15th December 1960, King Mahendra dissolved the first ever elected parliament, deposed and arrested all the ministers and banned all political parties. After taking this dramatic step, the King paid a long visit to China from 26th September to 19th October 1961. As a result, Arniko Highway (Kathmandu-Kodari) agreement was signed on 15th October 1961. India, on its part, expressed surprise at the King's move and protested. India was not happy with the Nepali decision to bring the Chinese close to Nepal.

In October 1962, the Chinese military forces moved across the Indian border at the extreme eastern North East Frontier Area (NEFA) and extreme Western Ladakh. But, by mid-December, peace was restored after the Chinese declared unilateral ceasefire. As a result, India changed its policy towards Nepal. The unofficial economic blockade which was being imposed from time to time was lifted. The Government of India advised the Nepali Congress leaders to suspend subversive activities against the King's rule.[8]

After the disintegration of Pakistan and the emergence of the new Republic of Bangladesh in 1971, India occupied a pre-eminent position in South Asia because of its size, politics, technology, economic potentials, military, and history.

The struggle for the liberation of Bangladesh evoked reactions in the international community. At the outset, Nepal, for its part, regarded the issue of Bangladesh an internal affair of Pakistan. For Nepal, friendship and understanding with India were very important but not at the cost of friendship with Pakistan. Certainly, Nepal's stand on this issue was considered by India as not friendly in Nepal's policy during this period.

The Ministry of Foreign Affairs announced on 16th January 1972 that Nepal had recognised Bangladesh, as an independent and sovereign nation. Thus, Nepal became the 4th Asian nation and the 8th nation in the world to recognise the new nation. Thus, this step had direct bearing on Nepal-India relations. In view of India's efforts for the creation of Bangladesh, it would definitely have favourable impacts in their relations. Nepal's foreign policy of non-alignment was appreciated in India. Nepal's adjustment to the changed context following the emergence of Bangladesh was an indication that India cannot be ignored by Nepal while pursuing it's policies.

In fact, despite the divergent attitudes reflected in Nepal's political circles regarding the Bangladesh issue. Nepal-India relations were shaped in accordance with time and the new context. The treaty of peace and friendship of 1950, the emergence of India as a preeminent power in South Asia after the Bangladesh issue, India's security concern, the economic interdependence, and Nepal's realisation of its limited maneuverability were some of the basic points of convergence of mutual national interests.

The Indian aggressive posture revealed itself in the early 1970s, particularly when Mrs. Indira Gandhi's government decided to annex Sikkim to India on 4th September 1974. The Indian Lok Sabha granted the status of an Associate State to the tiny Himalayan Kingdom of Sikkim. Nepal's reaction over the Sikkim affair found expression both in official and non-official circles. The Nepali Foreign Minister made a statement in the National Panchayat expressing "Nepal's opposition to outside interference in internal affairs of any nation."[9] The pro-government Nepali students' union Rastravadi Swatantra, Vidyarthi Mandal had organised anti-Indian demonstrations breaking some window panes of the Indian library and some shops run by the Indians. The procession went to the Indian Embassy and handed over a memorandum demanding that India should not encroach upon the independent existence of Sikkim. Even an effigy of Mrs. Gandhi was burnt; pictures of Mahatma Gandhi and Nehru were torn. Anti-Indian demonstrations were organised in all the big cities of Nepal. Former Prime Minister, Tanka Prasad Acharya said, "India has gone beyond the limit. This has posed a danger even to Nepal." Similarly, former Foreign Minister, Rishikesh Shah said:

> India has declared itself as the champion of independence in the world. But the action taken by it with regard to Sikkim was not democratic.... There is no reason for us to feel disturbed because Nepal's internal condition and international status are different those of Sikkim.[10]

Indian indignation at the Nepali reaction was demonstrated through a number of moves. Girija Prasad Koirala, leader of the banned Nepali Congress, was reportedly allowed by the Government of India to move about in his car in India using the flag of the Nepali Congress in retaliation to the anti-Indian demonstrations held in Kathmandu on the Sikkim issue.

The Foreign Office spokesman in New Delhi observed that India did not see any legitimate grievance with Nepal over the Sikkim issue. He added, "We have consistently held that Indo-Sikkim relations do not concern any third countries."[11]

India had also sent a strong protest note to Nepal regarding the strikes and demonstrations organised against India's policy towards Sikkim. The Indian Embassy in Kathmandu issued a press note contradicting reports that India was trying to block the normal flow of essential commodities to Nepal. The press note added that Nepal's request for additional allocation of certain essential commodities for 1975 had only recently been received.[12] Consequently, Nepal's search for alternative sources for petroleum products was legitimate. It was materialised after the Nepali Prime Minister Nagendra Prasad Rijal's visit to Iran in 1975. Iran had agreed to meet Nepal's requirements of petrol.

Apart from this, when the Nepali side had mounted anti-Indian expeditions after the Sikkim incident, Nepali politicians living in self-exile in India were seemingly trying to cash in on the Nepal-India differences. The former Prime Minister B.P. Koirala, who had declared himself as the leader of the armed revolution that he undertook after 1969, stated:

> If the Government of India and the Indian people do not strengthen democratic forces in Nepal, one fine morning they will see that China has launched a military attack on Nepal and occupied it. A big democratic movement has started in Nepal under the leadership of the Nepali Congress. Clashes are occurring between army men and the revolutionary groups. For this purpose, a liberation army has been formed in eastern Nepal with ex-servicemen.[13]

In fact, B.P. Koirala's statement was neither good for Nepal-India relations nor for Nepal-China relations and neither for Sino-Indian relations. Anyway, the declaration of emergency of Mrs. Gandhi on 25th June 1975 gave consolation to Nepal that the parliamentary democracy abandoned by Nepal in 1960 was being repeated in India as well. But the psychological satisfaction that was evident in Nepali government circles following the declaration of emergency in India was affected by the Indian government's move to impose restrictions on the entry of Nepali nationals into Assam, Darjeeling, Sikkim, and Dharmashala regions of India.[14] Nevertheless, the flow of visits by the high dignitaries of the two countries continued in order to improve their relations.

In the midst of minor controversies, Prince Gyanendra, Princess Komal, and Prince Dhirendra visited India officially on 5th November 1976. During their visit Prince Gyanendra declared:

> Nepal's aim has always been to strengthen its relations with India on the basis of understanding and trust, mutual benefit and aspirations. We will be friends both in name and reality if we understand, respect, and recognise each other's growing needs for development, and our aspirations for peace, peace in our country, peace in the region, and peace in the world.[15]

This visit helped in adding strength to the existing bonds of friendship. Talks were held also on the question of restrictions imposed by India on the movements of Nepali nationals. Subsequently, India's new ambassador to Nepal, N.P. Menon, presented his credentials to His Majesty King Birendra.

Basically, the declaration of a state of emergency in India seemed to have created some great impact on Nepal. HM the King promulgated on 12th December 1975 the Second Amendment to the constitution of Nepal. Nepal also introduced press legislation for the prevention of publication of objectionable matter on more or less the same line as India had done. The Nepali democratic opposition particularly the Nepali Congress elements were shocked by the declaration of emergency in India. This step seemed to have weakened their hopes of restoring democracy in Nepal.[16]

It had been realised that the Indian emergency rule had put restrictions on the activities of Nepali opposition leaders living in self-exile in India. 'There alleged connections with the Indian opposition leaders, Jaya Prakash Narayan, and other Socialist's help to Nepali politicians seemed to have created a kind of misunderstanding between the Nepali Congress leaders and Mrs. Gandhi's government. When B.P. Koirala and Ganesh Man Singh, two Congress leaders found that their stay in India would not help them any longer, they advanced the idea of national reconciliation and national unity between the King and the democratic forces. Later accompanied by their party colleagues, they returned to Nepal on 30th December 1976, but they were arrested on their arrival at the Tribhuvan Airport of Kathmandu.

Mrs. Gandhi's emergency regime was equally taken with suspicions in Nepal. The authorities were fearful of the growing aggressive posture of India particularly since its decision to integrate Sikkim into India. On the question of Nepal's Zone of Peace proposal, India politely but firmly rejected this proposal. Thus, the relationship between Nepal and India during the emergency period was not as cordial as they appeared.[17]

The Janata Party which was a coalition of five parties had come to power following its landslide victory in the 1977 poll. But the Janata experiment started showing cracks immediately after its formation. The Socialist leaders and Jana Sangh elements often quarrelled over the party's role with each other showing a feeling of competitiveness. After two years, the Janata experiment failed when the Prime Minister and Deputy Prime Minister, Morarji Desai and Charan Singh respectively, could not work together in the government. Consequently, the Janata coalition broke down giving way to the coming of Mrs. Gandhi to power after a year. Charan Singh who claimed himself as the architect of the Janata Party preferred to run a coalition government with the grace of Mrs. Gandhi when the circumstances favored in 1979. His government collapsed after her withdrawal of cooperation creating conditions for a fresh election. In January 1980 general elections, the Congress (I) recaptured power by an overwhelming mandate from the electorate.

During the election campaign, Mrs. Gandhi had raised foreign policy issues pertaining to India's small neighbours. She had time and again stated that even small countries like Bhutan (obliquely Nepal) had been challenging India due to the weak policy pursued by the Janata Government.

In fact, the public level relations between Nepal and India were controversial during the Janata Government because of the frequent interference of some Janata Party leader in the domestic affairs of Nepal. Reacting to the Indian parliamentarian's demand of B.P. Koirala's release, nine members of the National Panchayat of Nepal issued a statement on 11th April 1977 stating that, "...Our friends in India should realise that no nation can tolerate violent and subversive activities."[18]

The period was also marked by political uncertainty in both Nepal and India. The hanging of the deposed Pakistan's Prime Minister, Z.A. Bhutto in 1979 by the Pakistani military junta and Nepali students' demonstration against Bhutto's hanging created a new political climate in

Nepal. The Nepali students while protesting the hanging picked up the issue to start a movement in Nepal. When the Nepali authorities failed to contain the discontent of students, the movement picked up its momentum. As a result, H.M. King Birendra declared the holding of a national referendum on 24th May 1979 on the basis of universal adult franchise through secret ballot for which "all eligible citizens will be asked to vote on the two choices: whether we should set up a multi-party system of government or we should retain the present Panchayat System with suitable reforms." In the referendum, the Panchayat won the election in 1980.[19] This was the turning point in the political history of Nepal in terms of real democracy. Thus, the government and the people level relations with India also improved.

The government-to-government level relations between the two countries were characterised by cordiality during the Janata regime. The exchange of visits of government leaders of both countries and the signing of the two separate treaties on trade and transit and the steps taken for controlling floods were some of the examples of cordial relations.

It was a matter of profound satisfaction that the two countries held similar views on events that were taking place in these regions, but India had not openly demanded the withdrawal of Soviet troops from Afghanistan. Due to the Soviet's intervention in Afghanistan, the Olympic Games had been a major issue not only in Nepal but also in other countries. On 14th March 1980, the Assistant Minister of Education, Mrs. Kalpana Bista inaugurated a photo-exhibition on the Olympic Games organised by the Nepal Soviet Cultural Association in Kathmandu. On that occasion, she declared that "Nepal would participate in the Olympic Games commencing in Moscow in July 1980."[20] As a result she had to resign on the ground that her remarks about Nepal's participation in the Olympic Games were unwarranted. It was amazing that Nepal participated in the Games.

In the 1980s, Nepal-India could not maintain good relations owing to the Nepal's Zone of Peace proposal, different from India international issues like in Afghanistan and Cambodia, decrease the trend of economic dependence on India from 95 per cent to 39.5 per cent up to 1988, Basic Needs Program of Nepal, Work Permit System in three districts (Kathmandu, Lalitpur, and Bhaktapur), and import of the Chinese arms including anti-aircraft guns from China in August 1988.

In fact, there was no need for India to be alarmed when Nepal imported some defensive weapons, such as anti-aircraft guns. Since Nepal did not need to use Indian territory for those imports, authorities in Kathmandu did not find it necessary to inform India about the consignments coming overland via Tibet. But New Delhi considered it an offence, and accused Nepal of breaching the spirit of the 1950 Treaty. Subsequently, the Indian Government imposed a trade and transit blockade on Nepal, at the start of 1989, which lasted 15 months. As a result, many governments, political leaders, mass media, students, and intellectuals openly opposed the blockade. However, the two countries exercised several actions, reactions, counteractions, and counter reactions both in domestic front and international field. Besides, several times, high dignitaries exchanged their visits between the two countries, but the relations could not be improved.

During the blockade period, Prime Minister Rajiv Gandhi's Secretary Mr. G. Sen had proposed a six pages draft to Nepal. After going through the six pages draft proposal of India, the then HMG of Nepal did not discuss on it. Because, the draft was not concerned to national interests of Nepal. As a result, India became furious with Nepal.

A 10 member's Indian official delegation, led by Foreign Secretary S.K. Singh, arrived in Kathmandu on 31st March 1990 on a four day visit with the mandate to work on a comprehensive solution to all outstanding issues.[21]

Basically, his delegation had brought five pages Secret Treaty of 1990 to pressurise the HMG of Nepal to sign on it. The Treaty was proposed to King Birendra. But the King flatly refused and rejected the Treaty. Hence India supported the political parties, ex-servicemen, students, and teachers against the Panchayat System. Subsequently, the movement reached its climax. As a result, King Birendra called the Congress and Communist leader at the Narayanhiti Royal Palace to discuss about the system change. Thus, Multi-Party System announced with the Tripartite Agreement (King, Congress, and communist) on 8th April 1990. After the declaration of the system, the political situation reached its climax on 23rd April. An excited mob attacked on several persons including the policemen. Six policemen were beaten to dead at Teku of Kathmandu. The mob paraded two dead bodies and six injured persons in a push-cart in Kathmandu city. Hence, a curfew was imposed in Kathmandu from

23rd April, to Lalitpur on 25th April, and to Kirtipur the next day. The curfew continued up to May second week.

During the interim period, Krishna Prasad Bhattarai became Prime Minister to make the New Constitution and to success general election. He alongwith Sahan Pradhan, Dr. Devendra Raj Pandey, and senior officials of the government were visited to New Delhi from June 8 to 10, 1990. At the end of the visit, Nepal-India Joint Communique signed by the Prime Minister and the Prime Minister of India, Mr. Vishwanath Pratap Singh in New Delhi on 10th June 1990. Relations became normal only after June 1990.

After the victory of Nepali Congress in the general election, Girija Prasad Koirala became the Prime Minister. He followed the Joint Communique of the former Prime Minister. Besides, he signed on the Tanakpur Treaty during his visit to India. Anti-Indian feeling increased owing to the Tanakpur Treaty. The Supreme Court of Nepal also defeated the then Government of G.P. Koirala in several cases like Labor Act, Citizenship, and Tanakpur. Despite many efforts, Nepal-India relations could not good.

In the Mid-term General Election which was held on 15th November 1994 had bagged 88 seats out of 205 by the CPM (UML) and formed the minority Communist Government by the support of whole Parliament. Man Mohan Adhikari became the Prime Minister during 9 months period. After the fall of this government, Sher Bahadur Deuba formed the tri-partite coalition (Congress, NDP, and some independent Members) government. Prime Minister Deuba visited to India on the invitation of his Indian counterpart Mr. Rao. Both of them signed a Treaty on the Mahakali Integrated Development Project, the Sarada Barrage, the Tanakpur Barrage, and the Pancheshor Project on 12th February 1996. The leaders of 7 leftist parties published a joint statement describing the new Nepal-India Treaty on the Integrated Development of Mahakali River as a betrayal of the interests of the nation.

A new NDP, CPN-UML and NSP coalition government was formed under the Prime Ministership of Lokendra Bahadur Chand. On 19th March 1997, the House of Representatives passed a motion of confidence to the coalition government. Prime Minister I.K. Gujral visited to Nepal on 7th June 1997 and explained that India had been agreed to provide the Phulbari transit route to Nepal on a trail basis for 6 months because of the heavy traffic.

The leader of the Nepali Congress, G.P. Koirala tabled a non-trust motion against the Chand's Government on 2nd October 1997. Prime Minister Chand could not secure his position. Then, Surya Bahadur Thapa, President of the NDP became Prime Minister of Nepal. Owing to the political instability, again G.P. Koirala, S.B. Deuba, L.B. Chand and S.B. Thapa became Prime Minister respectively. However, none of them solved the Maoist problems.

II

National security in its conceptual frame work cannot be observed independently since it is related to the concepts of national interest, national power, and national stability. It is an interdependent notion, shaped by the existence of social forces, international interactions, and the presence of other security reference and the problematic nature of the state.[22]

Historical development of security studies does not build a universally accepted theory to be applicable for all nations. It is influenced by internal and external security environment. The policies adopted by global and regional actors influence over the national security issues. States formulate national security applying foreign policy as its tools. This is an instrumental to demonstrate international commitment. At the same time, understanding other's intention remains as a fear of national security. Small and weak states remain vulnerable from big and strong powers as an organic nature of power hunger. Many states have been victimised in the past because of unknown intention of others. Individual security is assured by the guarantee of universally known fundamental freedoms by incorporating them in the constitution. Therefore, this helps to assess national security. Social harmony, capable defence force, and stable economy are some of the master indicators to view a nation's security. National vision, mission, goals, objectives, and operational strategies provide bases for the formulation of national security and defence doctrine. In sum, each nation's security is surrounded by the perceptions and realities of the history.[23]

The unifier of modern Nepal, Prithvi Narayan Shah had a clearer vision of the characteristics of geography in relation to national security. According to his great instruction:

> This country is like a yam between two rocks. Maintain a treaty of friendship with the Emperor of China. Keep also a treaty of friendship with the emperor of the southern sea (the East India Company). He has taken the plains. He will realise that if Hindustan unites, it will be difficult, and so he will come seeking places for forts. Prepare forts, without burdening the people. Set traps in the trails. One day that force will come. Do not go down to the plains to fight. Withdraw to the hills to fight. Chure Pass will be much-used.[24]

His policy was based on defensive, but when Prime Minister Bhimsen Thapa did not follow and adopted the policy of offensive, had to sign the treaty of 1816 with British India. However, he tried to foil British attempts to bring Nepal into orbit of British sphere of influence by cleverly managing to keep up a show of Nepal's alliance with China in accordance with the terms of the treaty of 1792. After the rise of Jung Bahadur in September 1846, seemed the triumph of British diplomacy.[25] He earned the British appreciation by making a trip to England in 1852 and concluded an extradition treaty with British India in 1855. He also convinced the British government of his friendly and cooperative attitude by sending Nepal's army during India's first struggle for freedom in 1957-58.

Thus, Nepal had long standing relations with British, but owing to British withdrawal from the Indian sub-continent in 1947, some adjustments were necessary. On 9th November 1947, a Tripartite Treaty concluded between Nepal, Independent India, and the British. Under this treaty, Nepal allowed India and British to recruit Gorkhas or Nepali for their respective armies which still exist in practice. In fact, indirectly Nepal and India are members of the NATO. The both countries can be benefited from this treaty if cleverly managed according to time and situation. Moreover, Nepal and Indian signed a Treaty of Peace and Friendship and a Treaty of Trade and Commerce on 31st July 1950. In fact, this Treaty is not equal. Hence it should be amended according to the international environment. Avatar Singh Bhasin, editor of books comprising documents on Nepal-India relations, describes the treaty-bound relationship as feudal and suggests that New Delhi to modernise it. "The sooner it (treaty) is replaced, revised or abandoned the better..." he writes.

The Sino-India War of 1962 had impact on Nepal-India security. The Government of India advised the Nepali Congress leaders to suspend subversive activities against the King's rule. Thus, King Mahendra became successful both in withholding Indian economic pressure and resisting his domestic opposition with the solid backing of the Chinese leaders with whom he had established very good relations.

One of the most irritant factors in Nepal-India relations was the presence of the Indian Military Liaison group in Kathmandu and Indian personnel's in the northern border of Nepal. There were altogether 50 persons including officers who had come to Nepal for training purpose but this number had increased to 300 to assist the Government of Nepal. Moreover 17 northern check posts supervised by 75 Indian personnel. In 1969, Prime Minister Kirtinidhi Bista challenged the validity of the existing mutual security arrangement between the two countries and asked for the withdrawal of the check posts as well as the liaison group. He also referred to the ineffectiveness of the Treaty of Peace and Friendship of 1950 and Arms Assistance Agreement and added that "Nepal could not compromise its sovereignty for India's so called security".[26]

Some Americans felt that India was attempting to circumscribe Nepal's independence. However, the Indians believed that the Americans were upsetting the natural relationship between Nepal and India. Their rivalry was reflected in the village development project.

The friction between the two countries became inevitable on 2nd January 1958, when they joined the Government of Nepal in forming the Regional Transport Organisation (R.T.O.).[27] On the other hand, the Soviet Union was directly involved in the intraregional affairs in South Asia in the mid 1960s. It played a crucial mediatory role between India and Pakistan by negotiating with them in Tashkent. Later the agreement arrived at between India and Pakistan under the Soviet auspices was called the Tashkent declaration in 1965. In fact, India won the war of 1965 by destroying the American patent tanks near the Akhanur bridge of Jammu city. Nepali in Indian army played a great role by sacrificing their live in the war on the one hand and the government of Nepal maintained the neutrality on the other. Earlier, Nepal and India had also signed an Agreement of 1965 on 30th January 1965 in terms of security. But this agreement could not success. Nepal also played a neutral role during the Indo-Pak War of 1971. Many Nepali in the Indian army were killed in the war. Nepal had to suffer refugees of Bangladesh.

The period of 1972 to 1974 has been not good between Nepal and India relations owing to the violent incidents. In the night of 24th August

1972, about 100 persons in military uniform, who were armed with rifles and SMG Gun, came from India and raided Haripur village in Saptari district. They had an encounter with the policemen of the Haripur Police Station. There was an exchange of fire, as a result of which one police constable was killed. They later fled towards Birpur of India, carrying their wounded comrades with them.[28] On 28th August, Indian's Minister of Foreign Affairs disclosed that Nepali living in India had been warned not to act against the declared policy of the Government of India.[29]

The first major incident in 1973 was the hijacking of a Royal Nepal Airlines Corporation plane on 10th June. It was hijacked when a large amount of money belonging to Nepal Rastrabank when it was on a domestic flight from Biratnagar to Kathmandu. It was flown to an unused airstrip near Forbesgunj of Bihar, from where the hijackers escaped with 30 lakh rupees in a jeep kept in readiness by accomplices.[30] Nepal expeditiously the assassination of Partap Singh Kairon, Suchcha Singh, was extradited to India under the extradition treaty but India failed to apprehend the hijackers. Another incident was the burning of the Simha Darbar (the lion palace) of Nepal's Secretariat building on 9th July 1973. Later there was also fire in the Army Headquarter Building in 1973.

The major incidents was took place in this year owing to grenade explosions in different parts of the country. On 16th March 1974, there occurred a hand-grenade explosion at Biratnagar. It took place only a few yards away from where His Majesty King Birendra himself was making his official visit of inspection to the local government offices. The explosion resulted in two deaths but the King was unharmed.[31] In connection of the bomb incident, Girija Prasad Koirala and Yagnya Bahadur Thapa from Forbesgunj make a strong criticism of India for its assurance that "no anti-Nepal activities would be permitted from India soil."[32]

Besides, 16 anti-national elements were reported to have been killed in an encounter with security forces at the Timure Bhot forest of the Okhaldhunga district on 16th December 1974. Captain Yagnya Bahadur Thapa, who was the ringleader of the gang, had been captured by the police. Later, he was sentenced to death by a special tribunal, but he and Bhim Narayan Shrestha shot to death at Kamala River in 1978.

The Indian Lok Sabha granted the status of an Associate State to the tiny Himalayan Kingdom of Sikkim on 4th September 1974. According to elite circle, this action is also directly threatened the security of Nepal.

The Royal Nepal Army (RNA) had to action against the Tibetan Khampa Guerrillas in 1974. The Khampas were well equipped with modern arms and ammunition. Their basic goal was to make Tibet free from the Nepali land with the help of external powers. The government of Nepal could not tolerate it owing to the threat for the security of Nepal from China. Hence, the RNA suppressed the Khampa guerrillas by capturing the Khampas and their weapons within few days. Many Khampas were killed in an ambush at Tinker in Darchula district of Nepal alongwith their leader General Wangdi. In fact, Nepal is fully aware of the activities of refugees of the past in Nepal in connection of the Bhutanese refugees. Against this background, King Birendra declared Nepal's Zone of Peace proposal on 25th February 1975 at the farewell reception hosted at the conclusion of his coronation. The King identified the objectives that:

> We adhere to the policy of Non-alignment because we believe that it brightens the prospects of peace. We need peace for our security, we need peace for our independence, and we need peace for our development. Our people genuinely desire peace in our country, in our region and everywhere in the world. It is with this earnest desire to institutionalise peace that I stand to make proposition that my country Nepal, be declared a Zone of Peace.[33]

The proposal became the major foreign policy objective when on 15th December 1980 through the third amendment it was incorporated in Nepal's constitution. During the 15 years period of Nepal's Zone of Peace since the declaration, 116 countries had formally supported it including 4 veto powers of the United Nations. But very close friend India, did not support it. After the restoration of democracy, the proposal removed from the foreign policy goal and the new constitution of kingdom of Nepal. As a result, Nepal has been suffering from the Zone of War instead of Zone of Peace.

Nepal's Maoist movement had begun on 13th February 1996. It was a fragment of United People's Front (Samyukta Jana Morcha), prior to that United People's Front (UPF) participated in the first parliamentary election in 1990 and had won 9 seats out of 205. Mid-term election was held in 1994. The UPF was vanquished in this election. It is not still clear to the Nepali whether it was an intention or a coincidence that during January/February 1996, Nepal's ruling and opposition parties were engaged in a controversial Mahakali Treaty. At the same time, splinted faction of UPF went underground declaring themselves as Maoist by declaring a People's War.[34]

Infiltration, hostage taking, indiscriminate sabotages, hijacking, destroying installations, indiscriminate killing, seeking desirable chain reaction, adopting the policy of hit and run tactics to engage the state in military confrontation are some terrorist activities all of which can have strategic implications. It may adversely affect the government's ability to adopt a flexible negotiating position. In an atmosphere of violence and threats to personal security, the government must take care of each incident. For combating internally generated terrorism, the government can take neither its hand off nor blame others. In Nepal's case, internal security has been threatened since the Maoist insurgency began.[35]

Initially Maoists support was primarily in the western highlands, but was growing in almost all of Nepal. At present, they are decreasing in their number owing to the internal unified command and external cooperation. A unit used to number 10 to 20 insurgents. .The insurgents steal money, arms and other valuables during raids, to acquire funds for purchasing arms, ammunition or training from supporters. For example, Maoists used automatic rifles and bomb in the assault. Significantly, Nepal and India agreed that Maoist support had come from Indian separatist groups such as the People's War Group in Andhra Pradesh and the Maoist Coordination Centre in Bihar. Nepali Police claim these groups have assisted Maoists in establishing training camps and programmes.[36]

After the tragic events of 11th September 2001, the United States have enhanced its concerned interest in Nepal's insurgency. It is difficult to say, but it is unusual that the US has suddenly chosen to increase contacts with the Himalayan kingdom that it has officially known for more than 55 years. Kathmandu and Washington established diplomatic relations on 25th April 1947 before independent India and Pakistan were born. And Nepal was never under British colonial rule. Rather Nepal fought the 3 years war with the British and the 3 wars with the North.

Nepal started to accept US assistance after the formal establishment of ties, adding up to about US $700 million in 50 years. The size of the annual package grew only recently US $ 38 million after the visit of US Secretary of State Colin Powel in January 2002. The military component in the package was allowed to be slightly increased in view of the need to make the RNA capable of effectively fighting against Maoist guerrillas. Some grant money was spent in procuring small arms from the US and Belgium. In fact, aid programmes are the outcome of present day dynamics of international power structure... Diplomacy of economic development has its relevance in the present day world order.[37]

About 9,000 people have lost their lives in 8 years of armed insurgency in Nepal. The victims include Nepalis working as guards at the US embassy in Kathmandu as well as in a US-aided development project in the western region. A ceasefire was agreed in last year between the government and rebels, but it is for from certain whether stuttering talks will bring peace to this largely mountainous country.[38]

In fact, the US assistance is very modest, and Nepal's present difficulties are real. But India is not happy at these developments. New Delhi's displeasure has been made public through periodic pronouncements, and by senior officials handling India's external affairs. Foreign Secretary Kanwal Sibal has spoken several times in Paris, New Delhi and elsewhere that Nepal must not take "outside assistance" to quell a domestic rebellion. But Indian ambassador Shyam Saran told a newspaper interview in Kathmandu, "The government of India is in close touch with the US government concerning the developments in Nepal, since both are friends of Nepal. There is no competition or rivalry between India and the US in Nepal".[39]

India wants Nepal not to buy defence supplies elsewhere, even if they cannot always give assurances that the goods made in India would maintain high quality. This means, they would like Nepal to spend the American grants to purchase weaponry from Indian manufacturers.

Naturally, 11 September has a great impact to fight against the Maoists in Nepal. After the help of machine and money alongwith training facilities have not only increased fighting capacity, but also boost the moral and morale of the RNA, Armed Force, Police, and other components. It is believed that if the 11 September had not happened Nepal would have been the rule of Maoists. In addition, the capture of Saddam in Iraq has also helped to fight against the Maoists. Moreover, India has also honestly handed over to politburo members alongwith other members to Nepal. As a result, about 700 Maoists have also been surrendered. Thus, the Maoists are unable to attack on the forces as before. It is better to come in negotiation for political stability by giving up their arms and ammunition. In short, the solution of Maoist problems will be an great achievement to both Nepal and India. Since the negotiation is a medicine to cure the disease of politics.

The hijacking of Indian Airlines plane IC 814 after it left the Tribhuvan International airport Kathmandu on 24th December 1999 once again brought for Indian vulnerabilities from its northern border. The airliner had 178 passengers and crew on board. Amid high drama in the air over Lucknow, it was flown to Amritsar, Lahore, and Dubai before finally landing at Kandahar, Afghanistan. However, the passengers were freed after eight days of negotiator on 31st December 1999. The hijackers had stabbed one to death by the time. This incident brought the main issue. Even as the drama was fast unfolding, Indian media consistently claimed that one of the hijackers was Gajendra Man Tamrakar, Nepali national. Nepal was quite helpless to deny the claim and come up with a proof that he was innocent of any wrong doing. The Indian satellite channels took advantage of this to falsely accuse a Nepali citizen, with no proof whatsoever to support their claim. It was also true that acknowledged the management failure its staff at the TIA in the media.

In a statement issued in Parliament, the then Foreign Minister, Jaswant Singh said:

> The hijacking incident has once again highlighted the complicity of Pakistan and of organisations patronised and supported by it in terrorist acts against India.... The hijacking was masterminded by Pakistan's ISI with the assistance of the Harkat ul Mujahideen.[40]

In fact, the incident not only illustrates the strategic significance of Nepal in India's security parameters but also exposes how serious were the security lacunae in the northern border. The relations between the two countries became uneasy owing to the incident. However, flights between the two countries were stopped and were resumed after Nepal agreed to allow Indian officials to carry out security checks at the airport.

India movie star Hrithik Roshan sparked riots in Nepal after he allegedly expressed dislike for the country and its people in an interview. He later denied making the remarks, but five people had died in the violence, several Indian businesses in Kathmandu were destroyed, and relations between the two countries took a turn for the worse. The Indian Embassy in Kathmandu had denied any statements against Nepal attributed to Hrithik Roshan in a television interview. The embassy said the text of the interview given by the star to former actress and TV presenter Simi Garewal on the STAR Plus channel on December 14, 2000 was available on the web sites indiafm.com and hrithikroshan.com/articles/simigare2.htm. The actor issued denials that any disparaging remarks were uttered against Nepal by Hrithik in the interview. Hrithik said he loved Nepal and had tremendous respect for its people. He said he had never given such an interview and this was a figment of imagination of some vested interests. In addition, refugees of Bhutan in Nepal has also been an irritant factor in terms of Nepal-India relations, and this issue can be solved through a mediation of India.

Vulnerabilities and Threats of Nepal and India

Land, people, and their properties are the physical foundation of a nation state. A combination of vulnerabilities and threats refers insecurity. If any danger imposed to its physical foundation, people and their properties is threat. Issues like poverty, illiteracy, diseases, unemployment, dishonest political leaders, corruption, weak constitution, insurgency, undisciplined forces, poor intelligence, demographic migration, open borders, disharmony among ethnic communities, and religions lead to vulnerabilities impact on both internal and external security.

In addition, interstate threats like nuclear war, chemical/biological weapons, conventional arms, border conflict, and proliferation of weapons of mass destruction are danger in the world. The transnational threats like organised crime, drug cartels, migrant smuggling, arms trafficking, money laundering, hacking of information, terrorist groups, national motives, political motives, illegal immigration, information disparities, sudden Refugee flows, financial market panics also slow poisons. The ecological threats like over-population, water shortages, food shortages, damage from seasonal flooding, wildfires, air and water contamination, emergent infectious diseases, invader species, diminishing bio-diversity, ozone depletion, climate change, global warming and its regional and local effects must be aware of in time so that they could be prevent from danger. Finally, autonomous natural threats like volcanic eruption, earthquake, hurricane or typhoon, tornado, drought and animal predation are difficult to control, but can be managed if properly considered them.[41] Taking into consideration the above mentioned different type of threats and vulnerabilities, more or less they are similar to both Nepal and India. Hence, the two countries must understand the prevention from these elements for the security of Nepal and India. But this does not mean that other countries are not allowed.

In fact, Indian security lies in maintaining territorial integrity and deterring threats emanating from neighbouring countries, especially nuclear powers like China and Pakistan, with whom wars have also been fought. Pakistani forces are allegedly fueling secessionist movements in Kashmir and northeastern India, both materially and morally. Toward the end of 2001, India and Pakistan deployed troops on the border following a terrorist attack on the Indian Parliament building.[42] India is watching closely the implementation of the pledge for peace from General Pervez Musharaf, the President of Pakistan.

Another aspect of Indian security is maintaining a say in the international order. When India tried to assert herself in the South Asian region in the 1980s, it proved to be oppressive to the neighbouring smaller states, such as Nepal, on which India imposed a unilateral embargo. Basically, Nepal's security perspective has been largely Indo-centric. India does not perceive a direct military threat from Nepal, but her major security concern is that a third party can have easy access by gaining a foothold in Nepal due to borders that lack any natural barriers. However, the difficult terrain leading to China has forced Nepal to rely heavily on India for access to sea. The 80s were a taxing period for bilateral relations between Nepal and India. It reached an all-time low when Nepal purchased military weaponry from China worth US$ 20 million in 1988. Taking into consideration the vulnerabilities and threats for the security of Nepal, the following tables 1 and 2 can be useful.

Table-1: Internal Threats of Nepal

1. Poverty,
2. Illiteracy
3. Unemployment
4. Rampant corruption
5. Political instability
6. Lack of check and balance in the constitution of 1990 of Nepal
7. Defective administrative machinery

8. Lack of big industries
9. Lack of sufficient road
10. Lack of transportation
11. Lack of sufficient communication
12. Lack of peace
13. Lack of security
14. Lack of fair election
15. Ethnic
16. Religion
17. Multi-culture
18. Multi-language
19. Different topography
20. Health
21. Population
22. Lack of management of natural resources
23. Lack of management of agriculture
24. Banking system
25. Violations of human rights
26. Artificial educational certificates
27. Girls trafficking
28. Regional inequality in the development budget
29. Weak intelligence department
30. Lack of able political leaders
31. Lack of nationalism of the political parties
32. Lack of proper man in proper place in political appointments

33. Break down of statehood
34. Designs attempts at turning into a satellite state
35. Espionage activities aimed at weakening the potential of Nepal
36. Threat to Constitution
37. Threat to Monarchy
38. Misunderstanding between the armed forces, police and army
39. Misunderstanding between the military and civilian population
40. Contradictions within the national leadership on issues of national security
41. Discloser of state secrets
42. Weakening state governance
43. Outbreak of famine and natural calamities
44. Lack of a uniform government policy
45. Failure to introduce world advanced technologies
46. Inability to make full use of the national intellectual potential and of trained personnel in the country
47. Use of the foreign mass media by any force as an instrument to increase tension in the country
48. Disregard for the cultures of other people
49. Emergence of an intellectual and young generation vacuum in the society
50. Smuggling historical and artistic value abroad
51. Spread of alcoholic and drugs addiction
52. Shortage of drinking water
53. Depletion of the forest
54. Drying up of rivers and lakes
55. Threat to Monarchy

56. Threat to Constitution

Table-2 : External Threats of Nepal

1. Armed aggression
2. Global crises
3. Provocative actions and pressures by other States in terms citizens right and freedoms
4. Disrupt the national unity of the people
5. Regional crises
6. Foreign interests
7. Pressuring the sovereign relations of Nepal with other states
8. Neighbours' crises
9. Emergence of dual citizenship
10. Organisation of terrorist against Nepal
11. Border violations
12. Dissemination of false information by outside sources
13. Espionage against Nepal
14. Flood
15. Influx of foodstuffs, chemicals and consumer goods adversely affecting the health of the population
16. Imposition other countries policies on Nepal
17. Water resources
18. Raw materials for the industries
19. Attempts to resolve disputes by force
20. Migrations
21. Refugees
22. Imposition of ideological control over Nepal

23. Citizenship crises
24. External debt
25. Political control
26. Ecological calamities
27. Threat to Monarchy
28. Economic control
29. Spread of infectious human and animal diseases
30. Terrorists activities
31. Military control
32. Making use of ethnic and religious differences of opinion
33. Entrapping of Nepali citizens by foreign agencies and services through brainwashing and using them to the detriment of Nepal's interests

Apparently Nepali are getting experiences from the past like the Dasdhunga Incident in which Madan Kumar Bhandari, the then General Secretary and Member Jivraj Asrit of the Communist Party of United Marxist Leninist died in a road accident at Dasdhunga, Chitwan district of Nepal on 16th May 1993. But the driver was safe without injury. Another incident which indicated at growing threat unfolded on 29th June 1998, Mirza Dilshad Beg, Member of Parliament of the Rastriya Prajatantra Party (RPP) was gunned down near his residence in Siphal, Kathmandu. However, this is one of the incidents which were thoroughly probed by the police. Besides, a Japanese monk, Yutaka Nawatame, was shot dead on the order coming from Abrar Ahmed, and Indian national in the first week of July 1997 in the premises of Buddhist shrine in Lumbini. Yet the most unprecedented incident was the Royal massacre at the Naranhiti Royal Palace in Kathmandu on 1st June 2001. Even in India, such incidents are happening time to time. Hence, the two countries must be fully aware of possible incidents in the future.

Global Strategic Vision

The entire world is moving from the realism to the neo-realism theory on the ground of the politically democratisation, economically privatisation, science and technologically transportation and communication, geographically environmentalisation, culturally socialisation, and strategically demilitarisation. An emergence of the United States of Europe, The victory of the Allied Forces led by the United States in the Gulf War of 1991, the end of Cold War, the down fall of communism, the break down of the balance of power after the disintegration of the Soviet Union, and emergence of unipolar world, have constituted the neo-realism.

According to Kenneth N. Wartz, neo-realism means different from the old realism. It proposes a solution to the problem of distinguishing factor internal to international system. It establishes the autonomy of international politics by showing in the form of a picture of international system as a whole. It immediately can distinct and connect with structural and unit level. Basically, dynamic density disrupts a simple society and transforms it into a complex one. It is a social force developing in society that, under certain circumstances, may first disrupt and then transform it.

Mackinder noted that mobility upon the ocean was the natural rival of the horse and camel mobility in the heart of the continent. The discovery of the Cape route to India and the Far East, had helped to connect the western and eastern coastal navigations of Euro-Asia, and thereby neutralised the strategically advantage of the grassland. Railways work the greater wonders in the grassland, because they directly replace horse and camel mobility, the road stage of development having here been omitted. Mackinder was clear in his mind that a sea power could, in the long run, be no stronger than the land base.

According to Mackinder's strategic formula:

Who rules East Europe commands the Heartland,

Who rules the Heartland commands the World-Island,

Who rules the World-Island commands the World.[43]

The United Kingdom became success to rule the most parts of the world after adopting the Mackinder's strategic formula, but after the Second World War, it could not maintain command neither in the East Europe nor in the Heartland owing to emergence of the Soviet Union as a Super Power. The Soviet maintained the balance of power up to 1990 with the United States of America, but it could not keep its power after the down fall of the communism and disintegration itself. At present, Spykman's Rimland Theory has replaced the Heartland theory in the 90s.

To Spykman, Mackinder's dictum about global strategy appeared to be false. He wrote that if at all, there is need for a slogan for global power politics, it must be:

Who controls the Rimländ rules Eurasia;

Who rules Eurasia controls the destinies of the world.[44]

The Heartland appeared less important than the Rimland. He was also convinced that it is a combination of land and sea powers controlling the Rimland that would in all probability control the essential power relations of the world, because this combination would emerge as the owner of far greater resources, manpower, and mobility than the Heartland or any other combination.

It is viewed that not only Nepal and India but whole Asia will be in danger of disintegration under the Rimland theory. In fact, time has come to think better way after the disintegration of the Super Power country the then Soviet Union. Everybody knows that more than 80 per cent conflicts are in Asia. In fact, all the countries are suffering owing to the theory of neo-realism and Rimland. Hence, India must understand to keep best understanding among the neighbouring countries for it security, because its security means security of South Asia. Another method of disintegration theory is the theory of Shatter belts of S.B. Cohen. It maintains that certain regions on the globe, because of their complex ethnic, religious, politics, ideological, economic, and physical composition, ,intrinsically stand out as areas of tension. They represent weak zones in international politics. Outside powers are attracted to them by virtue of their strategic location and resources. As regions that do not clearly belong to one or the other power bloc, they tend to become centres of international conflict.[45] This theory can be implemented through the NGOs and INGOs funded by the external powers.

Religion

When Nepali talk of only one Hindu State and only Hindu King in the world and also incorporated even in the constitution of 1990 of Nepal, but Nepal's national flag is belong to Vedas which is triangle alongwith the Sun and the Moon and different from the flags of the countries of the world. The triangle means-creator, preserver, and destroyer (Brahma, Vishnu, and Maheshwar) the meaning of the Sun and the Moon is no beginning and no ending. It is Sanatana. It means, Nepal will survive for ever, there is no ending of it.

We follow only foreign writer's books that turned and twisted our history and literatures very far from the facts of Nepal. The time has come. to demonstrate our indigenous religion, philosophy, and culture in the world so that the identity of Nepal could be linked up from Golden Age to present Age. In the Golden days, there was no any religion except the Sanatana Dharma. (46) The word Sanatana means from the beginning and the word Dharma means humanitarian knowledge. Sanatana Dharma has no beginning time but other religions have date (Buddhism-567 B.C.; Jainism-546 B.C.; Christianity-4 B.C.; Confucianism-551 B.C.; Taoism-604 B.C, Zoroastrianism-6th century; Islam-570 A.D.; Sikhism-1469-1538 A.D.; Bahai-19th century).

Vedas are the oldest scripture in the world which contain humanitarian knowledge. There are four parts of Vedas scripture. They are Rig Veda, Yajur Veda, Sama Veda, and Atharva Veda. The gists of Vedas are: "The Whole world is a family" (Vashudhaiva Kutumbakum), "No ending and no beginning of the universe", and "Aham Brahman Ashmi" (I am Brahman). Facts speak themselves that all the religions born under the umbrella of Vedic Sanatana Dharma. But in India, Sanatana Dharma became known as Hindu Dharma or Hinduism, while Buddhist people still practice as Buddhist Dharma. King Mahendra of Nepal, strategically incorporated Hindu religion in the 1962 constitution of Nepal, the same continued in the constitution of 1990. Hence, Nepal became only one Hindu State and only one Hindu King in the world. Basically, all the religions of the world were born from Vedic Sanatana Dharma. In fact, Shiva, Vishnu, Ram, and Krishna are not the Hindu, they are Sanatana. When we talk of King of Nepal, incarnation of Vishnu, how can we say Hindu King? King means not only the Hindu but the King of all religions, castes, and communities. It is my vision; the religion Hindu is not only the threat for security of Nepal but also to India. I believe, the time has come to replace the Hindu into Sanatana Dharma so that all the religions and castes could be accommodated for peace, security, and development. This is also a key to solve the problem of Hindu-Muslim in India.

Conclusion

Nepal's political and security relations with India begin since the time of Golden Age. Geographically, they are as old as the majestic

Himalayan range. Since time immemorial, water of Himalaya landmass of Nepal flowing down into India and Indian Ocean's water cycle for raining has been an unprecedented and incomparable relation between them. The interplay of these geo-socio-cultural factors is reflected in the manner of dress, language, food, and way of life of the people. Bhagawan Ram married with Sita, daughter of King Janak. Pandavas were also secretly resided at Morang district of Nepal near the palace of Birat King of Nepal. Bhagawan Krishna accompanied with his son Pradyumna and Gopala Bansha came in Nepal. Pradyumna married two wives at a time, one with Pravawati, sister of Mahendra Daman Giant, King of Chandana Giri and another with Chandrawati, daughter of Suryaketu King of Mrigrendra Shikhar to establish peace and security in Nepal. There are several exchanges of marriage between the two countries. Even today, Crown Prince Paras married with Ms. Himani Singh of India.

Politically, they are adopting the Multi-Party Democracy. Both are the members of South Asia, SAARC, NAM, and the United Nations. They have appealed to end hostilities anywhere in the world in favour of a negotiated settlement of disputes. Both have been opposing the colonialism, neocolonialism, racism, and intervention in the affairs of others. Economically, they are coming closer to each other in the field of economic cooperation like industries, trade, transit, and water resources. But Nepal is landlocked, nuclear locked, Hindu constitutional monarch, and least developed country. It is also small in size than India particularly in geography, population, army, development, and resources. India is also developing its nuclear power. It is secular and republic state. Apart from these facts, the following points are also important to understand to strengthen the political and security relations between the two countries:

- New Delhi has recognised Nepal's independence and sovereign status, but it has equally made efforts to bring Nepal under its defence umbrella by using the political parties. Nepal wants to correct it by pursuing a genuine policy of nonalignment and maintaining equidistance from India and China.
- Both countries have demonstrated their divergent approaches on some international issues. Yet such divergent lines do not clash with India's vital interest including its security interest.
- Nepal's political and security relations with India are close than any other countries, but India should take into

consideration that Nepal is also a close neighbour of China. Sometimes, when India fails to recognise this reality, an atmosphere of distrust arises.

- Nepal is a small landlocked country with no access to the sea. So it expects that a country like India should always sympathise with the economic interest of Nepal by allowing Nepal to diversify its trade with other countries. Major irritants exist in relations owing to this issue like embargo.
- Whether imported from India or other countries, all goods in Nepal are foreign. Non-Indian goods have been imported into Nepal and are redirected to Indian market by traders. India is always lodging its complaints against Nepal's inability to stop such illegal flow of foreign goods from Nepal. Yet the Indian border authorities and tourists, besides black marketers and smugglers, are creating much difficulty in their relations. Unless the two countries take effective joint steps for overcoming this problem by regulating the 1760 kilometers open borders, their relations are likely to suffer.
- Another aspect that has been generating problems in their relations is the issue related to the water resources. India maintains that the rivers flowing from Nepal to India should be harnessed jointly thereby prohibiting any third country from entering into the arrangement. India's relations with Bangladesh are also equally disturbed by this issue, as Bangladesh wants to include Nepal for harnessing the river flowing in the territories.
- A Tripartite Treaty of 1947 between Nepal, Independent India, and the British has been playing a foundation role of security relations among them. Indirectly, Nepal and India are the members of the NATO. Nepali recruitment in Indian army under this treaty is an important in terms of security of the two countries. In addition, Nepali in Indian army has been playing a role of integration. In addition, the Treaty of Peace and Friendship, 1950 has been irritating factor since the very beginning, so it must be amended according to the time and situation. Nevertheless, military relations between two countries have been an example since the very beginning.

- There must be reciprocal in terms of extradition. Recent hand over of Maoist Politburo and general Members from India to the government of Nepal was an example of the Extradition Treaty.

- The two countries must be aware of the Heartland theory, Rimland theory, and Shatter Belts theory to prevent from disintegration. Because these theories are slowly implementing not only in two countries but also in the entire Asia.

- Their vision must be cleared in the present environment so that missions, goals, and objectives can be achieved through their political and security strategy based on tactics. The changes of negative attitude of the authorities can be possible after understanding universal vision. Then only, the two countries can win the political stability and security without using the politics and security.

- Another basic threat factor is Hindu religion. For security of Nepal, it should replace the Hindu religion by adopting the Sanatana Dharma in the Constitution. There must be Sanatana State and Sanatana King instead of Hindu State and Hindu King. Because Sanatana is the umbrella Dharma of the world. This factor is also applicable in India taking into consideration the fact of Ram Janmabhumi's Mandir. Ram is not Hindu. Ram is Sanatana. So the vision must be cleared in this context.

References

1. Mukti Nath Khanal (Translator), Nepal-Mahatmya, Kathmandu: Nepal Rajakiya Pragnya-Pratishthan, 1972, pp. 75-87.

2. Jitendra Dhoj Khand, Nepal's Relations, Cooperation, and Peace: A Study of South Asia, 1971-1980, Kathmandu: Prava Khand, 1984 pp. 4-17.

3. —, "Neorealism and Nepal's Zone of Peace" in Astha (Journal of Nepal in Perspective), No. 1, Visheshanka, Year-1, Kathmandu: Nepal Graduates Association, p. 10.

4. —, Nepal's *op. cit.* p.10.

5. *Ibid.* p. 11.
6. *Ibid.*
7. *Ibid.*
8. *Ibid.* p.12.
9. The Rising Nepal, September 9, 1974.
10. The Samaya, September 19, 1974.
11. The Arpan Weekly, September 6, 1974. See also The Gorkhapatra, November 23, and The Weekly Minor, November 21, 1974.
12. The Samaya, September 19, 1974.
13. The Matribhumi Weekly, June 9, 1975.
14. Jitendra Dhoj Khand, Nepal's *op.cit.* p. 31.
15. The Times of India, November 6-7, 1976.
16. Paramanand, the Nepali Congress in Exile, Delhi: University Book House, 1978, pp. 47-89. See also Bhola Chatterji, Palace, People and Politics: Nepal in Perspective, Delhi: Ankur Publishing House, 1980, pp. 9-39.
17. Asad Hussin and Asifa Anwar, Conflict in Asia: A Case Study of Nepal, Delhi: Classical Publications, 1969, p. 69.
18. The Samaj, April 16, 1977.
19. The Rising Nepal, May 24, 1979.
20. The Gorkhapatra, March 15, 1980.
21. The Gorkhapatra, April 1, 1990.
22. Muthiah Alagappa, "Conceptualising Security: Hierarchy and Conceptual Travelling", Asian Security Practice: Material and Ideational Influences, Muthiah Alagappa (ed.) (California: Stanford University Press, 1998), p. 68.
23. Kama Bahadur Thapa, National Security of Nepal 1990-2000: A Study of Concept, Vulnerabilities and Threats, unpublished

Ph.D. Dissertation, Tribhuvan University, Kathmandu, 2002, pp. 32-33.

24. L.F. Stiller, S.J., Prithvi Narayan Shah in the Light of Dibya Upadesh (Kathmandu: Himalayan Book Centre, 1989), pp. 42-43.

25. Anirudha Gupta, Politics in Nepal: A Study of Post-Rana Political Development and Party Politics (New Delhi: Allied Publishers, 1964, 1964) pp. 11-13.

26. S.D. Muni, "India's Mutual Security Arrangements with Nepal", Institute for Defence Studies and Analysis Journal, Vol. IV (197 1), p. 61.

27. Eugene Bramer Mihaly, Foreign Aid and Politics in Nepal (London: Oxford University Press, 1965), p. 82.

28. The Gorkhapatra and The Naya Samaj, August 28, 1972.

29. *Ibid.*

30. The Rising Nepal June 11, 1973.

31. The Gorkhapatra March 17, 1974.

32. Dainik Nepal, March 28,1974.

33. His Majesty's Government of Nepal, Proclamation, Speeches and Message (Kathmandu: Department of Information, 1977), p. 121.

34. Kama Bahadur Thapa, *op.cit.*, p. 205

35. *Ibid.* p. 206.

36. www.media-watch.otp-/articles/1000/6.html

37. M.D. Dharmadasani, Indian Diplomacy in Nepal (Jaipur: Aalekh, 1976), p. 175.

38. www.times.com/atimes/South Asia/EH1 3Dfo2.html

39. *Ibid.*

40. www.observerindia.com/analysis/AO04.htm

41. Durch, William J., "Searching for National Security: Threat and Response in the Age of Vulnerability" (Report 30), (Washington DC: The Henry L. Stimson Centre, 1999), p. 48. Quoted Karna Bahadur Thapa, *op.cit.*, p. 154.
42. The New Delhi Television, "We the People", January 14, 2002.
43. Ramesh Dutta Dikshit, Political Geography, 2nd, ed. (New Delhi: Tata Mcgraw-Hill Publishing Company Limited, 1995), p. 108.
44. *Ibid.* p. 114.
45. *Ibid.* p. 140.
46. info@yogausa.com(*SANATNA DHARMA*-The word Sanatana means from the beginning and the word Dharma means humanitarian knowledge. In the olden days, there was no religion. People used to follow Sanatana Dharma which is based on Vedas. Vedas are the oldest scripture in the world which contain humanitarian knowledge. There are four parts of Vedas scripture. Nepalis, Indians and Chinese people believe that the Vedas scripture was given by the god to four holy saints. In other words, Sanatana Dharma means humanitarian knowledge given by the god. Before 300 years ago in India, Sanatana Dharma became known as Hindu Dharma or Hinduism, while Buddhist people still practice as Dharma).

6

Indo-Nepal Relations A Historical Perspective

V. Chandramouliswara Rao

Geo-Political considerations have compelled both India and Nepal to establish and continue the policy of good neighborliness in July 1950, Nepal signed two treaties with India, a treaty of Peace and friendship and a Treaty of Trade and Commerce. The treaty of Peace and Friendship required India and Nepal to consult mutually on matters relating to national security. The second Treaty deals with the special relationship between India and Nepal and India's direction and guidance in Trade and Commerce between the two nations.

Under the Treaty of 1950, both countries agreed not to: Tolerate any threat to the security of the other by a foreign aggressor. To deal with such contingencies both the Governments shall consult each other and devise effective counter-measures. The Treaty recognised Nepal's sovereignty, territorial integrity and independence.

Addressing Lok Sabha in December 1950, Prime Minister Nehru stated that India permitted Nepal to "develop other foreign relations". At the same time, India took up the stand that in view of the Chinese in Tibet, India had "special responsibility" with regard to Nepal. India took the position that no other country can have as intimate a relationship with Nepal as ours is and asked every other country to appreciate the intimate geographical and cultural relationship that exists between India and Nepal.

The waves of freedom and democracy sweeping India also spread to Nepal. Like the Indian Political movement, the Nepalese movement also had to socialistic texture. The Nepalese National Congress was formed in India in 1946 and depend on Indian National leadership for guidance and support. Though India restrained itself from interfering in the domestic matters of Nepal, it wants Nepal too, to develop into a democratic society.

There were a number of factors that called for 'special relationship' between Nepal and India. Factors like geographical contiguity, strong socio-cultural and ethnic identities between the two countries and Nepal's excessive dependence on economic front could be visited in this regard. Nepal's special relationship with India could be judged by the New Year broadcast in April 1953 of king Tribhuwan.

"I want to make a particular mention of our very cordial and affectionate relations with our neighbour, India. We are akin to each other in so many spheres: Religious, social, geographical, historical and so forth. Even Nepal's democracy is the result of an inspiration from India". India being the dominant partner in the special relationship, exercised immense and decisive influence over the affairs of Nepal. The Indian Government and leaders were often called on to resolve infights among the Nepali politicians. Even the Cabinet reshuffles in Nepal took place in accordance with the Indian advice in early 1950s. The appointment of M.P. Koirala as the New Prime Minister in November 1951 was said to have been made at the instance of Indian Mission in Kathmandu.

Nepal heavily relied on India in the crushing of lawless elements in Nepal by seeking Indian Police help. To find a permanent solution of the crossing by criminals on either side, Nepal and India signed the Treaty of Extradition in October 1953. Nepali Police Officers also received training in India. In the field of Civil administration also, Nepal sought Indian help for the administrative reorganisation to make the system amenasle for the tasks of development and welfare. The government of India also started giving economic assistance to Nepal in 1951. In May 1954 an "Aide Memoire" was signed between Nepal and India which stated as follows:

1. The Government Nepal would consult Government of India with regard to Foreign Policy and matters connected with foreign powers while India too would consult Nepal in all matters relating to the latter.
2. In particular, Nepal would consult India in all matters affecting Sino-Nepalese relations.

3. The Indian Missions, at the request of Nepal, would take care of the interests of Nepal and would give all possible help to Nepali nationals.

4. The two governments would, from time to time, exchange information relating to foreign affairs and relations with foreign powers in so far as they affected each other.

The Aide Memoire was not given the formal shape of an Agreementy the letter and spirit of it had been observed in practice between India and Nepal, throughout the Tribhuwan period. During the visits the king of Nepal and Government leaders the Prime Minister and Ministers, to New Delhi in early 1950s, it was again reiterated that the foreign policy of the Nepalese Government should be co-ordinated with the Foreign Policy of India. The then Foreign Minister of Nepal D.R. Regmi said in a press conference in New Delhi on 8 May 1954: "Nepal's foreign policy was similar with India's". We being very close to each other have to face several problems, difficulties and dangers and thus we will have to adopt a similar policy on many issued. India had very high stakes in the security and defence of Nepal. The strategic considerations that formed the basis of India's Policy towards Nepal in general were repeatedly stressed by Indian leadership.

The Treaty of Peace and Friendship (July 1953) had adequate provisions for mutual consultations to devise effective counter measures in case of any threat to security of either. By 1955, as the process of change in the domestic and external milieu advanced in Nepal the pattern of its special "special relations" with India also changed Alternatively, Nepal started evolving the policy of balance of power in relation to the neighboring region. The Panchasheel agreement between India and China prompted Nepal to normalise in relations with China. Prime Minister Nehru played an effective role in this accord. Nepal had cultural and historical ties with China and a 500 mile long common border with Tibet.

Consequent to the ascendancy of king Mahendra to the throne of Nepal, anti-Indian sentiments started expressing in Nepal. India was charged with interfering in the internal affairs of Nepal. In June 1951 there was the first black-flag demonstration when Nehru visited Kathmandu. In 1954 a second demonstration was staged against a visiting Parliamentary delegation from India. Nepal's anti-Indian attitude is partly the result of its size-psychology. Nepal is surrounded on three sides by Indian territory. Economically, Nepal is heavily dependent on India. The political leadership in Nepal realised that overwhelming presence of India toward the Nepalese sovereignty and its National stature. With the advent of the Nepali Congress Government headed by B.P. Koirala on 27 May 1959 Pro-Indian Foreign Policy initiatives started emerging. Koirala in his statement declared; "Nepal of today is not the Nepal of Yesterday. She is making new relations with different countries. Nepal's relations with India are historic and inseparable and they are growing closer.

The Sino-Indian Conflict of October-November 1962 had a most salutary effect on both India and Nepal. Indo-Nepalese border trade was resumed. India started entering into a new relationship with Nepal based on the understanding that it was for Nepal to decide for itself the type of government that it should have and that Indian territory was not allowed to be used for anti government activities. The Sino-Indian conflict of 1962 resulted in some hard thinking in both India and Nepal. India realised that any direct involvement on its part in supporting or opposing a particular government in Nepal was self-defeating. India espected Nepal not to lean towards China. India also wanted Nepal to take its strategic interests into account in following its own independent foreign policy.

Nepal maintained neutrality in the Sino-Indian conflict. Nepal even restrained itself from the pleas that it should moderate between India and China. While China was not averse to the Plea that Nepal should mediate between China and India, it held the view: "We know Nepal is limited in power and her efforts may not get the response from the other side (India)". While India did not favour Nepalese interventions in resolving its differences with China, for strategic reasons.

7

Nepal's Political and Security Relations with Special Reference to India

Amresh Kumar Singh

Nepal and India, since time immemorial have been linked by geography, history, religion, culture, language, beliefs and a number of factors.[1] However, the impact of this inheritance upon political, economic and strategic variables has also produce" a complex dynamics of intimate intervention, which has vast areas of rapport and understanding, co-existing with equally powerful expressions of conflicts and divergence between the two neighbours".[2] This paper focuses on some key issues of Nepal-India relations. The first section gives an overview of the relationship. The second section deals with the determinants of the relationship. The third section focuses on the 1950 treaty and the question of revision of the treaty. The fourth section is on security concerns and the last section provides the future prospects of Nepal's relation with India.

A Historical Overview

As a unified political and social system, the contemporary nation-state of Nepal is of relatively recent origin, dating back only to the latter decades of the eighteenth century. Nepal was not organised as a sovereign state till 1769 when Prithvi Narayan Shah brought about political unification of Nepal and established a monarchy. Another significant development took place in 1846 when Jang Bahadur Rana seized power and forced the king to become a nominal head of state. The Ranas became, and remained virtual rulers of Nepal till early 1951.

The domestic situation in Nepal changed in 1951 when a new government was established after the Delhi agreement of February 1951. It was not possible for the new ruling elites to continue with the policy of isolation. In fact, Nepal's sudden and unplanned debut into international society in 1951, although virtually unnoticed by the rest of the world at the time caused an immediate and severe crisis in its national self-identification.[3]

India, which had played an important role in overthrowing the Rana rule and eventually in the restoration of Monarchy, felt an urgent need for stability in the Himalayas so that its own interests were protected. Nepal laid emphasis on attaining the objectives of democracy, stability and development. India too was keen to establish co-ordial relations with Nepal and encourage the establishment of democracy and development however, was be seen more for its own interest them for Nepalese people. The relations thus established between the two countries were regarded by both as 'special'. Both the countries maintained close understanding on foreign policy issues and Nepal remained dependent on India on political and economic matters. Thus, in the early fifties India's positive role in shaping Nepalese nationalism and foreign policy was accepted.

After the accession to the thrown in 1955 King Mahendra took up the task of defining the fundamentals of Nepal's foreign policy. The king pin of his policy was nationalism and is manifestation found external expression in the diversification of Nepal's relations with countries other than India, in search of its separate identity and the domestic manifestation in the innovation of new political institutions. This objective became more pronounced after 1960, when the parliamentary system was abrogated. Along with its political assertion the monarchy also began to play the role of a modernising elite so as to legitimise is relevance in the changed context. King Mahendra believed that Nepal's identity and self-image were possible only by reducing its dependence on India. Although his policy of diversification has serious limitations because it was not possible to reduce Nepal's economic dependence over India beyond certain limits.[4] For the first time Nepal's 'special' relation sought serious jolt but it was all about to reflect its quest for self-identity and independence and to that extent satisfied Nepal psychology vis-a-vis India.[5]

The experiment with parliamentary democracy, however, proved to be short lived as King Mahendra dismissed the Koirala government and himself took power in December 1960. India's dissatisfaction with and open criticism of the king's action deteriorated relations between the two countries. In fact what Nepal wanted was that New Delhi should recognise the altered political situation in Nepal.[6] The cascade of events like deterioration in relation between Nepal and India, arise of anti-Indian sentiments and furtherance of Nepalese nationalism were major happenings which affected heavily the future course of action at political level between the two countries.

However, during the time of King Birendra, the hangover of India's dominance and Nepal's quest for national identity and quest for diversification of relationship continued, although he tried to deal with the issues in a different way. His idea of declaring Nepal, as a "zone of peace" was unique in this regard. During those periods Nepal made desperate efforts to distance itself from India by using the China card but the passion of the Nepalese rulers to seek the support of Indian governments for their own survival and sustenance still continue.

In the late eighties when the Indo-Nepal relations reached to a near collapse over the issues of trade and transit treaties were the real test of policy of diversification. India on the basis of Nepal's insensitivity towards its security concerns sought to pressurise Nepal.

Major determinants of Nepal-India Relations

The politico-strategic considerations are of prime importance in Indo-Nepal relations but the economic interests are also of considerable significance. Nepal is located in an important strategic position in the Himalayas. Lying along the southern slopes of the central Himalayas, it separates the avid Tibetan plateau from the Indian plains. Both India and Nepal have preferred on open border. The idea of a closed border is not acceptable to them because of age-old socio-cultural and economic relations.[7] This geographical situation has induced the pattern of relationship between the two countries.

India's political approach towards Nepal is clearly understandable. It believed that Nepal should have a stable government. It was considered essential to introduce certain political reforms in the kingdom in orders to avoid political upheaval.

However, though India condemned the autocratic rule in Nepal, it did not believe in forcing radial changes. Nehru said:

We have tried to advise Nepal to act in a manner so as to prevent any major upheaval. We have tried to find a way, a middle way, if you like, which will ensure the progress of Nepal and the introduction of or some advance towards democracy in Nepal.[8]

India believed that the political system of Nepal was bound to affected by the political changes taking place in the outside world. So it was considered desirable for Nepal to move in gradual steps, towards a representative and responsive political system. During the time of Nehru, he wanted to create a security zone around India's neighbourhood where cold war politics could be kept at bay. King Tribhuvan followed the policy of gradual democratisation of the country and maintained a closer understanding with India. But King Mahendra was ambitious and assertive. He tried to give new directions to Nepal's foreign policy. The same strategy was revived by the next monarch-Birendra, although he successfully maintained the co-ordial relations despite Rajiv Gandhi's intimidation of abrogating trade and transit treaty due to his personal problems.

India has many complex economic interests in the kingdom so is of Nepal in India. In fact for India, Nepal is one of its largest and most lucrative markets. For Nepal, Indian market is one of the keys which will unlock the gates of growth. Both need each other.

A new trade treaty came into force on 5th December 1996, which set the ground rules for growth in trade and investment for future. After the new treaty the trade has grown impressively in both direction, which is clear from the following table.

Table-I

	Post Treaty 1997/98	*Post Treaty 1998/99*	*Post Treaty 1999/2000*
Growth in Nepal's Export to India	+68%	+49%	+79%
Growth in Nepal's Import to India	+50%	+19%	+40%
Change in Nepal's Trade Deficit	Improved by 11.4%		Deteriorated by 13%

Source: Padma Jyoti, "Nepal-India Economic Relations-a Practical Perspective", Policy Study Seires, Kathmandu, Institute of Foreign Affairs, 2000, p.67.

Thus, Nepal has immense economic dependence on India and their interests are closely interwoven. It naturally has bearings upon their bilateral relations.

Treaty of 1950

There have been very cordial and friendly relations between the people of Nepal and India. They have been active in promoting a mature understanding of continuing evolution of the ancient ties of friendship, keeping in view the changing demands and requirements of the globalised world. India since its independence in 1947, has shown keen interest in ensuring the security of its northern borders and signed treaties with Bhutan (August, 1949, and with Nepal (July, 1950). On July 31, 1950 Nepal and India signed the Treaty of Peace and Friendship followed by the Exchange of Letters (EOL) at the court of Nepal to regulate certain matters of details through it.[9]

The Treaty, in particulars, letters accompanying it, were kept secret for nearly a decade in both the countries and the smell of the Treaty with accompanying letters came out only on November 27, 1959, when Indian Prime Minister Nehru, in course of his speech on international affairs in the Lok Sabha, referring to Sino-Indian border troubles, stated: "may I just repeat what we had declared that any aggression on Bhutan and Nepal will be considered by us aggression of India."

The Treaty of Peace and Friendship concluded between India and Nepal in July 1950, provides the basic framework for friendship between the two countries. Though its main thrust is on political and security matter, it goes much beyond these parameters and covers essential aspects of people to people relations as well.[10] But the several questions come at its scathing attack, one; does the context of cold war still exist against which the treaty was signed? Second; is it a just treaty it was signed between the Ranas and India who were overthrown from power in 1951? Third, does it not seem as a mask of peace and friendship treaty while India has usually tried to conceal its security perceptions by bringing Nepal under its security umbrella? Fourth, Does it follow the Vienna convention 1961, which stipulates that a treaty must be flexible in nature to cope with the changing time and situation. Fifth; Have India and Nepal honestly implemented all the provisions and articles of faith of the Treaty? Sixth; Does India equally provide Nepal all information pertaining to security as Nepal has abided by this treaty or not. As Nepal did so in 1989. Seventhly, Does it not against the spirit of the 1990 constitution whose articles clearly stipulates about the course of action of Nepal vis-a-vis other nations of world on the basis of equality and mutual interests/welfare and peaceful co-existence against the 'special' treatment with anyone including India. Finally, in the present globalised world, which encourages concepts like "global village", the world is moving towards interdependence and the nation-states, the weaker ones in the third world under pressure have to adjust with international regimes like IMF, WB and MNCs. And when in the present changed situation, security today is mostly people centered and is interdependent. In such a situation today is mostly people centered and is interdependent. In such a situation is there any need to change of 1950s treaty: if yes then how can this be possible?

Over the years, the framework of 1950 treaty, which perhaps benefited India more than Nepal, has guided the Nepal-India relations basically at political and strategic level.

For the time being if we curve out the questions like. Why India seems reluctant towards revision of the Treaty? A host of convincing arguments be put forth:

- Termination of Treaty will deny India the advantage of exercising unilateral, option (implied though not stated under the treaty) of meeting unforeseen security contingency in Nepal. Abrogation of the Treaty would certainly increase China's expansionist urges South of the Himalayas. As things stand today, though India has erected a credible structure of defence along its border with China, the structure of deterrence against any possible Chinese onslaught. Potential credibility of this already weak deterrence would be drastically undermined with the abrogation of the treaty. Of course, there does not appear to be any prospect of such a Chinese move in the near future, particularly in view of improving Sino-Indian relationship which have gained new momentum after Prime Minister Atal Bihari Vajpayee's visit in 2003 to China, but the Chinese may not have direct interest in dominating Nepal military per se, but the possibility of using Nepal as a pawn in their policy towards India and the subcontinent as a whole, can not be dismissed. If the unrest in Tibet was to take turn for the worst.

- Abrogation of Treaty would also necessitate a drastic redefinition of the totality of Indo-Nepalese relations. In order to protect Vital Indian security and economic interests, the entire Indo-Nepalese border will have to be closed with adequate defence preparedness which may require raising of 4 to 6 additional divisions of armed forces with other related financial and institutional burdens. China's presence behind Nepal, with the former's military consolidation in Tibet will naturally make Indo-Nepalese border much harder even as compared to Indo-Bangladesh and Indo-Burmese border.[11]

- The consequences of the abrogation of Indo-Nepalese Treaty would not be confined to India's relations with Nepal alone. It will strengthen pressures from Bhutan also, which is already trying its best to diversity its diplomatic and economic relations with various countries. And if it happens the India's stand would be weakened in South Asia.[12]

- It is not too far fetched to say that India's strong and assertive role in South Asian region is an important factor in containing fissiparous tendencies and forces (ethnic sub national and regional) within India. A weakening of India's position in Nepal would indirectly encourage these divisive forces within the country. In view of all these factors India has put its deaf ears forward.

Despite Nepal's big hue and cry, (Article 10 of the Treaty clearly stipulated to abrogate it by giving one year's notice to India, Nepal could not declare the termination of the treaty. To understand the reasons a couple of factors need to borne in mind.

- Former Prime Minister Man Mohan Adhikari, during his visit to India in 1995 for the first time officially requested the Govt. of India to revise the 1950 treaty. But the request was wisely declined by India. It justified the pretension of both sides although it was no way sensuous attempt to put the Treaty more relevant in the present context.

- Nepal's strategy seems to be that of perpetuating an atmosphere of ambiguity with regard to its exact position on the Treaty. The ruling elites however, have always tried to sustain the state of ambiguity and parallelly arousing the anti-Indianism to consolidate their regime.

Nevertheless, the 1950 Treaty has provided the basis of Nepal-India political and security relations for more than 53 years, however, some practical revisions need to be done so that two countries remain happy with its prevailing status in operational terms. While doing do, those provisions that still have validity in immediate or long term future for the enlightened interests of both the countries, will have to be reiterated and, if need be, strengthen. In review of this nature, the two sides may have to keep in mind the spirit of mutual interests, reciprocal obligations and inherently interdependent nature of their relations.

Security Concerns

India's security concerns become pronounced when smugglers, militants, terrorists and criminals misused its open border with Nepal.

One the most serious problem that India sees as a threat to its security is the alleged presence of the Pakistani ISI on Nepalese soil to carry out anti-India activities. An Indian security expert commented: "Pakistan has been funding mosques and madrasas in Indo-Nepal border areas with a view to building up a constituency of pro-Pakistani Muslims who could later be used for supporting their operations".[13] Pakistan ISI is alleged to has penetrated well into Nepal, particularly in the Terai region and are involved in activities such as pumping fake Indian-currency to destabilise the Indian economy; rendering financial assistance and providing transit facilities to the Kashmiri and Sikh militants, etc.[14] The hijacking of Indian Airlines plane IC 814 after its departure from Kathmandu in December 2000 has increased its security concerns in Nepal and the alleged role of Pakistan ISI in the incident. The then Indian Foreign Minister, Jaswant Singh, in a statement issued in Parliament said, "The hijacking incident has once again highlighted the complicity of Pakistan and of organisations patronised and supported by it in terrorist acts against India... The hijacking was master minded by Pakistan's ISI with the assistance of Harkat-ul-Mujahideen".[15]

Nepal has consistently assured India its full cooperation on issues such as terrorism and extremists group. As early as 1992, the then Prime

Minister G.P. Koirala had assured his governments cooperation to resist terrorism and to deter terrorists from using Nepal as a transit camp.[16] In order the control the misuse of open border, Nepal had cooperated with India to strengthen mechanisms for monitoring at airports, terminals and border crossing. A joint working group was established to formulate modalities to monitor the border. In the same year, Uttar Pradesh-Nepal Border Police force was raised to check illegal activities along the border.[17]

Since the Nepal Maoist's activities began in 1996 and the establishment of linkages with Indian ultra-leftist groups, the Government of India has shown concern over this developments. The creation of a Compact Revolutionary Zone (CRZ) by the Nepal Maoist and India's Naxalitics which extends from Nepal and stretch across more the five Indian states, "hold certain advantages to the insurgents and, thus significant security implications for India.[18]

The deployment of SSB force along Indo-Nepal border after the Kargil war with Pakistan was primarily at resisting any threat emanating from the north and to secure its border with Nepal.

Nepal's threat perceptions were defined by a new elite in power that equated regime security with state security[19] and the treaties and agreements with India were "conditioned more by short strategies of regime survival than by genuine national interests".[20] But most of Nepal's security concerns emanate from inside the country such as the political instability, poor governance and economic development, and the Maoist insurgency.

Future Prospects

Unlike Nepal's relations with other neighbours, there are irritants coming up from time to time in Nepal India relations. In order to further strengthen the ties between the people and government of the two countries, it is essential to analyze why such irritants crop up and how they can be removed. What are the major reasons for that? How should Nepal prepare itself to face the challenges and reap opportunities of the new century? As we have seen that how critical variables that have been influencing the dynamics of India-Nepal. At the dawn of twenty-first century besides other dominant variables, two are of immense important-(a) the internal politics changes of two countries (b) the nature of regional and international political environment impinging upon relations between them.

The domestic political situation in Nepal has been witnessing major upheavals and transform as well as character of governments.

The anti-Rana revolution of 1951, the arrival of King Mahendra on the scene of 1955 and his coup against the elected parliamentary multi-party government in 1960, the success of anti-Panchayat democratic struggle of 1990 and finally the most atrocious Royal massacre in June 2001 and eventually incarnation of Gyanendra as the king whose unfailed motive to throw the future democratic of transition in deep dark and deeply penetrative Maoists insurgency, are all major landmarks in Nepal's political evolution which influenced the content and contours of Indo-Nepal relations.

So far as future of strategic relations of Nepal with India is concerned, both has become conscious of the fact that global strategic and economic relations in post-cold war order has created new compulsions as well as incentives for forging closer regional ties and understanding.

Finally, in the 21st century, Nepal, instead of losing everything in each and every case, as is happening these days, should muster political will, self confidence and self-reliance in negotiations and feel that there are many small powers in the world than Nepal in respect to size, shape, population, resources which are successful even with the so-called big or super power and have achieved their national interests without surrendering their well being and benefit.

References

1. Ram Kumar Dahal, 'Review of Nepal-India Relations: Issues and Challenges (1950-1999), Policy Study Series, Institute of Foreign Affairs, Kathmandu, November 2000, p. 2.
2. S.D. Muni, India and Nepal: A Changing Relationship, Konark Publishers, New Delhi, 1992, p. 4.
3. Leo E. Rose, Nepal Strategy for Survival, OUP, Delhi, p. 279.
4. B.C. Upreti, Uneasy Friends, Kalinga, Delhi, 2001, pp. 56-59.
5. *Ibid.*
6. *Ibid.* p. 60.

7. M.D. Dharamdasani, Indian Diplomacy in Nepal Jaipur, 1976, p. 4.

8. A.S. Bhasin, Document on Nepal's Relations with India and China, Siba Publications, Delhi, 1994, p. 23.

9. Ram Kumar Dahal, *op.cit.*, p. 3.

10. S.D. Muni, *op.cit.*, p.32.

11. S.D. Muni, *op.cit.*, p. 60.

12. *Ibid.*

13. Satish Kumar, 'India's Stratagic Neighbourhood', in India's National Security Annual Review 2001, Vakash Publishing House, New Delhi, 2002.

14. See *Ibid.*, and Sangeeta Thapliyal, 'Contesting Mutual Security: India-Nepal Relations', at http://www.orfonline.org

15. Quoted in S. Thapliyal, *Ibid.*

16. *Ibid.*

17. *Ibid.*

18. P.V. Ramana, 'PWG Naxal-Nepal Maoists Nexus' at http://www.orfonline.org

19. S. Thapliyal, *op.cit.*

20. Lok Raj Baral, 'India-Nepal Relations: Continuity and Change', Asian Survey, Vol. xxxii, No.9, September 1992, p. 816.

8

Nepal's Role in SAARC

Deepak Prakash Bhatt

A Historical Overview

The foundation stone of modern Nepal laid down by the Gorkha King Prithvi Narayan Shah, in 1768-69. Nepal has always been an independent and sovereign country. After the defeat in the war against East India company of the British Empire Nepal was forced to sign a unilateral treaty, known as Sogawlee Treaty in 1816, resulting in the loss of almost three quarters of Nepal's fertile land in Terai, including Tista, Darjeeling, Kumaon and Garhwal. In addition Nepal's external relations were also restricted to some extent. Since then, Nepal virtually remained a protectorate of British-India. The Rana families of Nepal, who ruled the Kingdom for 104 years till 1950, maintained cordial and loyal relationship with British government for their own survival. They were continuously threatened by internal rivalries and growing demands for democracy in the country.

The independence of India-Pakistan in 1947 was a major breakthrough for Nepal's internal politics and its changing role in the region. The colonial era had ended and in Nepal politically in fighting, associations and forcible transfer of power was ended. Nepal first experienced democracy in this period and international relations too took a quantum jump.[1] And than democracy was forcibly replaced by a state system called Panchayat for another 30 years and in 1990 successful people's movement reintroduced multiparty system-a limited version of democracy with the constitutional monarchy.

A rapid growth of the regional cooperation phenomenon in South Asia in mid 1980s Nepal plays a constructive role, where many of the fears and mistrusts were in the existence. Nepal has successfully maintained a climate of good relations with all SAARC members.

Regionalism: a Theoretical Perspective

The core concept of regional cooperation or regionalism conceived that states would cross over the limitation imposed by the national borders and work together.[2] The need of regional cooperation have two determinants-economic and political. The economic determinants such as deterioration in international economic situation, inflation, shrinking foreign aid flows and the spiralling price of western technology. The universal recognition of the need for cooperation among developing countries as expressed by the group of 77. Report of the Brandt commission and empirical study done by Raul Prebisch influenced the leader's in different region. The constructive idea for regional cooperative framework in South Asia was mooted by the then President of Bangladesh Zia-Ur-Rehman in 1980.

Genesis of SAARC

President Zia-Ur-Rehman said that, "the countries of South Asia share many common values that are rooted in their social, ethnic, cultural and historical traditions. Perceptions about certain specific events or political situation of the world may differ, but such differences do not seem to create a gulf between them that cannot be bridged. In fact, the beginning of co-operation on a regional basis may be a positive force in generating a climate of harmony conducive to a better perception of what the countries in the region have in common and the value of this shared heritage.[3]

However, because of India's preoccupations with global political and Nehru's personal ambitions of India s status in world politics, India could not give proper attention to the regional dimensions. But the smaller states of the region, because of their own problems took interest in regional cooperation. It was with the eighties that their idea took a concrete shape. The South Asian Regional cooperation was finally inaugurated in April 1981. Since then it has already had six meeting till 1985, at the foreign secretary level – April 1981 Colombo, November 1981 Kathmandu, August 1982 Islamabad, March 1983 Dhaka, July 1983 New Delhi and

February 1985 Male. Three meetings had already been held at Foreign Minister level – August 1983 New Delhi, July 1984 Male and May 1985 Thimpu. Various issues of common interest have been discussed in these meeting.[4]

South Asian Association for regional cooperation (SAARC) was established when its charter was formally adopted on 8 December 1985 by the Heads of state of Bangladesh, Bhutan, India, Maldives, Nepal, Pakistan and Sri Lanka, where two were military regimes, two monarchies, one dictator and two democracies. This shows regional cooperation even there without democracy.

SAARC is an association based on consciousness that in an increasingly interdependent world, the objectives of peace, freedom and economic strength can achieve in the region by cooperative relations and meaningful efforts. It aims to accelerate process of economic and social development in the member states. This cooperation is based on the respect for the principles of sovereign equality, territorial integrity, political independence, non-interference in the internal affairs of member states and mutual benefits.

Nepal's Role in South Asian Regional Cooperation

Nepal began to take interest in regional cooperation in South Asia, after late seventies. At the Colombo conference of the non-aligned countries held in August 1976, Nepal emphasised the need for regional cooperation among the neighbouring countries. King Birendra inaugurating the Colombo Plan Consultative Committee meeting held in Kathmandu in December 1977, urged for cooperation with the Asian countries particularly with China, Bhutan, India and Bangladesh. King Birendra's approach of regional co-operation received appreciation from the President of Bangladesh during his visit to Dhaka in 1978. when the President of Bangladesh formally put forward the proposal of regional cooperation. Nepal obviously endorsed it promptly.[5]

Nepal's Objectives Behind Participation

Nepal's longtime status as buffer state between South and East Asia make cautions about two great neighbours circumstances seemed to dictate. Nepal's interest in South Asian cooperation seems to have been primarily between because of its identity problem also. And in search of alterative to its economic dependence upon India, where Nepal-India have an age old socio-cultural relationships. The border between the two countries is porus and people have a frequent movement across the border. Inspite of special relationship with India there are number of complications, which showed some stresses and strains in political relation between India-Nepal.

The sheer size of India in the middle, bordering on each South Asian country, non of which borders each other – it seems as a single challenge to regionalism in South Asia. India has looked towards the Himalayan states from its own perception of security.[6] Nehru placed Nepal within India's security orbit after Chinese attack over Tibet and link between India-China. Peace and friendship Treaty in 1950 postulates for common security arrangement between Nepal-India. India started to play a big role in Nepalese affairs giving aid to construction of a temporary landing strip at Kathmandu in 1952. Nepalese appreciations have been that India's overwhelming influence is overshadowing its national identity. Rishkesh shah wrote, 'India's dominance is so overwhelming that at times Nepalese as a way of reaction behave in a manner which appears different from India. They consider essential to maintain a separate identity.[7]

Nepal tried to woo with China after mid-fifties to balance India's influence and also tried to diversify its trade and aid so that dependence upon India could be reduced. King Mahendra succeeded his father has left a mark on Nepal's relation with neighbours. Nepal's status as a founding member of the Non-Aligned Movement gave it the status and space it needed to project its independent posture. During Panchayat days such position was always justified in Nepal as an instrument of enhancing security in relation to India, or at least, of asserting its independent national identity, while adhering to the principal of peaceful coexistence at the same time. For example, in Afghanistan and Cambodia Nepal opposed the Russian and Vietnamese actions respectively. And on the question of the recognition of Israel, too, Nepal took a line opposite to that of India. These steps were appreciated in China and the US.

When King Birendra publicly announced his zone of peace proposal in 1975 as clear and potentially most effective instrument of concretising the equidistance policy vis-à-vis the two neighbours, India's irritation reached in a new height.[8] Specially because Nepal did consult it prior to the announcement of this proposal. India did not discuss the matter while proposal was accepted by more than 100 countries including United States. This proposal was attempt for its acceptance by the countries of region as well as outside. As the idea of regional cooperation in South Asia was mooted Nepal came forward with its full cooperation. Not only the collective security arrangement could be possible through the SAARC, but Nepal could also reduce its dependence over India and economic development can be solved.

Economic Development

Simply the dominant Nepali perceptions sees the country suffering under the weight of Indian economy and Indian business houses, while in India it is generally believed that Nepal needs to be more grateful to India for the economic benefits it receives. As Nepal has a highly under developed economy and if now because of civil war situation waiting in the queue of failed state. High rate of population growth, lack of capital and technology to exploit the pool of natural resources are the factors or matters of aid and trade dependence. Economies of the South Asian states almost fear certain common characteristics such as poverty, exploitation, population growth, unemployment, structure of production, etc. But, now in tenth-five year plan (2002-2007) there is no increase in productive employment and economic development with the 2.4 per cent GDP growth rate which as lowest in SAARC countries. So far the prospects for Nepal's participation in regional co-operation for economic development is concerned; it can be possible in the following areas :–

(i) ***Trade:*** Nepal's major interest in regional cooperation is trade diversification. The treaty of trade and commerce 1950 signed almost simultaneously with Treaty of Peace and friendship made sure that Nepal would continue its extensive trade links with India. Nepal has been arguing for the decades that transit is a matter of right which should not require a periodic negotiations and agreement as in a trade treaty. Such Indian position accompanied by not so smooth bilateral relations between and Bangladesh has led Nepal to repose faith in the proposal for sub-regional cooperation hoping that somehow the question infrastructure and automatic transit for all parties will be part of a agreed scheme. Nepal has lacked heavy industries and trade deficit with India is about 5 times. Therefore, it provides ample scope for joint venture for the establishment of heavy industries in the field of cement, paper textile, etc. The now delayed graduation of SAPTA to SAFTA and the possible momentum of SAARC agenda and activities as a genuine regional economic community may produce good results. Till today tariff reductions by countries other than India have not led to an increase in Nepal's trade with them, so the SAPTA is not relevant for Nepal.

(ii) ***Exploitation of Water Resources:*** Nepal is rich in water resources. It's three big river systems-Karanli, Kosi and Gandaki have hydro-power potential of 75 MKW. It is estimated that 2.27 per cent of worlds hydro-power potentiality is in Nepal. The exploitation of water resources is only possible through regional cooperation especially with India and Bangladesh. Nepal does not have adequate capital and technology to harness the resource. Also the border region of Bangladesh, Bhutan, Nepal and India have significant scope for power generation and marketing surplus generated by hydropower plants in Nepal and Bhutan especially. Nepal have small market size and can capture big market in region through cross border trading. When wind, solar power or biogas cannot meet all the needs hydro power is the best choice in terms of cost effectiveness and environment safety. South Asian region has been exploiting hardly 11 per cent of estimated regional hydro power.

Table-I: Hydroelectric Potential in South Asia

Country	*Hydroelectric Potential (Mw)*	*Total Installed capacity (Mw)*	*% Harnessed of the total*
Nepal	83290	283	0.33
Bangladesh	75200	230	0.44
India	75400	21900	29.04
Bhutan	21000	355	1.70
Pakistan	38000	4825	12.70
Sri Lanka	2000	1129	56.45
Total	**271690**	**28722**	**10.57**

Source: Govt. of Bangladesh, Yearbook 1996, Seventh Five Year Plan 1992-97, Economic Survey, 1998-99, Govt. of India, His Majesty Govt. of Nepal Economic Survey 1996-97, MOF and Central Bank of Sri Lanka, Annual Report 1998, p. 75.

(iii) ***Ecological Issue:*** Ecological degradation – pollution of air, water and soil, loss of species and bio-diversity, destruction of the ozone layer, destablisation of the climate, soil erosion and deforestation are the most serious issues of South Asian countries. Nepal is faced with the problem of deforestation. More than 200 million meters of its fertile land is washed down every year, which creates the problem of siltation of India and Bangladesh. Plantation is necessary to chick this problem. Similarly the problem of floods is big problem in Nepal and India. These problems can be solved through an integrated development of the countries of the region.

(iv) ***Human Resources, Science and Technology:*** Nepal has to depend outside to borrow technology to execute its development projects. A marginal number of manpower, which is trained outside, is not in working conditions have not such enthusiasm. More than three million migrants are working in India and youth are forced to leave village because of the Maoist insurgency.

Nepal wants to cooperate with the South Asian countries of region to develop its manpower. In this regard it is possible to exchange engineering skills, expertise, scientific resource, development and communication and information and technology. Some more areas where regional cooperation is possible.

(v) ***Divergent Strategic Perceptions:*** Nepal demonstrated its insensitivity towards religious minorities by declaring itself a Hindu state, while the Plural and diverse society status to the Nepalese society. Maoist have divided people into different ethnic categories like the Khanbhuwan Chetra, the Limbuwan Chetra in Eastern Nepal and Madhesh Chetra in Eastern Terai and their demand for the formation of a Republican state by replacing the constitutional monarchy have changed the social landscape in Nepal. 'Networking with other insurgent groups in India and South Asia to create instability in the region'.[9] The establishment of a coordinating committee of, Maoist Parties and organisations of South Asia (CCOMPOSA) or Compact Revolutionary Zone (CRZ) in June 2001 provides an institutional structure is a serious security challenge to South Asian governments. The Maoists used violent method and their possible links with insurgent group in North-East India is significant security implication for India.

South Asia today has become a region of unending conflicting and violence. For Nepal approximately one hundred thousand refugees from Bhutan, unique reality of Porus border with India is also source of security problem. In the changing modern world-era of globalisation which have changed traditional ways of thinking, geographical distance have loses importance. The state is at once the power and non-power to deal with challenges confronting human security. South Asian countries namely India and Pakistan after May 1998 becoming nuclear power focused their security interest on the basis of military strength. Besides the subcontinent has common problems such as poverty, backwardness, unemployment, population explosion, cross border migrations and environmental degradation.[10]

Prospects

With a civilisation regarded as one of the most ancient the region South Asia derives its identity and uniqueness shared bonds of culture, history and the economics of neighbourhood. 'SAARC provides an opportunity to participate independently, discuss and take decisions on issues of common interest. It can also prove as a catalyst for the economies of the South Asian states by providing increased opportunities of trade, aid etc.'[11] Nepal like other member states maintain its national identity in SAARC as regional forum.

All the twelve SAARC summits are regarded as a successful and significant milestone's in regional cooperation. The declarations issued at the end of all the summits mentioned the collective views of SAARC members on a wide range of regional and international problems, the issues of nuclear arms control and disarmament, North-South/South-South dialogue, and economic problems. But the brief impression about all such deliberations held and decisions taken by the Heads of states or governments have never got serious intension to get the core of cooperation.

In all matters Nepal's participation have certain limitations. Because of Nepal's landlocked position it is mostly dependent over India for transit facilities. But 'the dynamics of Nepal-India relations will be directly affected by India's changing relations with extra-regional powers'.[12] Nepal's initiation for sub regional cooperation within the SAARC becomes controversial and Nepal recently become a member of BIMST-EC. Nepal want to project its, independent identity and manage its political and economic relations with India on the one hand and concrete formulation of regional cooperation on the other hand.

Social charter and SAFTA Agreement as well as an Additional Protocol to the existing Convention on the Suppression of Terrorism arc adopted at the 12th SAARC summit Islamabad 4-6, January 2004. implementation of such decisions again put challenge to follow the roadmap for South Asian cooperation and the establishment of South Asian Economic Union and common currency.

Thus Nepal's participation in South Asian cooperation is not without certain challenges. After initially focusing and solving internal problems, transcending its hyper independence on India and than deriving benefits from regional cooperation Nepal can think about necessicity of South Asian identity.

References

1. D.R. Pandcy, Nepal's Failed Development, p. 230.
2. B. Mahanan, The Politics of regionalism in South Asia', Atlantic Publishers and Distributors, New Delhi, 1992, p.11.
3. *Ibid.*
4. Enclopaedia of SAARC Nations, 5-Nepal, Ed. – Virender Grover.
5. *Ibid.*
6. S.D. Muni, 'Defence and Development in South Asia', Bhabani Sen Gupta (ed.), Regional Cooperation and Development in South Asia, Vol.-I, Delhi, 1986.
7. Rishikesh Shah, 'Nepali Politics, Retrospect and Prospect, New Delhi, 1978, p. 103.
8. D.R. Pandey, Nepal's Failed Development, The External Environment, p. 312.
9. Dhurba Kumar, Security in South Asia, "A Nepali Perspective", What vision for Security Future in South Asia"? Kathmandu, 2001, p.80.

10. M.P. Lohani, Comprehensive Security in South Asia, Delhi Policy Group, 2001, pp. 26-27.
11. N.P. Banskota, "Nepal-Towards Regional Economic Cooperation in South Asia." Asian Survey Vol. XXI, March 1981.
12. S.D. Muni, India and Nepal: A Changing Relation Shop, Konark Publishers, New Delhi, 1992, p.176.

9

The Role of 'Security' in India-China-Nepal Relations

Nabarun Roy

C.E.M. Joad had pointed out that socialism was like a cap that could be worn by anyone. Every person has a different understanding as to what socialism means. A similar trend can be seen in the context of security studies. In the post Cold War era, the word 'security' has come under a lot of scrutiny and consequently, the issues which can be included within the rubric of security studies have also generated a lot of debate. Scholars like Barry Buzan have spoken about the "wide" versus "narrow" debate in security studies[1].

To understand the dynamics of the India-Nepal China relations from the 1950s to the post-Cold War era, one has to understand how the quest for security has motivated each state. This means that one understand how security was viewed by each state and what this understanding led them to do at an inter state level in terms of forging alliances and entering into various agreements. The aim of this paper, hence, will be to examine the triangular relation between the above-mentioned countries from a security perspective, keeping in mind the change in the meaning of the term over a period of time.

Traditionally, Nepal has had close security ties with India. It was during the time of Maharaja Ranjit Singh that the Nepalese first joined the Punjab Army in Lahore[2]. In present times, there are around 40,000 Gurkha soldiers serving in the Indian Army[3]. In 1952, Nepal requested India to send a training team to help reorganise the Royal Nepal Army. India's

Gurkha connection has been described as "rich", "extensive" and one of the 'strongest trademarks of Indo-Nepalese relations'[4]. Security ties between India and Nepal were formalised by the 1950 Treaty of Peace and Friendship. This treaty was the outcome of the shared security apprehension that India and Nepal had vis-à-vis China. In the early fifties, military threat from China became prominent after it made claims on Tibet. Nepal's apprehensions found resonance in India, which was also disturbed by the political changes in the north[5]. The spirit of the treaty was underscored by Jawaharlal Nehru's statement in the parliament on 6th December, 1950 when he stated that, "...much as we appreciate the independence of Nepal, we cannot allow anything to go wrong in Nepal or permit that barrier to be crossed or weakened, because that would be a risk to our own country"[6]. A very important factor in the treaty was that there existed a common threat perception. If one had to examine the clauses of the treaty, it would be clear that Nepal hardly viewed India as a socio-economic threat. Clauses 6 and 7 of the treaty make this quite clear[7]. This is an important factor to note, as later it will enable us to see that even Nepal during the Cold War years was viewing security in the traditional sense.

However, the relation between the two South Asian countries was not without a sense of misgiving, especially on the part of Nepal. In collaborating with a much larger neighbour on as important an issue as security, Nepal risked undermining her own sovereignty. It has been observed that small nations generally face problems of survival as independent entities in the international system[8]. They appear too fragile in the company of larger states, thereby lacking the capability to perform all the tasks of self-rule, defence or security being an integral notion as regards self-rule[9]. Small countries, who can harbour no hope of strengthening their position through the military option usually try to reinforce their security by way of increasing their freedom of manoeuvrability in their dealings with the larger country.[10] In such a situation, 'balancing' serves as a handy tool.

The edifice of Nepal's strategy towards her larger neighbours was laid down in the mid 18th century when King Prithvi Narayan Shah had stated that being sandwiched between two larger neighbours, Nepal had to forge friendly relations with both India and China. During Jang Bahadaur Rana's rule (mid 19th century), Nepal had turned towards China whenever she faced difficulties in her dealings with the British in the south.

Two developments helped Nepal to edge closer to China in the mid 1950s.

One pertained to the domestic politics of Nepal. Nepal's threat perception was defined by the elite who equated regime security with state security. Being a monarchical polity, Nepal's decision makers had a sense of unease in their dealings with India as India was seen as the bastion of liberal democratic values in the region. Anti-monarchy pro-democracy forces were viewed as a threat to the regime and their ideological links with political parties and ideologues in India was seen as a threat to state security[11].

The second factor had to do with China.

Since her 'liberation', the People's Republic of China (PRC) has viewed India as a remnant of western colonialism. A successor state, India, according to Subrata K. Mitra, is keen to retain the *status quo,* which its leaders understand in terms of its relative power and territorial boundaries that it was privy to prior to the end of colonial rule. China contests this status quo, which it sees as tainted by imperial rule[12]. Also, the initial years of China's existence saw her viewing developments in the South Asian region, especially pertaining to India in a rather zero sum manner. This was the outcome of the quintessential 'Security Dilemma' as enunciated by John Herz[13]. As Swaran Singh points out, China's South Asia policy was being guided purely by its security considerations[14]. India's reach into Nepal in fact made China "paranoid" about its territorial integrity against a possible mischief from South Asia[15]. China as a result was defining her security in the politico-military aspect.

The triangular equation in terms of security thus becomes clear: China-a new nation state in the international system fearful of India's role as a mischief-maker (at the behest of the Western powers) and eager to blunt India's influence in the region; India-fearful of the threat presented to her by China in terms of her ideological zeal in terms of 'exporting' revolutions and generally dissatisfied with India's territorial acquisition / inheritance at independence; Nepal – rather fearful of China's intentions but unwilling to be used as a pawn by India. Nepal's physical distance from central China and the succession of weak governments there for centuries before 1949 caused Nepal in the past to think that India's interference and intervention in Nepal's affairs was a greater probability[16]. Obviously, the past had a bearing on how Nepal conducted her affairs with her neighbours in the second half of the 20th century.

In order to wean Nepal away from India, China's strategic, economic and political objectives were tailored keeping India in mind.

Strong political links were established with Nepal in the mid 1950s in the shadow of the 1955 Bandung Conference. It has to be remembered that Nepal had entered into the 1950 Treaty with India due to fears of the possibility of the formation of a 'Himalayan Federation' engineered by China. Hence, the Chinese leadership felt it necessary to assuage the fear of Nepal in relation to China. China was helped a great deal in her efforts by India's foreign policy, which in the 1960s was described as 'Militant Nehruvianism', where sub continental dominance became a cornerstone of Indian foreign policy[17]. The feeling that India behaves like a regional bully is a sentiment shared by many of India's neighbours to the present day. To wean Nepal away from India, China started sympathising with Nepal on matters specially pertaining to India, as also increasing aid and diplomatic presence in Nepal[18]. Between 1956 and 1973, nearly 20 per cent of China's total world aid was targeted to the South Asian countries[19]. China pulled off a coup of sorts when in 1960 the China-Nepal Treaty of Peace and Friendship was signed, which effectively blunted India's edge in Nepal as compared to China. Another example of Nepal edging closer to China was the construction of the Kodari-Kathmandu highway in 1967. It clearly increased Nepal's strategic options, especially as till that time, her capital was linked by road only to India[20]. When India made public her ire over the development, Nepal stated that the road had economic significance for Nepal and as it was an internal matter, it should be of no concern to India[21].

What in effect we have come across is the playing up of the security dilemma between India, China and Nepal. Why did China feel compelled to construct the Kodari-Kathmandu highway? One of the major factors was to even the skewed balance, which, strategically, was in India's favour as far as access to Nepal was concerned. Why did India react to the construction of the same highway? Because Nepal henceforth would be a 'level' playing field in relation to both India and China. Why did Nepal play the China card and seek closer relations with her? She was apprehensive of India's intentions. India's role in creating Bangladesh and annexing Sikkim shook the faith of Nepal on India's policy based on *Panchsheela* where non interference on the geographical integrity of other countries had been the key principle[22]. Such a zero sum approach is the result of viewing security in politico-military terms, the hallmark of the Realist school.

What we will see in the subsequent pages is how the relation amongst the three countries changed once security came to be viewed in a different light by the protagonists. China may be seen as the catalyst of that change once it embarked on the road to develop her economy along the liberal international economic order (LIEO).

The Deng period was to witness India-China rapprochement and a gradual shift of China away from other smaller South Asian countries from the late 1970s onwards[23]. Once China had evolved a long-term economic plan to catch up with the western countries, regional Byzantine politics seemed to pale in comparison. Being involved in the regional political intrigues was seen by China as a waste of precious resources. It was better for her to evolve some sort of cooperative mechanism with her rival, India rather than to adopt a confrontationist approach. One of the clearest manifestations of this was the reflection of China's 'shift' which was conveyed during Li Peng's visit to Nepal in 1989. China refused to be drawn into making any comments on the India-Nepal Trade and Transit treaty. The treaty had strained relations between the two countries. In fact, Li Peng told the then Prime Minister of Nepal to 'maintain good relations with India'[24]. An even greater move towards improving relations with India was made in 1996 when the Chinese President Jiang Zemin on a visit to Islamabad advised Pakistan to shelve historical problems and bilaterally 'mend their ties' with India[25].

Sans a strategic lever, Nepal had to normalise relations with India. The very next year after China refused to be drawn into the Indo-Nepal Treaty dispute, Nepal gave an implicit assurance to India that Nepal would not use its policy of equidistance to violate Indian security sensitivities[26]. In 1995, Nepal agreed to fully respect India's security concerns and not to allow any activities on its soil prejudicial to Indian security and to consult each other on reaching mutual agreement over defence related matters[27]. It would be naïve to ascribe the change in Nepal's behaviour towards India simply on the basis of China's shift in priorities. Domestic politics has had a role in bringing Nepal closer to India. Thapliyal avers that a shift in the perception of Nepal was visible after the multi party democracy was established in Nepal in 1990. Democratic Nepal has not been overtly concerned with regime insecurity[28].

Chinese scholars identify the urge to develop a strong economy as one of the main reasons for the improvement in relations amongst the South Asian countries. It is pointed out that the East Asian region has not only seen very high rates of growth but also a high degree of regional cooperation. This has led the South Asian nations to consider emulating the East Asian experience. In July 1991, India agreed to Nepal's request to have separate agreements on trade and transit, and to reopen fifteen transit trade ports[29].

In terms of the discourse on security, it is being realised that with development, there is a need to view security from a wider spectrum as compared to the narrow politico-military prism that was used during the Cold War to analyse security. Attaining security through the development of the economy is recognised by countries like India as a viable strategy. Under the LIEO, nations can develop only by evolving a complex interdependence in the economic sphere where a country's prosperity is hinged on the prosperity of other countries in the region. This logic resounds in the traditional security sector too. Sridhar Khatri, a Reader in the Tribhuwan University avers that a powerful India, which is both confident and secure, can invariably contribute to a greater sense of regional security[30].

With a shift in the emphasis of security from matters political/military to economic, the relation between India and China as regards Nepal has moved away to large extent from a zero sum approach. In the absence of internal weaknesses, the region should remain free from external interference. Both the powers realise that an underdeveloped, unstable Nepal would not add to the overall stability of the region and that there could be spill over effects on both China and India. Therefore it is in the interest of both the countries to allow Nepal to develop, with aid and other benefits from the 'other' side is necessary.

References

1. Barry Buzan, Ole Waever, Jaap de Wilde, *Security A New Framework for Analysis,* Lynne Rienner Publishers: London, Colorado, 1998, p. 2.

2. Shook Mehta, "India's Security Concerns and Nepal", *USI Journal,* Vol. 131(545), July-Sept 2001, p. 335.

3. *Ibid.*, p. 335.

4. *Ibid.*, p. 336.

5. Sangeeta Thapliyal, "Contesting Mutual Security: India-Nepal Relations", *AGNI,* Vol. 6(4), Jan-April 2003, p. 43.

6. Quoted in M.R. Josse, "Nepal's Strategic Balancing", *South Asian Journal,* Vol. 3, Jan-March 2004, p. 84.
7. Thapliyal, n.5, p. 46.
8. Mohammed Arif, "National Security: South Asian Perspective", *Journal of Peace Studies,* Vol. 8(3), May-June 2001, p. 6.
9. Barry Buzan, *People, States and Fear,* Lynne Rienner Publishers: Colorado, 1991, p. 66.
10. Sridhar Khatri, "Security Issue in South Asia: A Nepalese Perspective", *South Asian Survey,* Vol. 2(2), Jan-July 1995, p. 107.
11. Thapliyal, n.5, p. 43.
12. Subrata K. Mitra, "The Reluctant Hegemon: India's self perception and the South Asian Strategic Environment", *Contemporary South Asia,* Vol. 12(3), Sept 2003, p. 399-400.
13. John Herz writes that the self-help attempts of the nations to look after their security lead to the rising insecurity for other nations. Nations interpret their own actions as defensive and the actions of others as potentially threatening. In this particular instance, China saw India's security relation with Nepal undermining her own security.
14. Swaran Singh, "Sino-South Asian Ties: Problems and Prospects", *Strategic Analysis,* Vol. 24(1), April 2000, p. 32.
15. Swaran Singh, *China-South Asia: Issues, Equations, Policies,* Lancer's Books: New Delhi, 2003, p. 333.
16. Josse, n.6, p. 83.
17. Mitra, n.12, p. 405.
18. Narayan Khadka, "Chinese Foreign Policy toward Nepal in the Cold War Period: An Assessment", *China Report,* Vol. 35(1), Jan-March 1999, p. 66.
19. Singh, n.14, p. 33.
20. Josse, n.6, p. 83.

21. Thapliyal, n.5, p. 40.

22. Mahendra P. Lama, "Newer Dimensions in India Nepal Relations", *World Focus*, 21(10-11-12), Oct-Nov-Dec. 2000, p. 45.

23. Singh, n.15, p. 336.

24. *Ibid.*, p. 337.

25. *Ibid.*, p. 338.

26. Thapliyal, n.5, p. 45.

27. Khatri, n.10, p. 105.

28. Thapliyal, n.5, p. 44.

29. Du Youkang, "South Asian Security and its Impact on China", *China Report,* Vol. 37(2), Apr-June 2001, p. 145-146 .

30. Khatri, n.10, p. 108.

10

SAARC's Conceptual Framework and Realities

Anup K. Mishra
G.S. Kushwaha

Background of the Study

Geographically speaking South Asia is a compact region. All the seven members have either common boundaries or are joined by the sea. Historically India, Pakistan and Bangladesh were one nation prior to their independence – all part of one political-social and economic unit till 1947. Politically speaking all the seven South Asian was either under British Empire or under its influence in one way or the other. India, Pakistan and Bangladesh constituted British India. Sri Lanka was under imperial possession. Bhutan was a protectorate and it had only strategic value for the British. Similarly Maldives was an important strategic outpost of British Empire. Thus, South Asian countries have geographic proximity, historically they are close, ken and have cultural and socio-economic commonalties. And till very recently had political dominance of the British. In fact like the six original members of European Union had common political suffering.

The South Asian leaders are conscious and aware of the situation and therefore are in favor of regional cooperation. It is important to quote from the First SAARC Summit held in Dhaka in 1985, felt that bound as these countries were by many common values, rooted in their social, ethnic, cultural and historical tradition, regional cooperation provided a logical response to their problems. They were conscious of their individual and regional strengths, their potential as a huge market, their substantial human and natural resources and the complimentary of their economies. They were confident that with effective regional cooperation, they could make optimum use of their capacities for the benefit of their peoples, accelerate the pace of their economic development and enhance their national and collective self-reliance.

With this favorable aspect, it is necessary to mention that all the countries of the South Asia are facing one or two other kind of centrifugal violent forces. The matter becomes worst by external involvement in their movements.

India is suffering from cross-boarder terrorism and separatist movements in Jammu and Kashmir.

Pakistan is suffering from its own creation of sowing the seed of terrorism. President Musharraf escaped two assassination attempts within a fortnight during December 2003.

Bangladesh tacit support to India separist movement by giving shelter to terrorist groups within its own territory is subject to tension between India and Bangladesh.

Nepal is facing violence of Maoist guerrilla movement.

Bhutan acting bravely against the militants from the Indian State of Assam is facing threats.

Sri Lanka is facing and suffering from the movement of LTTE.

Maldives, although free from any of the above type of troubles, is facing internal resentment owing to long-term office of president of Abdul Gayoom.

The basic problem is that South Asians countries are facing one or the other type of Terrorism engineered by external forces. These countries need a strong and determined political will to effectively curb this trend otherwise the consequences for not only to the member countries but also for the region as a whole. It is in this background we have to discuss and examine ***SAARC's Conceptual Framework***.

Conceptual Framework: Evolution of SAARC

It was in November 1980, the idea of regional cooperation was first mooted. The foreign secretaries of the seven South Asian countries met for the first time in November 1980. Thereafter, foreign secretaries met in April 1981. A committee of the whole was established, the committee identified five broad areas for regional cooperation. In august 1981, the Foreign Ministers of the South Asian countries, at their first meeting (held in New Delhi) adopted the Declaration on South Asian regional Cooperation (SARC). An Integrated Program of Action (IPA) was formally launched in the five agreed areas – Agriculture, Rural Development, Tele communications, Meteorology, and Health and population. Some other areas like Transport, Postal services, scientific and technological cooperation, sports, arts and culture were also added. In the First SAARC Summit which was held in Dhaka on 7th and 8th of December, the charter formally establishing the South Asian Association for Regional cooperation was adopted. The Seven South Asian Countries are now known as SAARC members. Thus the SAARC as a region was born in December 1985.

PRINCIPALS, PROVISIONS AND OBJECTIVES

Principals

SAARC's Principles are as follows-

- Cooperation within the framework of the association is based, territorial integrity, political independence, and non-interference in the internal affairs of other states and mutual benefit.
- Such cooperation is to compliment and not to substitute bilateral or multilateral cooperation.
- Such cooperation should be consistent with bilateral and multilateral obligations of member states.

General Provisions

- Decisions at all levels in SAARC are taken on the basis of unanimity.

- Bilateral and contentious issues are excluded from its deliberations.

Objectives

- To promote the welfare of the peoples of South Asia and to improve their quality of life.
- To accelerate economic growth, social progress and cultural development in the region and to provide all individuals the opportunity to live in dignity and to realise they're full potential.
- To promote a strengthen self-reliance among the countries of South Asia.
- To contribute to mutual trust, understanding and appreciation of one another's problems.
- To promote active collaboration and mutual assistance in the economic, social, technical and scientific fields.
- To strengthen cooperation with other developing countries.
- To strengthen cooperation among themselves in international forums on matters of common interests and
- To cooperate with international and regional organisations with similar aims and objectives.

These objectives, principles and general provisions of SAARC are undoubtedly just, reasonable and in the best interests of people of the region. But the conceptual framework will not be complete without referring to institutional framework.

Institutional Framework of SAARC

SUMMIT

The highest authority of the Association rests with the Heads of States and Governments, who meet annually at Summit levels. To date 12 meetings of the Summit have taken place. The first was at Dhaka in the year1985 and the 12th at Islamabad in the year 2004.

Council of Ministers: Comprising the Foreign Ministers of member States, the council formulation policies, decides on other area of cooperation, consider additional and other measures and mechanism of cooperation and reviews program. The council normally meets twice a year and can meet earlier also by agreement under extra-ordinary circumstances.

Standing Committee

It comprises foreign secretaries of Member States and is responsible for overall monitoring and coordination of programs, considers modalities of financing, determining inter sectional priorities, mobilising regional and external resources and identifying new areas of cooperation. It may meet as and where necessary but normally meets twice a year. The committee submits its reports to the council of Ministers. It may also set up Action Committee comprising of Members States concerned for implementation of projects.

Technical Committee

The technical committee, comprising representative from member state formulates programs and prepares projects in their respective fields which make up the I.P.A under SAARC.

SAARC Secretariat

It was established at Kathmandu in January 1987. It coordinates and monitors the implementation of SAARC activities, services the meetings of the Association and serves as the channel of communications between SAARC and other international institutions. Secretariat being the headquarters is being utilised as the venue for various SAARC meetings.

This is in nutshell the basic conceptual framework of SAARC. Regarding regional cooperation within the framework of SAARC, there are three important features. Regional cooperation among all the SAARC members, regional cooperation among a few members (may be bilateral or multilateral) and SAARC's relation with other international institutions. We will in brief give some salient aspects of agreed areas at cooperation before coming out with our comments. We begin with international institutions.

Agreed Areas of Cooperation

SAARC and the International Institutions

There are some cooperation agreements and Memorandum of understanding. We are giving a few examples:

- Cooperation agreement was signed between SAARC and UNICEF in December 1993.
- Framework agreement for mutual cooperation between SAARC and ESCAP in February 1994.
- Cooperation agreement between SAARC and Colombo Plan Bureau in April 1995.
- Memorandum of understanding between SAARC and UNCTAD, Feb. 1993.
- Memorandum of understanding between SAARC and Asia Pacific Telecommuting (APT), Feb. 1994.
- Memorandum of understanding between SAARC and UNDCP, Aug 1995.
- Memorandum of understanding between SAARC and EC, July1996.
- Memorandum of understanding between SAARC and CIDA, July 1997.

These few examples indicate the effectiveness of SAARC at the international level.

Bilateral and Sub-regional Level Cooperation

SAARC has made programs and is in the process of increasing cooperation at the bilateral and sub-regional level. Some of the agreement is infect unilateral initiative. For example India has increased her investment limit from US $ 15 million to US $ 30 million in 1999 for SAARC countries and from Indian Rs. 60 crore to Indian Rs. 120 crore in 1999 for investment in Nepal and Bhutan. Further India's unilateral offer to dismantle import restrictions on around 2307 import products from the SAARC countries.

Among the sub-regional agreements, we have Indo-Bhutan and Indo-Nepal cooperation Treaties and recently formed. Indo-Sri Lanka Free Trade Area. There are two other sub-regional agreements in which more than two countries are participating and in one-two members of ASEAN are also signatories. The first is Bangladesh – Bhutan – India – Nepal quadrilateral Growth initiative and the second is India – Myanmar – Sri Lanka – Thailand economic cooperation. Later on Bhutan and Nepal also become members. This arrangement has taken a very significant decision in Feb. 2004 to create a FreeTrade Zone by 2017. The countries have reached only a framework agreement setting a time frame for creating a Free Trade Area for goods and services in addition to promoting investment. India, Sri Lanka and Thailand are categorised as developing countries and Bhutan, Myanmar and Nepal as Least Developed countries.

Thus, at the sub-regional level, the program must be considered reasonably satisfactory.

Regional Level

SAARC's performance as a region is not very effective and progressive. In certain areas regional agreements exist but are not properly implemented and in some area particularly the South Asian Free Trade Area only in the 12th Summit a decision has been taken to form it by 2006 spread over a period of twelve years. In brief, we will mention these steps. But before proceeding further a reference must be made to the poverty of the SAARC. Economically South Asian Region, among the low and middle income Regions of the worldS are most unfavorable placed. A sixth of the world people receive about 78 per cent of the world income and average of 470 a day. Three fifth of the world's people in the poorest 61 countries receive 6 per cent of the world's income – less than $2 a day. According to 'World Development Report (2000-01)', percentage share of people living on less than one dollar a day in South Asia has gone down from 44.9 per cent (1987) to 40 per cent (1998) while the number of poor has increased from 474.4 million in 1987 to 522 million in 1998. By any estimate the number in 2004 will be greater. The other low and middle income regions of the world have different trends' The East Asia took the lead reducing at from 29 per cent to 24 per cent (1982-1998), Sub-Saharan Africa had 46 per cent. Latin American and Caribbean had 16 per cent. Thus, among the regions, south Asia is just above sub-Saharan region. The situation in

SAARC regarding poverty is not at all satisfactory if not alarming. Invariably the same situation exists in Human Development Index. We are excluding these points, as they are not directly related to our present topic.

SAARC has the distinction of taking many steps at the regional level. Let us begin with regional agreement/ Conventions:

- Agreement on establishing SAARC Food Reserve, signed during the third SAARC Summit in Kathmandu in November 1987 came into existence on 22Aug. 1988.
- SAARC regional convention on suppression of Terrorism, signed during the Third SAARC summit in Kathmandu in November 1987 came into existence on 22 Aug. 1988.
- SAARC convention on Narcotic Drugs and Psychotropic substances signed during the sixth SAARc summit in Mali in Nov. 1990 came into force on 15 Sept. 1993.

SAARC Regional centers are existing, for example :

- SAARC Agricultural Information Center (SAIC) established in Dhaka in 1988.
- SAARC Tuberculosis Center (STC) established in Kathmandu in 1992.
- SAARC Documentation Center (SDC) established in New Delhi in 1994.
- SAARC Meteorological Research Center (SMRC) established in Dhaka in 1995.

SAARC Youth Awards Scheme

SAARC youth Award Scheme has been established following the adoption of the SAARC Youth Resolution by the Ministerial Conference on Youth (Male, July 1994). It aims to encourage and recognise the skills and talents of Youth of the region. The first award was made in 1997 in the field of 'Outstanding social service in Community Welfare'. 'New Inventions and discoveries' followed it.

There is SAARC Audio Visual Exchange (SAVE) program. A number of Designated SAARC years were adopted, e.g. SAARC year for combating drug abuse and drug trafficking (1989). SAARC year of the girl child (1990), SAARC year of environment (1992), SAARC year of poverty eradication (1995), SAARC year of literacy (1996). The decade 1991-2000 AD has been designated as the 'SAARC Decade of Girl Child'.

There are a number of Regional Apex bodies, SAARC chambers of commerce and industry (SCCI) is doing excellent work in promoting regional cooperation. Besides, there are SAARC recognised bodies like South Asian Federation of Accountants (SAFA), SAARC Federation of University Women (SFUW) and the Association of SAARC speakers and Parliamentarians. Under the SAARC Visa Exemption Scheme 21 categories were conferred under the scheme.

Thus, these are a number of success points at the SAARC's regional level.

SAARC as a region has not done well with respect to poverty eradication and fighting terrorism. The real problem is regarding trade and economic cooperation with the operationalisation of SAARC Preferential Trading Arrangements on 7th Dec. 1995, These were great hopes and expectations that very soon SAFTA will be formed

Till now three Rounds of Tariff Negotiations have taken place. Total concessions were made in 5550 commodities, out of which 3456 were LDC's and 2094 for all members. The important point is that not only large number of concessions was given to LDC's but also the extent of tariff cuts was greater for them.

SAPTA was hailed as a positive and constructive achievement of SAARC. It marked the success of one decade of regional cooperation. But there were some shortcomings also. Concessions were granted in the commodity where Trade was non-existence or negligible. Infect it did net increase intra-regional trade to the desired extent. But it was considered as a major step towards south Asian Free Trade Area. The ball starts rolling.

SAARC's transformation from SAPTA to SAFTA took time. There were many ups and down. Its formation depended upon Indo-Pak relations to be very frank. The hard fact was and the doubts of the heads of state or Govt. Nepal, Bhutan, Bangladesh, The Maldives and srilanka that no substantial progress can be achieved unless India and Pakistan move away from their adversial relationship to solving issues between them in a pragmatic way. This was the crux of the problem. This explains why it was deferred earlier despite the heads of the States or Govt. at the 9th SAARC Summit recognised the importance of achieving a Free Trade by year 2001. And reiterated that steps towards trade liberalisation must take into accounts the special needs of the smaller and the LDC's and that benefits must accrue equity.

However in January 2004 things changed. The 12th SAARC Summit held in Islamabad (Pakistan) adopted the SAFTA agreement as well as an additional protocol to the existing convention on the suppression of terrorism. As per agreement, SAFTA will come into force from January 01, 2006 and the "Developing countries" in SAARC will reduce their tariff between zero and 5 per cent for LDC's beginning from January 01,2006. Describing SAFTA as a major milestone, the declaration said it is important to maintain the momentum and move provides further broadening of economic cooperation and to ensure equitable distribution of benefits of trade.

Prof. Muchkund Dubey discussed the signing of the SAPTA agreement can be regarded as a landmark in the evolution of the SAARC. This represents a movement away from the mere tinkering with tariff under SAPTA. The SAFTA agreement has the potentiality of going beyond its stated objective of freeing trade in goods. It can make South Asia a magnet for vastly enhanced foreign investment and lead to a restructuring of the economies making the region one of the fastest growing and most competitive economic blocks.'But he also observes, ' Although the treaty marks a breakthrough and a great potential, it falls short from the vision projected by the Eminent persons group laid out in a roadmap with distinct milestone – FTA by 2008, a customs Union by 2015 and economic Union by 2020'. One Editorial (Economic Times, 6th June 2004) was a bit cautious. 'Historic is perhaps an exaggerated description of the decision taken by the leaders of South Asia to make the region a free trade bloc by 2006. This is the Third and not the first time that the member countries of the SAARC have laid down a target for setting up a free trade Area'.

However, now the things are more optimistic and the two major players are willing to play following the rules of the game.

Conclusion

One may be surprised why despite unanimous recommendation and suggestions; the SAARC did not take off. The SAARC provides that ' Bilateral and contentious issues are excluded from its deliberation'. Unfortunately, although such issues were excluded but such issues prevented trade cooperation at a regional level. There are unilateral, bilateral and even multilateral programs of cooperation. But at the regional level progress was prevented.

The fact is that political expediency overweighs economic rationality. The economic wellbeing of the people goes to the back seat. There was nothing wrong into the conceptualisation of SAARC. It wanted that all people should be better off and nobody is worsening. In SAARC Governments were not trading but people were trading. The unofficial trade (particularly between India and Pakistan) was much greater than the official trade. The poor were suffering because of the political whims of the governments. Things are changing. Now there is realisation that united South Asia will help in solving the basic and fundamental problems of the region. Even in European Union there were problems at the initial stage during the sixties. The very existence of EEC was endangered when France boycotted the proceeding. But it was on account of economic factors, which had political implications. In South Asia it was the reverse. However, well begun is half done.

The brief review of SAARC activities (based primarily on SAARC publications) is a clear indication of the progressive success of economic cooperation among the seven members. It will be too much to expect something concrete from the SAARC as compared to EU. SAARC has its own limitations and problems besides internal differences. *Consider the circumstances their achievement must be considered outstanding the SAARC has taken off from SAPTA to SAFTA. It will move forward as the basic infrastructure has been created, it now needs superstructure for concrete results.*

Infact there is no alternative but to set together, forget the past, think of the future. SAARC's conceptual framework is reasonable and realistic and if necessary it can be amended to suit new challenges.

References

* UN Publications have classified Low and Middle income regions of the World as follows:

1. East Asia and Pacific 2. Europe and Central Asia 3. Latin America and Caribbean 4. Middle East and North Africa 5. South Asia 6. Sub-Saharan Africa.

For details see 'Dynamism of South Asian Preferential Trading Arrangements (SAPTA), studies in Humanities and social sciences, journal of inter university center IIAS, Shimla, Vol. X No.2, winter 2003, pp. 99-100.

11

The Role of SAARC : with Special Reference to IXth and XIIth SAARC Summit

Manju Kumar

Prime Minister of India Shri Atal Bihari Vajpayee's projection of the South Asia Union may appear to be a dream but not an unrealistic one. It has its roots in Nehruvian vision of Asian resurgence, which had got lost in the Cold War and Intra-Asian conflicts. Today, the people are more than prepared for such a South Asian Community.

The Vision of Pt. Jawahar Lal Nehru in his words that the countries of Asia are very backward and the standard of living appallingly low. These economic problem demand urgent solution or else crisis and disaster may overwhelm us. We have, therefore, to think in terms of the common man and fashion our political, social and economic structure so that the burdens that have crushed him may be removed and he may have full opportunity for growth.[1]

This was the vision for unity peace and progress in South Asian of Pt. Jawaharlal Nehru, can be taken as the genesis of cooperation in this region which ultimately gave to the birth of the South Asian Association of Regional Cooperation (SAARC) in 1985 in Dhaka.[2]

Prior to that it was at the initiation of President Zia-Ul-Rahman of Bangaladesh the idea of SAARC came into existence in 1980. The however the emerging trends of regional organisations in Europe, Africa and Latin America, and then important role in the development of the region were hardly overlooked by the statesmen and leaders of the South Asian Countries. In August 1983 the area of cooperation for regional cooperation were identified by the foreign minister of seven countries, namely Bangladesh, Bhutan, India, Nepal, Pakistan, Shri Lanka and Maldives to attain self reliance through economic growth, Social progress and cultural development. To give it a final shape to the idea of SAARC all heads of states of the seven Asian countries met at Dhaka in 1985. SAARC has been established is gaining a new momentum with gradual widening of the areas of cooperation among the seven South Asian Nations and imparting of greater strength to the institutional structure that has come up for promotion of multilateral interaction.

A series of SAARC summit followed:-First summit in Dhaka (1985), Second Summit in India (1986), third summit in Kathmandu (1987), fourth summit in Islamabad (1988), fifth summit in Maldives (1990), sixth summit in Shri Lanka (1991), seventh summit in Bangladesh (1993), eighth summit in India (1995), ninth summit in Maldives (1997), tenth summit in Shrilanka (1998), eleventh summit in Kathmandu (2002) and twelth and latest summit in Islamabad (4-6 January 2004).

At the first summit held in Dhaka on 7-8 Dec. 1985, the charter establishing the South Asian Association for regional Cooperation (SAARC) was adopted. The main objectives were as follows:[3]

(i) To promote the welfare of the people of South Asia and to improve their quality of life; (ii) To accelerate economic growth, social progress and cultural development in the region to provide all individual the opportunity to live in dignity and to realise their full potentials; (iii) To promote and strengthen collective self-reliance among the countries of South Asia; (iv) To contribute to mutual trust, understanding and appreciation of one another's problems; (v) To promote active collaboration and mutual assistance in the economic, social, cultural, technical and scientific fields; (vi) To strengthen cooperation with other developing countries; (vii) To strengthen cooperation among themselves in international forums on matters of common interests; and (viii) To cooperate with international and regional organisations with similar aims and purposes.[4]

The Principles were: (i) Cooperation within the frame work of the Association is based on respect for the principles of sovereign equality, territorial integrity, political independence, non-interference in the internal affairs of other states and mutual benefit. (ii) Such cooperation is to complement and not to substitute bilateral or multilateral cooperation. (iii) Such co-operation should be consistent with bilateral and multilateral obligations of the member states.[5]

Its General Provision were: (i) Decisions at all levels in SAARC are taken on the basis of unanimity and (ii) bilateral and contentious issues are excluded from its deliberations.[6]

SAARC was officially born in 1985 as an association of States whose aims were to "promote the well-being of the populations of South Asia and improve their standard of living; to speed up economic growth, social progress and cultural development; to reinforce links between the countries of this area; and lastly, to promote mutual collaboration and assistance in the economic, social, cultural technical and scientific fields". The primary objectives of SAARC was to benefit the participating countries by identifying an exploiting potential areas for economic social and cultural cooperation and resolving outstanding problems between the member countries.

SAARC groups seven countries: Bangladesh, Bhutan, India, The Maldives, Nepal, Pakistan and Shri Lanka. With 1.3 billion inhabitants in 1999, these countries represent almost 22 per cent of the world population, but only 1.97 per cent of world GNP (575 billion US$ in 1999). Average per capita income is $441 (World Bank, 1999). Indeed, poverty is one fundamental element characterising the situation in South Asia.[7]

If we look at the figures of SAARC countries:-[8]

Sl. No.	*Countries*	*Population*	*GNI*	*Per Capital Income*
1.	India	1,032 m.	GNI $ 477b	$460
2.	Pakistan	141 m.	GNI $ 60b	$420
3.	Bangladesh	133 m.	GNI $ 49b	$360
4.	Nepal	24 m.	GNI $ 5.8b	$250
5.	Bhutan	0.82 m.	GNI $ 0.5b	$640
6.	Shri Lanka	19 m.	GNI $ 16b	$880
7.	Maldives	0.28 m.	GNI $ 0.59b	$2,090

GNI: Gross National Income in $ billion; figures 2001.

It seems that share of Asian Countries in world trade has been increased and steadily growing whereas the member state of SAARC in significant in the total trade of the world. Among SAARC countries India ranked first in foreign trade followed by Pakistan, Shri Lanka, Bangladesh, and Nepal. India had also made significant structural change in the economic and trade structure. However, in low index of trade complimentary among SAARC countries indicates a pressing need to search out some area of joint cooperation for investment and production activities.

Some Reflection on XIth and XIIth Summits

Nepal had played very important role in SAARC since beginning. Nepal hosted the IIIrd SAARC summit in 1987.[9] Nepal had the honor for the establishment of the SAARC Secretariat in Kathmandu. Nepal among the South Asian Countries had interest in SAARC because of its social, economic, political and environmental problems. Its sovereignty, territorial integrity and national interest to be more guaranteed through SAARC. The Third summit held in 1987 in Kathmandu was significant in view of its agreements which reflect a consensus and provide the basic frame work for collective endeavors to eradicate poverty and hunger from the region. One of the major achievements of this summit was establishment of a regional ford security reserve. The summit had also recorded in major breakthrough in the fifth against menace of terrorism. The Third summit unlike the previous summit did not avoid the issues of extending regional cooperation in the basic areas of development Trade, Industry, Money and financial areas of cooperation were fully discussed and efforts were made to strengthened the cooperation.

Nepal hosted XIth SAARC Summit in January 2002,[10] "Nepal is the country which chaired SAARC for the last two years. What Nepal had tried to do is to keep the SAARC issues alive. Even during the period when there was a one social charter, poverty alleviation commission report, issues related to trade which probably suppresses all over issues specially SAPTA and SAFTA and terrorism,"[11]. In an exclusive interview to the People's Review on Monday, prior to leaving for Lahore, Pakistan, for the 12th SAARC Summit, Thapa said; "All these have been updated, brought in the line for consideration of the Summit including in the area of terrorism where a convention was adopted in Kathmandu. A progress report on what is happening on those major fronts where we expect cooperation between the countries to expand and grow. That has been the contribution made by Nepal during the time when Nepal has chaired the organisation. So, we didn't waste time and we kept the whole momentum alive." "In other areas, achievements have been made on various fronts. The social charter should be adopted, the Poverty Alleviation Report, which was initiated when KP Bhattarai of Nepal was chairperson, has been update."[12]

SAARC has been gradually building its identity as a regional organisation among the peoples of our region. However, in a frank admission of the truth, our endeavours to fight poverty, economic backwardness and a myriad of other social problems have yet to bear the desired degree of success. The growing menace of terrorism has added a new dimension to the problems we have been facing in the region.

We all agree that poverty is our common enemy. We have made and reiterated our commitments to eradicate poverty time and again in the past. I am happy to recall that as directed by the Eleventh SAARC Summit, the Ministerial Meeting on Poverty Alleviation was held in Islamabad in April 2002. The need for adopting a comprehensive and multidimensional approach to poverty eradication in South Asia together with a set of internal and extern policies to be adopted in Independent South Asian Commission on Poverty Alleviation (ISACPA) has also held two meetings so far and their work is in progress. Likewise, considerable progress has been reported in the preparation of the Regional Poverty Profile, a task which was entrusted to the Secretary General by the Eleventh Summit. I believe, these exercise will enable us to undertake poverty alleviation measures on a more sound and surer footing in the days ahead.[13]

It has been widely felt that regional economic integration with more liberalised trade among the Member States is one of the core areas of cooperation. It would not only lead to economic growth but also constitute the fundamental pedestal from where to effectively address the problem of poverty in our region. Increased trade means additional opportunities for people in terms of fresh entrepreneurial initiatives, more employment and more income and this will ultimately lead to the betterment of the lives of the people in the region. Our Leaders have envisaged a step-by-step approach to the ultimate goal of South Asian Economic Union. Unless we make rapid progress in the negotiations for trade liberalisation under SAPTA, and thus pave the way for progression into the South Asian Free Trade Area by early finalisation of the text of the Draft Treaty Framework for SAFTA, our efforts to increase the volume of trade and accelerate the pace of economic integration within SAARC do not seem to make much headway. We are hopeful that the next meeting of the 4th round of trade negotiations under SAPTA would be conclusive.[14]

At the eleventh summits as discussing about the challenges of social development from home to more than a quarter of all humanity that we face in South Asia are no less formidable. At the Eleventh Summit, two Regional Conventions-one each of Preventing and Combating Trafficking in Women and Children for Prostitution and on Regional Arrangements for the promotion of child Welfare in South Asia-had been signed. While these are in the process of ratification by the Member States, measures for their effective implementation have to be considered. The SAARC Social Charter, once it is prepared and finalised, would also be a significant step in addressing the challenge of social development in South Asia. Likewise, the formation of a SAARC Autonomous Advocacy Group on Women Personalities would be an important step in the area of Women empowerment and gender related issues.

The Most Important issue of terrorism was taken up in Eleventh SAARC Summit. Terrorism has been acknowledged by our Leaders as a challenge to all states and to all of Humanity, and cannot be justified on ideological, political, religious or on any other ground. Our Leaders have also agreed to redouble efforts, collectively as well as individually, to prevent and suppress terrorism in all its forms and manifestations by waging a comprehensive and sustained fight against it. We already have a SAARC Regional Convention on Suppression of Terrorism the enabling legislations for which are being worked by the Member States. In view of the growing seriousness of the terrorism problem in South Asia, and the threat it has posed on the security, stability and development of the entire region, it would be timely to accelerate the process whereby the Convention could be brought to implementation with a view to suppressing terrorism with full force.[15]

On the occasion of the SAARC Charter Day, Kathmandu, 8 December 2003, H.E. Mr. Q.A.M.A. Rahim, SAARC Secretary General in his statements said at the Eleventh Summit Kathmandu, the Leaders solemnly renewed their pledge to strengthen the Association and to make it more result oriented and forward looking by adopting clearly defined programmers and effective implementation line with popular expectations. The pronouncement made during the last Summit to give effect to the Shape for a more prosperous South Asia and to work for realisation of the vision of a phased and planned process leading to a South Asian Economic Union is a testimony to our collective will to move forward.[16]

He also suggests for the forthcoming Summit could be a watershed development for the region for several reasons. I would mention a few. First, a framework treaty for the South Asian Free Trade Area (SAFTA), which is being be considered by the next Summit. If signed, this will pave the way towards the eventual creation of a Socio Economic Union, as envisioned by our Leaders. Second, the text of the SAARC Social Charter and encompasses a broad range of targets to put across the region in areas of poverty eradication, empowerment of women, youth mobilisation, human resource development, promotion of health and nutrition, protection of children etc. Third, the reconstituted Independent South Asian Commission on Poverty Alleviation (ISACPA), as per the directive of the last Summit has been Worked Report and is ready with it for submission at the summit. Their recommendations will go a long way in the struggle against the scourge of poverty in the region. Fourth, the Summit will consider proposals for establishment three new regional centers, namely the SAARC Cultural Centre in Sri Lanka, the SAARC Centre for Cooperation Management in the Maldives and the SAARC Media Centre in Nepal.[17]

A conducive environmental development is of utmost important the promotion of South Asia through more people-to-people contact may go a long way in creating such an environment. We at the fully committed to realising this objective. You will be happy to know that this year we are not only celebrating in Kathmandu at the Secretariat but in some other capitals as well through the various SAARC regional Member States have been requested to organise special events to commemorate this day. We have also some Member States to consider celebrating this day in various non-SAARC capitals though their Missions and South Asian Communities.[18] Over the last two years Nepal as a chair hosted number of SAARC events to keep the momentum generated by the Kathmandu Summit alive. This was the background prepared in Kathmandu for the coming twelth SAARC Summit in Islamabad.

The XIIth SAARC Summit (4-6 January 2004),[19] concluded on 6th Jan 2004 after the signing of a historic agreement on free trade, an additional protocol on terrorism and a social charter. Under the agreement the Member State pledged to create a just and equitable partnership in the region and to work towards the creation region and to work towards the creation region and to work towards the creation of a South Asian Economic Union. It pointed out that the least developing countries had been given special and differential treatment under the present agreement.

The declaration concluded, with the remarks of Pakistan Prime Minister Mr. Zafarullah Khan Jamali, the declaration contained the road map for South Asian Cooperation and had a historic significance.[20]

Under the social charter the seven nations have pledge to work together in themes much as poverty alleviation, population stabilisation empowerment of women and human resources development.[21] The SAARC heads of state and government signed the social charter, which calls for pooling resources of the member states for the uplift of the peoples in South Asia. It also envisages the protection of children's and women's rights, as well as the development of health, education, culture and other sectors. Nepalese Prime Minister Surya Bahadur Thapa called on Prime Minister Jamali. The Two Prime Ministers exchanged views on trade and diplomatic relations between the two countries. They expressed satisfaction over the process of SAARC during the Twelth Summit.[22]

The South Asia free trade area agreement and the additional protocol on terrorism were signed by the foreign ministers of the Member States in the presence of their heads of State and Government.

The protocol on the view of SAARC convention of suppression of terrorism 1987-which pledges itself to elimination of terrorism in all its forms and manifestations in the regions as another "landmark" agreement the protocol deals with tackling the problem of the financing of terrorism. Clauses 29-32 of the declaration deal in the combating terrorism and indicate the seriousness with which all SAARC Countries, including Pakistan are now looking at the issue. The additional protocol reiterates the condemnation of terrorism by all SAARC countries and their commitment to implement all the relevant international convention to which they are party. It adopted the 'Islamabad Declaration' affirming the commitment of member nations to fight terrorism and promote regional trade. The next summit is in Dhaka in January 2005.

If South Asian Union is Strong the west would feel competitive, if not threatened. The West has always been interested in the subcontinent and if a common thread emerges from it in a form of a single brand they would gain too. Trading with or traveling through the union, with a single currency make life easier. After all Brand South Asia should not be about power, but about making life better.

Inspired by the successful experience of regional groupings like ASEAN and EU, the SAARC was conceptualised with a hope of opening a horison of collective prosperity and cooperation in South Asia. The founding leaders of this regional grouping must have visualised the SAARC as a vehicle of momentous change in this region. They might have expected it to help in making use of the expertise, resources and technological development to grapple with poverty and forge closer cooperation in the field of economy, culture, education, science, regional peace and other host of issue.

However, with the constraints in SAARC, the future would depend on how strategic relations in South Asia evolves with the entry now of Nato into Afghanistan, the evolving geo-economics in Central Asia, China's interest in the Bay of Bengal, and last but not least, the level of global and intra-regional inequalities and the plight of the poor. Having Afghanistan in SAARC will open a new window of opportunity for SAARC's resilience and further innovation towards additional avenues for sub-regional cooperation as well as engineering inter-regional cooperation.

References

1. Nehru, J.L., India's Foreign Policy: Selected Speeches, Sept. 1946 to April 1961, New Delhi, pp. 249-252.
2. Sreedhar, (1985) "Prospect for SAARC: A Novel Venture, Strategic Analysis." New Delhi, pp. 12-16.
3. Charter of SAARC, Articles.
4. *Ibid.*
5. *Ibid.*
6. *Ibid.*
7. The EU & South Asian Association for Regional Co-operation (SAARC)-Overview.
8. Asian Survey.
9. IIIrd SAARC-Summit in Kathmandu on 2-4 September 1987.
10. Eleventh SAARC-Summit in Kathmandu on January 2002.
11. Dr. Vek Bahadur Thapa, Ambassador-at-Large.
12. *Ibid.*

13. Hon. Minister for Health Mr. Sharat Singh Bhandari and the Chairman of the SAARC Council of Ministers, Kathmandu, 21 Aug. 2002.
14. *Ibid.*
15. *Ibid.*
16. H.E. Mr. Q.A.M.A. Rahim, SAARC Secretary General on the Occassion of the SAARC Charter Day, Kathmandu, 8 December 2003.
17. *Ibid.*
18. *Ibid.*
19. Twelth SAARC Summit held in Islamabad on 4-6 Jan 2004.
20. Times of India. Com.
21. Twelth SAARC-Summit, 2004.
22. *Ibid.*

12

Nepal's Trade Relations with SAARC Countries: An Appraisal

V.K.L. Srivastava
Anil Kumar Srivastava

Introduction

Nepal Government started its planned development process in 1950. Since then various efforts were made to establish economic relations, i.e., trade with other countries, especially South Asian neighbour countries. In spite of all development efforts Nepal could not achieve self-reliance in the field of economic development. More or less the same situation was prevailing in other South Asian countries. Hence, in order to accelerate economic development and to promote trade among neighbour countries, an organisation namely South Asian Association for Regional Co-operation (SAARC) came into existence in December 1985 as per decision of Dhaka Summit. India, Maldiv, Pakistan, Bangladesh, Bhutan, Sri Lanka and Nepal became its members. SAARC has proved to be a powerful engine of economic progress especially trade as well as strengthening security among member countries. The Minister of External Affairs, Sri Yashwant Sinha visited Nepal from August 19-24, 2002 to participate in SAARC Council of Ministers' meeting and he categorically stated that India has condemned the Maoist violence and continues to extend assistance for the strengthening of the Nepalese Security Forces.[1]

Major Trading Partners

Though the economic integration in South Asian nations is still at infant stage. However, the member countries of SAARC had striven to accelerate trade and aid relations among themselves. Consequently, Nepal adopted trade diversification efforts in 1960, 1970 and 1990 decades. Trade diversification and export-oriented trade strategy were the basic objectives of Nepal's foreign trade policy. Nepal has trading tie up with more than hundred countries of the world. Presently, Nepal's major export and import trading partners besides SAARC countries are Japan, USA, Germany, China, Singapore, Korea, New Zealand, Hong Kong, etc.

Table 1 reveals that Nepal exported the largest chunk of Rs. 5672.8 million to USA in 1995-96, which enhanced to Rs. 14973.7 million in 2000-01. Besides, Nepalese export to Germany, United Kingdom and Japan also surged. However, the export to Korea was meagre. Thus, the countries with which Nepal had trade relations were mostly developed countries.

Table-1: Nepal's Major Trading Partners (Rs. N million)

Sl. No.	*Country*	*1995-96*	*1996-97*	*1997-98*	*1998-99*	*1999-00*	*2000-01*
Export							
1.	USA	5672.8	5930.2	5106.4	9520.3	13677.7	14973.7
2.	Germany	6751.3	7651.7	8813.5	7820.7	7510.6	6178.5
3.	United Kingdom	289.4	297.7	318.2	521.8	1192.4	980.6
4.	Belgium	309.9	231.2	152.7	283.3	812.1	392.0
5.	France	175.6	241.9	486.6	479.2	735.5	676.0
6.	Japan	79.0	100.3	178.5	230.8	705.0	1341.0
7.	China	549.3	625.1	621.1	558.7	514.3	—
8.	Hong Kong	28.6	21.1	17.8	31.0	504.3	—
9.	Switzerland	445.2	346.5	234.9	281.5	418.5	—
10.	Spain	182.9	156.6	198.4	180.5	301.3	—
11.	Italy	356.6	348.3	461.8	385.0	300.0	—
12.	Canada	112.0	164.7	97.0	156.1	285.0	—
13.	Netherlands	127.6	174.2	129.8	159.1	193.3	—
14.	Austria	196.4	309.2	329.4	330.9	187.5	—
15.	Singapore	40.9	22.8	28.7	17.6	174.8	—
16.	Australia	40.4	58.5	81.7	101.6	109.9	—
17.	Sweden	71.8	170.9	151.5	78.8	95.7	—
18.	Korea	28.1	33.8	17.3	6.4	61.5	—

Import							
1.	China	4067.4	4334.5	5268.4	5252.1	12530.1	6274.6
2.	Switzerland	119.5	2321.2	1885.5	7545.2	10139.4	—
3.	Singapore	10563.3	9943.4	12640.4	9679.0	8013.4	12083.3
4.	Hong Kong	11706.1	20242.5	9283.7	4947.1	6801.3	5577.5
5.	Kuwait	1222.0	87.2	1602.5	1242.1	2974.9	—
6.	Japan	4551.2	3955.3	2751.6	2251.5	2891.9	3305.2
7.	Korea	1099.6	993.9	1862.0	1956.2	2794.8	—
8.	Indonesia	563.3	865.0	1351.4	1157.7	2242.9	—
9.	Thailand	1030.3	1631.3	1735.8	5565.9	2211.0	3306.2
10.	Malaysia	607.1	818.5	1163.3	1779.8	2203.9	3153.9
11	UAE	923.1	5572.4	1322.2	2763.3	1991.3	—
12.	Saudi Arabia	1042.0	1691.8	1901.6	1431.0	1979.5	4957.8
13.	France	513.7	317.6	463.4	1043.3	1920.3	—
14.	USA	765.6	862.3	1357.7	1317.9	1713.0	—
15.	Germany	2455.0	1148.6	1498.6	1463.4	1499.7	—
16.	New Zealand	2357.2	2203.2	1515.3	1785.3	1470.2	—
17.	United Kingdom	1024.3	3147.0	1312.6	1639.5	1462.5	8827.2
18.	Italy	186.2	346.8	1367.6	603.7	909.7	—
19.	Argentina	367.1	190.1	92.1	1106.0	834.8	—

Rs. N = Nepalese Rupee.
Source: Nepal and the World: A Statistical Profile. 2001, FNCCI, Kathmandu.

Nepal's imports from major trading partners increased during the aforesaid periods. The largest imports were from China, Switzerland, Singapore, Hong Kong, Kuwait, Japan and Korea from 1995-96 to 2000-01. The import from Argentina was paltry as compared to other countries. Nepal Government imported kerosene oil, petrol and other medium oils from UAE, Kuwait and Saudi Arabia. According to the available information, Nepal had trade relations with almost all developed and developing countries. The whopping foreign trade of Nepal in recent years is a result of liberalisation and globalisation measures adopted in various countries.

Composition of Exports and Imports to SAARC Countries

Moreover, Nepal had close trade relation with SAARC countries. Nepal exported various commodities like rice, spices, leather from goat, kid, bags, sacks of textiles, oilseeds, jute and other textiles, bast fibres, etc. The commodities like rice, refined sugar, spices, tobacco, unmanufactured wool, animal hair, kerosene oil, petroleum, soyabin oil, cotton fabrics, fertilisers, passenger cars, buses were imported by Nepal.

Nepal Trade with South Asian Countries

The foreign trade of Nepal rose considerably during the past several years. The trade partners were mainly India, Bangladesh, Pakistan and Sri Lanka.

Table 2 shows that Nepal's major foreign trade was with India among SAARC countries. The import had been higher than export and the balance of trade had been quite adverse from 1986 to 1995. Indo-Nepal trade had increased because India unilaterally removed all quantitative restrictions on imports of around 2300 items from SAARC countries with effect from August 1, 1998. The move is expected to give considerable boost to the eventual establishment of a South Asia Free Trade Area (SAFTA).

Table-2: Nepal's Trade with India (1996-2002)

(Rs. crores)

Year	*Imports*	*Exports*	*Balance of Trade*
1996-97			
1997-98			
1998-99			
1999-00			
2000-01			
2001-02			

Source: Statistical Abstract, India 2002.

Nepal could not maintain continuity in export trade with Bangladesh. There was only 6 million US dollars exported by Nepal from 1986 to 1995. However, the import was 89 million US dollars during the same period. The notable thing was that the import trade had taken place every year. The position of balance of trade of Nepal with Bangladesh was completely unfavourable.

Table-3: Exports and Imports of Nepal with SAARC Countries

		INDIA			*BANGLADESH*			*PAKISTAN*			*SRI LANKA*		*TOTAL*	
Year	*Export*	*Import*	*Balance of*	*Export*	*Import*	*Balance of*	*Export*	*Import*	*Balance of*	*Export*	*Import*	*Balance of*	*Export*	*Import*
1986														
1987														
1988														
1989														
1990														
1991														
1992														
1993														
1994														
1995														

Source: Statistical Year Book for Asia and the Pacific, 1997.

Likewise the foreign trade of Nepal with Pakistan was not able to feel good because the export and import of Nepal to Pakistan was minimal and sporadic. The balance of trade was favourable in 1986, 1991, 1992 but it was against in the years 1987, 1990, 1994 and 1995.

Nepal's trade with Sri Lanka was very scanty only in few years like 1986, 1987, 1988, 1989 and 1992. The balance of trade reveals a mixed position, since it was favourable in 1986, 1987 and 1992. Nevertheless, it was against in 1988 and 1989.

The total foreign trade of Nepal with SAARC countries shows that the exports were lesser and imports were higher. Consequently, the balance of trade was perfectly adverse except in the year 1988.

India is the biggest country in SAARC region. Therefore, Nepal's 40 per cent trade is being done with India.

It is evident from Table 3 that the balance of trade had been adverse from 1996-97 to 1998-99. Thereafter, it took shape as a favourable trade from 1999-2000 to 2001-02. The Nepalese and other SAARC countries except India were probably the least globalised in the world. Hence, it affected the entire economic gamut of these countries.

Conclusions

After analysing the facts and figures regarding Nepal's trade with SAARC countries, the following conclusions may be drawn:

1. Nepal has a very old tradition of foreign trade.
2. Nepal has exported both canalised and non-canalised goods to developed and SAARC countries.
3. The economic conditions of all SAARC countries are almost the same. This is the main reason of SAARC to come into existence.
4. SAARC is still in an infant stage. However, member countries have developed the idea of co-operation among themselves.
5. Nepal exported goods mainly based on agriculture and allied sectors.
6. Nepal made the greatest trade with India. About 40 per cent of its total trade is executed with India.

7. All the member counties of SAARC had adverse balance of trade. But Nepal's balance of trade had been against with all trade partners.

8. The new economic order could not get momentum in SAARC countries. Thereby the economy of these countries is lagging behind.

Suggestions

Nepal's trade with SAARC countries may be enhanced to adopt some economic policies, which are as under:

1. Nepal should pursue the global economic policy within certain period.

2. The export commodities should be diversified so that export may be increased.

3. In order to make balance of trade favourable, import substitution should be implemented.

4. To accelerate trade with SAARC countries, terrorist activities should be strictly controlled.

Select References

1. India 2004, Ministry of Information and Broadcasting, Government of India, New Delhi, p. 406.

2. Nepal and the World: A Statistical Profile 2001, FNCC, Kathmandu, October 2001.

3. Statistical Year Book for Asia and the Pacific, United Nations, Bangkok, Thailand, 1997.

4. Statistical Abstract, India 2002, Ministry of Statistics and Programme Implementation, Government of India, New Delhi.

5. Report on Currency and finance, 2002-03, Reserve Bank of India.

13

Terrorism and Mao's Insurgency in Nepal and it's impact on India

Shafiuzzaman

The Himalayan kingdom geographically, strategically and culturally is very important country of this region. In the SAARC frame work Nepal occupies an important position and in the Indian context this country is more important and it's stability or de-stability, it's economic growth or poverty, it's social troubles or political disturbances are directly associated with India's security concern. Detailed and special study is required for all these fields and experts are supposed to do this academic and tiresome job.

In this brief study an attempt has been made to focus on issues of terrorism and Mao's insurgency which directly leave deep consequences on India. In general, any bordering country if suffers from any problem, it's mark can easily be observed on the neighboring country. In this case the problem is more complex because Nepal's cultural scenario is more or less same and less guarded borders make the situation easy for those outfits which are dissatisfied with the system and to achieve there means they use terror tactics.

Firstly, I shall take the issue of terrorism. Terrorism, no doubt, is a direct threat to stability of Nations. It's different definitions and it's different interpretations, what so-ever it may be, can't deny, even in the pretext of human rights or state repression that India and Nepal both are suffering from this menace, though the faces and causes of terrorism are different for each country.

In Indian context terrorism is due to political frustration as in the cases of Jammu & Kashmir and North-Eastern states and due to intervention in to religious social and personal freedoms of people as in the cases of Mumbai blast and blast in other parts of India and due to economic deprivation and regional disparities as in the cases of Naxallite movement and different movements for separate states.

As for as Nepal is concerned Mao's insurgency is a kind of revolutionary terrorism. "This form of terrorism aims at achieving political and social change. It is directed not only against defeating the enemy by military means but has the mass support of people as a crucial factor" [1].

Nepal's 2.5 million population deeply suffers from poverty. The country of 52,800 sq. miles is not very rich in natural resources, only 17 per cent of land is worth farming. The population growth rate annually is 2.29 and per capita income is 250 US dollars per anum. 81 per cent labour force is associated with agriculture, 16 per cent is with services and only 3 per cent with industry. Nepal's army is comprising of 46000 personnel.[2]

In such dismal economic conditions slogans of jobs security, fooding and lodging security can easily draw the attention of masses and masses can easily be allured to the dreams propagated by outfits which have ulterior motives and to make masses in there favour they coin such types of slogans and they inculcate in the hearts of masses that there poor condition is due to mis-governance and usurping and looting the natural resources by the rulers. This sustained propaganda supported by foreign interest leads to social disturbances in the country and the suffering country is derailed from it's growth, trade development etc. Mao's insurgency, Nepal experts may agree, is a movement born out of deep economic frustration.

Although both countries are suffering from terrorism, yet the faces of terrorism are different. Nepal a tiny state is demographically any culturally more harmonious and it's national integration is in no way under threat from present disturbances. Fast economic growth and certain political reforms can easily uproot the terrorism say more political power to the representatives of masses more involvement of people in governance, poverty alleviation programmes and distribution of lands for cultivation among the landless people.

In contrast with Nepal, India is a country where inhabitants follow different religions, use different languages and are of different races. After the partition the constitution makers tried to give the aspirations of different people suitable place and tried that beyond all these contradictions India may develop as a strong Nation. India is successfully governed since 1952 by elected representatives of people but certain issues like land reforms, corruption, partial attitude of some element in government machinery, growth of communalism and unsolved issue of Jammu & Kashmir have paved the way for growth of terrorism in India, In the way that India was compelled to enhance it's military budget manifold and the social sector was pushed behind in the budgetary provision. Violation of human rights, frequent out break of communal riots, delayed action of government machinery in such volatile conditions and growth of certain communal organisations compelled a section of people to think about there respectful existence and this dissatisfaction proved a handy for anti-national elements. Cross-border terrorism may be a reality in Indian context but the social, economic and religious issues are important factors for the growth of terrorism. Without taking steps to change the internal situation terrorism can't easily be wiped out from Indian soil. Cross-border terrorism becomes successful when the social and religious condition are conducive. Cross-border terrorism is a well defined reality in Jammu & Kashmir but India's bordering areas with Nepal are suitable places for infiltration of money and man power both. News papers often publish stories about the construction of religious centers in the district of Uttar Pradesh bordering Nepal and Nepal's borders areas. This development creates doubts and there are reports that antinational and terrorist groups very easily use these religious centers as their transit camps. Illegal trade and smuggling are other attractions. Intelligence agencies reportedly have pointed that several terrorist attacks on India were planned, financed and managed through Nepali soil.

Going through the above described situation one can easily draw that Nepal's political and social stability has a direct bearing on India especially when Nepal's insurgent groups are in league with terrorist outfits operating in India. Nepali terrorist groups are dangerous for India in the way that they collaborate with Indian groups. If Nepal's problem is solved at least it can minimise India's problem and in greater sense the situation can become useful for whole SAARC nations because India as it is a biggest country in the region, if it is disturbed the whole region can not be aloof from it's effect. That's why realising the intensity of the problem 12th SAARC summit in Islamabad agreed on the inclusion of the additional protocol on terrorism. The seven member SAARC reached to include the additional protocol to the regional convention on suppression of terrorism.[3]

References

1. Dr. P.K. Agrawal, Gensis of terrorism. The Meerut Journal of political science and public administration, Vol. 6, No. 1 p. 23 to 26.
2. Urdu bi-weekly DAWAT, 10 Jan., 2004.
3. Front line 30 Jan., 2004.

14

Maoist-Insurgency in Nepal

S.B. Singh

The last few years have witnessed a dramatic upsurge in terrorist activity in all corners of the world. So much so that the magnitude of global terrorism is compared to the plague in the middle ages, frightening both leaders and citizens. It is a syndrome that has fast spread and there is hardly any cure in sight.

The Himalayan kingdom of Nepal, a constitutive unit of South Asia, too, has not been free from the common scourge of terrorist violences. She has been experiencing the heat generated by the Maoist terrorists since Feb. 1996. The hardcore Maoist leaders are demanding overthrow of the constitutional monarchy and establishment of people's democracy, which they called Naulo Janbad (new democracy). The chief aim of the paper is to analyse the various factors responsible for the ascendancy of Maoist, insurgency in Nepal and its cumulative impact on India-Nepal Relations.

II

Nepal, a country blessed with breathtaking natural beauty, is facing a civil strife caused by the Maoists, who are the consequence of political instability and socio-economic underdevelopment in the country. The failure of the successive governments to effect change in socio-economic conditions and meet minimum needs of people and provide a stable political order led to a situation in which the political system of Nepal had to facre insurgency organised by the radical communists. The historicity of these hard core Maoist Communists goes back to 1991, when they organised into a political organisation known as United People's Front, participated in 1991 general elections. They contested seventy seats, and won nine seats in new parliament. However, the hardcore Maoists realized it soon that only through a violent movement a complete social transformation could be possible in the country.

It was during the mid-nineties that Maoist began to indulge in violent activities against the government establishments and the Maoist insurgency became a regular feature after February, 1996. It appears that the Maoist have taken advantage of intra-party hostility and inter party feuds that failed to provide an effective and stable government much to the disappointment of common people, who had participated in the movement for restoration of democracy in the country with great expectation. The arrival of multiparty democracy, far from empowering the common people, had only made their plights worse. The political instability was so strong that during fourteen years following restoration of democracy in 1990, as many as thirteen governments were toppled. The growing corruption, increasing gap between the rich and the poor and bad governance has led to a situation in which the Maoists have emerged as a powerful force to reckoned with. Consequently many Nepalese, disillusioned with the democratic process, them as the only real hope, if their problems are to be addressed.

The Maoist insurgency has gradually widened in the country in the background of communist movement which started there as early as 1948-49. The communists never liked compromising attitude of the political parties like Nepali Congress which had been as tourch bearer of democracy in the country. They were not happy with the democratic political parties reaching to an understanding with the royalists and surrendering before the feudalistic forces. During the long thirty years of Panchayat dispensation in Kingdom, it were the communists, who never stopped their underground activities against the authoritarian forces. Although the communists joined hands with the Nepali Congress and other democratic forces to end the Panchayat System yet very soon more radicals in the block got frustrated with the establishment of constitutional monarchy. A Maoist leader stated in an interview thus:

> *"Our war is aimed as destroying the current regime which is based on two hundred years old coalition between feudalism*

> *and imperialism and to establish people's republic. During this long period, political systems have changed with different names coming into existence but the fundamental structure of the regime remains the same ."*[1]

At the same time, socio-political discrimination generated a sense of alienation among the ethnic minorities in the country. The unique cohesive structure of Nepalese society was shaken in 1990 when the new constitution declared Nepal a Hindu State and Nepali the only official language. Minority groups like the Tibeto-Burman community, questioned the propriety of declaring Nepal a Hindu state, as they do not consider themselves Hindus. Though pre-domination of the dominant groups and castes in education, employment, etc., was prevalent during the Panchayat regime as well, the commencement of democracy and new constitution brought the problem to the fore by guaranteeing freedom, of expression and thereby giving voice to the people who were earlier silent expectations. This enabled ethnic groups to organise themselves against socio-economic and political discrimination including the imposition of Sanskrit as compulsory subject in school or Nepali as the country's official language.

The Maoist leadership successfully exploited the popular mood of discontent to their advantage by promising the Nepalese people a much better future. They promised to remove the monarchy and the survile government, replacing it with a communist state, which would end the exploitation of poverty stricken farmers and labourers. They further proclaimed for the establishment of a 'people's government' through the means of 'people's war'. At the same time, the Maoists began to use the ethnic cleavage to its advantage by promising self rule and autonomy to ethnic minorities in their respective majority areas. They also committed for recognition of ethnic minorities's culture and language. In his statement chairman Prachanda, made it clear "We want to clarify once again that we are committed to guarantee party freedom in the new state power to be constructed after the destruction of feudal authority. The state envisaged by us will not be a one party dictatorship. The freedom to operate political parties according to one's ideological convictions and contest elections will be guaranteed. There only be activities of such elements up holding feudalism and inviting foreign domination will be curbed. We are committed to established and develop a people's democracy of the twenty-first century.[2]

To fulfil its objectives, the Maoist formally announced in Feb. 1996 the necessity of bloody war. Simultaneously, they also submitted a Forty Point charter of their demands to the government then led by Prime Minister, Sher Bahadur Deuba, which included the abolition of royal privileges, promulgation of republican constitution and abolition of Mahakali Treaty with India. When the government did not pay attention to their demands, they attacked government installations, indulged in loot and arson and killed local bureaucrats, village headmen and influential people in the western, central hill areas and the eastern terai. Starting from six western districts-Rukum, Rolpa, Jajarkot, Salyam and Gorkha, and Sindhauli in the east in 1996, the Maoist insurgency has engulfed sixty-six of country's seventy-five total districts, especially in the poverty stricken and economically backward areas.

It is ironical that what Maoists called 'people's war, the royal Nepalese Army was left untouched in the initial stages of the insurgency, but became favourite target later on. Starting with confiscation of land from the wealthy persons and its distribution among the landless class, the Maoist gradually assumed multifarious activities of governmental sphere such as living taxes, establishing schools and courts in order to provide education and justice much to the relief of the hapless populace. At the same time, socially supporting the cause of weaker sections enabled the Maoists to extend their traditional social support base from the upper castes (Brahmin, Kshatris and Newar) combined to new group such a Rais, Limbus, Barungs, Mangars and Tamngs etc. Even the women have also participated in violent activities. It is an indication of social as well as geographical expansion of the Moists's violent movement in the kingdom.

The gravity of the situation can be gauged from the fact that more than seven thousand people have been killed due to the insurgency problem in the kingdom, which entered into tenth years. The severity of clashes and violence between the Maoist rebels and the Royal Nepalese army and police had led to the postponement of mid-term general elections and dismissal of elected government of Prime Minister, Deuba in October, 2002. Having become a big challenge to the successive government of the country, the initial response from different governments have been of law and order problems, and using force to bring it under control. They dubbed it as a new terrorism in the country.

III

To tackle the Maoist challenges to it security and integrity the, Nepalese government has used force and negotiation and persuation. However, these strategies have hardly been effective so for. The police miserably failed against the better-armed and well organised Maoist insurgents in the beginning itself. In 1998, the then government sponsored operation was carried out in 18 districts. But the government failed to re-establish its writ in areas under the Maoist rebels. This compelled the government to initiate peace process with the Maoists by constituting the Ganesh Man Singh Peace Campaign in July, 1999. But this mechanism of government to convince the rebels to give up arms did not make any progress. Likewise, the 'Carrot and stick' policy applied by G.P. Koirala Government, too, proved to be unsuccessful.

Sher Bahadur Deuba, who became Prime Minister in July, 2001, following the shock of royal assassinations, entered into a serious attempt to return peace in the country. To take wind out of maoist's soils, he offered peace talk with a series of policy measures pertaining to land reforms, unsociability and gender discrimination. Deuba, however, firmly ruled out any chance of conceding to the maoist demands for the abolition of the monarchy, and an interim government and a new constitution.

With these fundamental differences, chances of the talks succeeding, had always been in doubt and do the violence never really ended even as the talks were hold. Ending their four month old ceasefire, Maoists, once again attacked more than 35 districts in November 2001. The army barrack were attacked for the first time. Moreover, they declared the formation of a 'Revolutionary government' with its capital at Rolpa and 37 members People's Revolutionary Council to run their government.

This compelled Deuba government to tender advice to King Gyanendra to proclaim an emergency. According the emergency was declared in Nov. 2001 and it gave army authorization to cope with the situation. In the beginning, the army seemed to be more than a match for the Maoist insurgents but it soon became clear that the military would not be able to defeat the rebels decisively. On the contrary, democracy and human rights suffered badly under the state of emergency.

Though more than 3000 Maoists were killed after the imposition of emergency, heavy losses for the security forces as well. In addition, the Maoist changed their tactics. More and more, they attacked public institution and property eg. airports, power stations, telecommunications facilities, administrative buildings, water pipes and so forth. A growing number of attacks was also made inside the Kathmandu Valley. This meant more civilians were affected by the Maoist insurgency than before. The senseless killing and destruction contradicted the people-orientation ideals expressed in many of the Maoist's original demands. These demands were related to nationalism, public well being, and people's living conditions and standard. Most of these demands corresponded to the state policy as prescribed by Article 26 of the 1990 constitution.

Up to the end of Oct. 2002, a total of 5111 Maoist have been killed. But a high price was paid for the vigible and statistical success of the army and police, because more than, 1189 security forces and 773 civilians had also lost their lives in six and half years of clashes, according to official figures. Share of civilians killed many have been higher, as deliberate killings of suspected Maoists were nothing unusual. Just since the imposition of emergency in November, 2001, another 4,366 persons had been killed.[3] In a special report in early April 2002, Amnesty International expressed fears that there may have been many civilian killing among those counted as Maoists rebels.[4]

Prime Minister Deuba's politics of Militant Maoist suppression found support abroad, most of all in Western countries such as the United States and the United Kingdom. Both countries saw the Maoist insurgency as an integral part of global terrorism, as defined by American President George Bush after the September 11, 2001, attack on the World Trade Centre in New York. India also extended its diplomatic support to declaration of emergency in Nov. 2001 and condemned violence by the Maoist. More importantly, both the countries had agreed upon the traditional system of joint management of border. Also when the Nepalese Prime Minister Deuba visited India in March, 2002, New Delhi offered him help to face the on going insurgency in Nepal. The India has supplicated also INSAS rifles at heavy discounts in various Army-run counter-insurgency schools in the kingdom.

IV

As the border between India and Nepal is more open and links between peoples on both sides of it are also strong, neither can be unaffected by an upheavals in the other. This is particularly true in the context of Maoist insurgency in Nepal. Moreover, the Maoist, functioning under various names such as People's War Group and Maoist Communist Centre, are very active in Indian states of Andhra Pradesh, Bihar and Jharkhand. The timing of the attacks by the PWG in Andhra Pradesh with end of Maoist's ceasefire in Nepal was noteworthy. It is said that the Maoist got electronic detonators and explosives from the PWG, while pistol, ammunition and high quality detonators were provide by the M.C.C. OF late, they have establish their foothold in West Bengal and Bangladesh too. As the Nepali Consul-General in Kolkata pointed out to the West Bengal Chief Minister, Maoist from not just India and Nepal but also from Bangladesh have been holding conclaves in Places like Siliguri. Besides, there are reports that Maoist are providing bases to insurgent groups such as United Liberation from Assam (ULFA) in India's north-east and getting arms and tactical training in return the other side of the coin is that the Nepali Maoist, as and when under pressure from the Nepalese Army, try to escape and to adjacent Indian territories and seek sanctuary in the hideouts of their soulmates.

The socio-political turmoil in Nepal has thus a spil over effect in India. India has a very justifiable need to take a deep interest in domestic turmoil affecting its neighbour like Nepal, but it does not have the primary responsibility to resolve their problem. It is for the political forces of Nepal to get their act together and deal with the Maoist menace. They must first clearly point out whether this Maoist insurgency is a terrorist problem, a political problem or a socio-economic one. The Nepalese government has to assess its own strength while dealing with Maoist be on seeking external support or its own negotiating strategy.

V

To conclude, it can be safely observed that in view of the ground realities, the future of Maoists insurgency appears hanging in a balance. Its perpetrators must understand that large scale violence, indiscriminate killings, even women and children and destruction of public properties are evil means to achieve their political objectives. Hence, the Maoists should lay down their arms and agree for the peaceful resolution of their problems, there must be joint strategies and actions involving all the major democratic forces. The Monarchy and the Maoist rebellions through negotiation. Therefore, both ways may be applied: the truce for a dialogue and the dialogue for a truce in order to establish permanent peace in the country. There is great need for realisation to the all concerned parties. Monarchy, the political forces and the insurgents that this meanace of insurgency can be resolved only through a peaceful settlement of disputes problem which, of course, must be tackled domestically.

References

1. Kathmandu Post, Feb. 12, 1997.
2. Economic and Political Weekly, Sept. 7, 2000, 3315, 16.
3. Kathmandu Post, Nov. 1, 2002.
4. Asian Survey, Vol. XLIIII, No. 1, Jan-Feb. 2003, p. 210.

15

Dynamics of Nepal – Japan Relations : Past, Present and Future

Siddhi Laxmi Vaidya

Nepal-Japan relations rests on the twin bedrocks of tradtion and modernity.[1] It has gone through several changes in recent decades alongwith changes in time and circumstance. Major factors behind this new shape of Nepal-Japan relations are the changes of Japan's status in international community due to its great success in its economic development. Japan has become not only a global economic super ppower but also the largest donor in absolute dollar terms. It is a net creditor nation, with Japanese companies continuing to expand their operations around world and its banking sectors have strong impact on the world economy. Japan's global political activity has also grown enormously and is set to rise, especially as new world order emerges following the demise of the cold war. For example, Japan is a serious candidate for a permanent seat on the United Nations Security Council; while some of its younger politicians, who are gaining ground domestically, argue strongly that Japan should become politically active in the international community. Japan is also a leading regional power. Its influence in East and Southeast Asia is already enormous and is constantly rising. Japan's economic influence is obvious, and politico-security ties are being established through a number of regional multinational institutional organizations such as the Asia Pacific Economic Cooperation forum (APEC), the ASEAN post ministerial meeting, ARF (ASEAN Regional Forum).[2] In recent decades, Japan has become the top donor in South Asia as well. It began to play a significant role in all the countries of South Asia in their economic development. This changing scenario has, naturally great impact on Nepal-Japan relations. As Japan has changed so has Nepal. Many changes occurred specially in the area of political and economy. Transformation of the status of monarchy into the constitutional monarchy, policy of isolation into the present nonaligned foreign policy, restoration of democracy alongwith the poor economc condition and its membership in the United Nationa etc. have brought profound changes in Nepal's position both in domestic as well as in internationa rena which has naturally brought the changes in its internationa relations including Japan. Despite such changes on both sides, relations between the two countries is becoming very closed and intimate day by day which has attracted the world.

Nepal-Japan relations begins from the 6th century alongwith the birth of Lord Buddha in Lumbini, Nepal. However, direct contact between the two countries started only in the 19th century with the visit of the scholar Rev. Ikai Kawaguchi in 1899 for research on Buddhism on his way to Tibet.[3] Beside this, he had also visited Nepal on 1903, 1905, 1912 and 1913.[4] Officially recorded first visit took place in the year 1902 when eight Nepalese were sent to Japan to study engineering. During the Russo-Japanese War of 1904-1905, the Nepalese students were still in Japan.[5] A few year later, in 1912, another Japanese scholar, Junjiro Takakusu[6] undertook research work on Sanskrit for about a year in Nepal. After that, for some time, there was not so much interaction between the two countries due to the outbreak of thr first and second World War. The beginning of Nepal-Japan relations was cultural in nature.

The postwar relations between the two countries reached a new level in 1953[7] with the arrival of the Japanese expedition to Mt Annapurna led by Dr. Eijaburo Nishihara, former chairman of Nepal-Japan Friendship Association. Since then growing number of Japanese have been visiting informally in Nepal as trekkers, mountaineers, researchers, tourist and travelers. In 1956, the diplomatic relations between the two countries was established. Thus the year 1956 is a turning point in the history of modern Nepal-Japan relations. From this year onward, the exchange of visits between the two countries has been increasing steadily at the governmental level as well as people's level. Such heart to heart contact between the people of the both countries provided the foundation for strengthening the friendly relations between the two countries. Also it helped in enhancing more mutual understanding and trust between each other. This is unique and significant aspect of Nepal-Japan relations.

It was only after the establishment of the diplomatic relation, there was, for the first time, exchanges of visits between the two countries at the highest leve. In the year 1960, the late King Mahendra and the Queen Ratna paid the state visit to Japan. In the same year, Japanese Crown Prince Akihito and Princess Michiko visited Nepal. In 1965 the Royal Nepalese Embassy was established in Tokyo. In 1967, the then Crown Prince Birendra studied in Tokyo University. A year after this, the Japanese Embassy was established in Kathmandu. Though the formal relations between the two countries have been increasing, the pace was very slow during 1950s and 1960s because of Nepal's involvement of its own domestic problems and Japan's priority of economic recovery and regaining of international status. Due to these reasons, both the governments could not pay much attention to make closer relationships in spite of their strong desire to do so. But unlike in the past decades, the 1970s were remarkably better in strengthening the relations between Nepal and Japan. During the 1970s there was frequent exchange of visits between the two countries not only at the highest political levels but also at the official and ministrial levels, which indicated growing relations between the two countries in political level too.

For the first time, the Nepal-Japan Society was founded in 1970 which was renamed as the Nepal-Japan Friendship and Cultural Association in 1980. In the same year, Prince and Princess Hitachi of Japan came to Nepal in order to attain the Wedding Ceremony of the then Crown Prince Birendra. From Nepal the late King Mahendra and the Queen Ratna visited Japan at Expo'70 in Osaka. This visit was also no less important for introducing Nepal in Japan. This has helped quite a lot in strengthening their relationships. In 1973, Japan's Students Trainee's Alumni Club was found which was later changed as Nepal-Japan Students Trainee's Club. In 1974 Rastriya Panchayat Chairman Swanr (Nayan Bahadur) visited Japan. This visit broke the trend in the exchange of visits between the two countries. The reason is that until that year, there was an exchange of vistis either at the highest level or at the people's level. So that was something unusual. In 1975, Crown Prince Akihito and Princess visited Nepal on the coronation of late King Birendra. Among the several exchanges of visits during 1970s some of the notable and very significant visits were Japanese Parliamentary Vice Minister for the foreign affairs Keiwa Okuda's visit to Nepal in 1977, the first ever Japanese foreign minister Hatoyam's visit to Nepal in 1977, and the state visit to Japan by their Majesties the King and Queen of Nepal in 1978. These visits have contributed tremendously in strengthening the relations between the two countries not only at the political level but also at the economic level.

Parliamentary Vice-minister for foreign affairs of Japan, Mr. Keiwa Okuda's five day official visit to Nepal at the invitation of His Majesty's Government was considerably significant from the political point of view because this was the first ever visit to Nepal by a Japanese political figure. During this visit, he disclosed Japan's deep understanding and high appreciation for the proposition that Nepal, be declared as"Zone of Peace". The visit has helped substantially to enhance the scope of future Nepal-Japan Cooperation. Japan understood the significance of the reason behing the declaration of the Peace Zone proposal as an important diplomatic policy of Nepal that will contribute to the regional peace and stability. As the maintaining the peace and stability in the world is one of the major objectives of Japanese policy, its support to such proposal will not only help Nepal but also achieving its foreign policy objectives. The support of the Zone of Peace proposal by the government of Japan was an example of political cooperation to Nepal.

Few months after Mr. Okuda's visit, the visit to Nepal by Japanese Foreign Minister Hatoyama added more significance and a new chapter in the political history of Nepal-Japan relations. Mr. Hatoyama's visit was the indication of the increasing concern and an active interest of the Japanese government to the people of Nepal to enhance the cordial and friendly relations between the two countries. The visit had focused attention on the possible trends in Japanese foreign policy considering that this visit to Nepal followed by Japanese parliamentary Vice Minister for foreign affairs and this had encouraged the Nepal-Japan ties in particular. The visits had contributed well for the promotion of cooperation in both economic and political fields. Considering the establishment of the diplomatic relations between Nepal and Japan in 1956, the trade and mutual contact between the two countries have seen a noteworthy increase since then. These visits not only further explored such areas of co-operations but shows Japan's strong desire to further promote the relations. In return the Nepalese Foreign Minister Krishna Raj Aryal visited to Japan in the same year.

The year 1978 is another epoch making year in the history of Nepal-Japan relations. In May 1978, King Birendra and Queen Aishwarya paid state visit to Japan. The visit was a great success. Regarding the contribution of this visit in strengthening Nepal-Japan relations, former Japanese Ambassador to Nepal Mr. Sasaki said "Japan has so many guests, but it is not possible to welcome so many of them in a year. But Japan itself had invited their Majesties the King and the Queen that speaks the volumes of the good relationship."[8] One of the most substantial outcome of the 1978 visit was, among the others, Japan's expression of its complete understanding and support of the concept that Nepal be declared a Zone of Peace. In the same year, Nepal-Japan Parliamentary Friendship Association was established. Since then frequent visits to Nepal by Japanese political figures have been increasing. Some of the noteworthy visits among them were the Japan-Nepal Parliamentary Friendship Association's President Mr. Kasuga's visit in 1979, Parliamentary Vice Foreign Minister Mr. Aichi's visit in 1980, Nepal-Japan Parliamentary Friendship Association's President's visit in 1982, former Prime Minister Takeo Fukuda's visit to Nepal in 1986, the visit of Mr. Hideo Edo, Vice President of Japan Association for Tsukuba Expo'85, Crown Prince Hironomiya's visit in 1987, HRH Crown Prince Dipendra's visit to Japan in 1990, Finance Minister Ryutaro Hashimoto's visit 1991, nine member Japanese Parliamentary delegation's visit in 1998 and so forth. Such frequent visits had contributed for better understanding and that the leaders in Japan increasingly understood the typical geo-political situation of Nepal.

In terms of economic development Nepal and Japan seems as an unusual partner. Japan in one of the world's leading aid donor nations while Nepal is one of the top recipients of this aid. The cordial friendship between two such unequal power is unique in many respects. There were no fundamental differences to be resolved between the two countries perhaps because of similar culture. Though Japan is not a non-align country like Nepal, both the countries have similar views regarding peace in the world. Both Nepal and Japan believe that the peace and stability in Asia and the prosperity of the region are of utmost important for the maintenance of peace and prosperity of the world. Both the countries have stong faith in the objectives and principles of the United Nations and similar views on the matters relating to respect for territorial integrity, non-interference in each other's internal affairs, prohibition of the threat or use of force and disarmament in accordance with the United Nation's charter. Also both the countries have been totally opposed to colonialism, racism and apartheid and held the view that such policies should be terminated as soon as possible.

Economic Relations

Nepal has economic relations with Japan even before the Second World War. At that period of time Nepal used to import the cheap cotton textiles goods from Japan[9]. Postwar Nepal-Japan economic cooperation started when Japan indicated her interest in assisting Nepal in the latter's development efforts only after the establishment of the diplomatic relationship in 1956. The postwar Nepal-Japan economic relations begins with the visits of agricultural survey group in 1970. The first exchange of notes to extend 36 million Yen loan assistance was signed between the two governments in March 1970. It was provided to Nepal Industrial Development Corporation by the Export-Import Bank of Japan for industrial development of Nepal. The second and third loan assistance of 4.0005 billion-Yen was extended by OECD for the construction of Kulekhani Hydro-Electric Project (first phase). Since 1970, as to other developing country of the wrold, Japan is providing assistance to Nepal for developing her economic and non-economic sectors. Now Japan has become one of the top donor countries of Nepal. Economic cooperation here will be classified into three categories, i.e., aid, trade and investment.

Nepal-Japan economic cooperation can be divided into three periods. Until 1969, Japan had extended only technical cooperation through Overseas Technical Cooperation Agency (OTCA). From 1970, financial assistance, grant and loan, and volunteer services were added to it. Since 1978 when their Majesties the King and Queen's paid the state visit to Japan, financial assistance to Nepal has substantially increased. The reason behind the incresement of Japanese aid to Nepal was partly due to changes in Japan's policy towards Asia as well as partly at the request of the Government of Nepal. Though Nepal is getting Japanese aid since 1950s but up to 1975, there was no regularity of Japanese aid to Nepal partly because of then Japanese foreign policy and partly because of the "Nixon Shocks of 1971, normalization of China-Japan relations in 1972 and the "Oil Shocks" of 1973. Besides it, there were less interactions between Nepal-Japan in official level and also lack of much information. As a result, in the beginning year, the flow of Japanese aid in Nepal was small. The total flow of Japanese assistance to Nepal from 1970 to 1977 are as follows :

Table 1: The Official Japanese Assistance to the Kingdom of Nepal for the Period of 1970 to 1977

Grant Assistance		*(Unit : Million-Yen)*
FY	1970	72.0
	1972	169.4
	1974	113.8
	1976	1,061.14
	1977	480.0
	Total	**1896.34**
Loan Assistance		*(Unit : Million-Yen)*
FY	1969	360.0
	1975	3,000
Technical Assistance		*(Unit : Million-Yen)*
FY	1954-1978	3,532,613
	Grand Total	**8788.953**

Source : Nepal-Japan Economic and Technical Cooperation Exhibition. Nepal-Japan Students and Trainees Club Embassy of Japan, JICA and JOCV offices in Kathmandu.

Table 2: Japan's ODA performance to Nepal during 1978 to 1991

Year	*ODA ($ million)*	*Increase %*	*ODA/GNP %*	*DAC Average ODA/GNP %*
1978	2,215	55.5	0.23	0.35
1979	2,638	19.1	0.26	0.26
1980	3,304	25.3	0.31	0.37
1981	3,171	4.0	0.27	0.35
1982	3,023	0.7	0.28	0.38
1983	3,761	24.4	0.322	0.36
1984	4,319	14.8	0.34	0.36

Contd.

Year	*ODA ($ million)*	*Increase %*	*ODA/GNP %*	*DAC Average ODA/GNP %*
1985	3,791	12.1	0.29	0.35
1986	5,634	48.4	0.29	0.35
1987	7,454	32.3	0.31	0.35
1988	3,134	22.5	0.32	0.36
1989	8,965	1.8	0.31	0.34
1990	9,222	2.9	0.31	0.35
1991	11,034	19.6	0.32	0.34

Source : Japan's ODA 1992. Annual Report. p. 72.

Table 3: Japan's ODA Disbursement to Nepal ($ million)

Year	*Grant Aid*	*Technical Cooperation*	*Total*	*Loan Aid*	*Total*
1979	80.30	41.43	121.73	43.65	165.38
1980	57.66	8.05	65.71	0.00	65.75
1981	62.48	9.81	72.29	73.44	218.02
1982	83.50	11.98	95.48	48.06	143.54
1983	58.10	12.97	71.07	0.00	71.07
1984	58.85	12.14	70.99	0.00	70.99
1985	62.12	9.27	71.31	0.00	71.31
1986	65.12	16.10	81.22	0.00	81.22
1987	71.84	18.89	90.73	187.70	278.43
1988	55.50	0.00	55.50	0.00	55.50
1989	47.21	15.53	62.74	0.00	62.74

Source : Official Development Assistant 1993. (Annual Report) Ministry of Foreign Affairs, Tokyo, 1994.

Table 4: Japanese ODA to Nepal ($ million)

Year	*Grant*	*Technical*	*Total*	*Loan*		*Total*
1987	49.98	14.74	64.72	13.06	12.05	76.78
1988	41.37	14.56	55.93	7.75	6.43	62.36
1989	42.24	14.57	56.81	21.99	20.58	77.39
1990	34.27	12.86	47.13	9.38	8.04	55.17
1991	44.33	15.52	59.85	69.14	67.69	127.54
1992	52.32	24.83	77.16	33.87	29.51	106.67
1993	68.11	35.28	103.39	13.82	7.50	110.89
1994	83.96	31.18	115.14	10.48	3.61	118.75
1995	95.38	29.42	124.80	10.27	2.80	127.60
1996	64.36	30.21	94.57	0.68	-5.78	88.79

Source : Official Development Assistant 1997. (Annual Report) Ministry of Foreign Affairs Tokyo.

The above tables shows that the Japanese Oversease Development Assistance (ODA) to Nepal rapidly increased specially after 1978. Between 1978 to 1982, Japan secured first place among developed countries giving aid to Nepal. Since then, the trend has been continuing. The main reason of this increment to Nepal was due to increment in ODA fund according to the "Three Years Plan" of Japanese government and the changes on Japanese policy regarding ODA etc. As a result, not only the total volume of Japanese ODA had been increased but also the per cent of grant aid to LLDC. As Nepal also fall under this category, the increment is the natural outcome of it. Besides this, Japan has been also providing aid on the request of HMG/Nepal from time to time on different areas like electricity, agriculture, health, transportation, the manpower development program, Radio and telecommunication etc.

Aid to Nepal from Japan comes within three main categories i.e. grants, loans and technical assistance. Among them grant assistance is the most important. From 1970 to 1977, Japanese total grant aid to Nepal was 1,896.34 million-yen. Table No. 2, 3, 4 shows the trend of flow of Japanese aid in Nepal since 1978 to the present.

Both flow and magnitude of Japanese aid to Nepal was changed over the time in Nepal. The flow of aid increased from US $ 62.36 m. to

US $ 127.60 m. in 1995. The flow of Japanese aid dropped sharply for developing countries of the world especially after the decade of 1990 because of financial crisis caused due to economic recession in Japan. Consequently, the Japanese aid to Nepal dropped from US $ 127.60 m. in 1995 to just US $ 88.79 m. in 1996. Nepal received additional US $ 585.45 m. worth grant aid, US $ 151.94 m. worth of loan aid and US $ 231.39 m. worth of technical assistance in ten years period (1988-1997) from Japan. The share of Japanese grant element to her total aid to Nepal have been found at the highest level (60 per cent) followed by technical aid (23.88 per cent) and the loan aid (15.68 per cent). It is quite surprising that Japan which had a very small percentage share in total Nepalese assistance scenario during 1969-70 emerged as the second largest aid donor in 1971-75 and 1987 to till now, it became the largest bilateral single aid donor country granting US $ 968.79 m. worth of economic aid which is supposed to be more than 35 per cent out of the total aid received by Nepal in ten years period. For the past couple of years, Japan's annual economic assistance to Nepal has totaled US $ 100 m. annually.[10] At present, Nepal is the 15th largest recipient of Japan bilateral aid (based on cumulative aid net disbursement up to 1997). Japan's ODA Annual Report 1988 spells about Japan's ODA policy to Nepal as well. The report indicates that ever-growing volume of aid to Nepal is being provided on the basis of Nepal's amicable relations with Japan, its strong demand of foreign aid, and the assessment of the impact of Japanese aid in its economic development and its overall impact on its GDP, expenditure, savings, investment and trade gap.

Beside economic assistance, another important factor is *trade* between Nepal and Japan. No doubt trade between the two countries has been increasing day by day which are shown in the following table.

Table 5: Japan's trade with Nepal ($ Million)

Year	*Export*	*Import*	*Balance*
1970	13.81	2.57	+ 11.24
1975	13.91	1.75	+ 12.12
1976	9.25	3.65	+ 5.58
1977	13.56	5.19	+ 8.37
1978	32.58	6.87	+ 25.71
1979	22.34	6.69	+ 12.65

Contd.

Year	*Export*	*Import*	*Balance*
1980	30.70	8.49	+ 13.21
1981	44.23	2.27	+ 41.96
1982	54.11	1.41	+ 52.72
1983	42.36	0.90	+ 41.46
1984	39.38	0.54	+ 38.84
1985	60.99	1.12	+ 59.87
1986	71.26	2.88	+ 68.38
1987	79.30	2.63	+ 76.67
1988	61.84	2.28	+ 59.56
1989	71.77	1.84	+ 69.93
1990	58.85	2.58	+ 56.28
1991	97.51	1.70	+ 95.82
1992	59.43	2.22	+ 49.21
1993	67.78	4.14	+ 63.63
1994	66.00	3.20	+ 62.80
1995	58.78	1.79	+ 59.05

Source : Japanese Custom Statistic, 1987. Saiking no Neparu no Jyoho to Nihon Neparu kankei, Southwest Asia Division, Asian Bureau, Gaimushu, Tokyo, Nihonkokuzei Kyokai Gaikoku Boeki Gaiko, 1993. 4.

The table has clearly shows that the trade has been favorable only for Japan and Nepal has been earning huge deficiency year by year from the very beginning. Nepal continued to increase its imports from Japan even while the level of its exports to japan started to decline, inevitably enlarging the trade imbalances between the two nations. So time has come to Nepal to think critically on this regard Nepal still lag behind in the export of her goods to Japan. Nepal's hand woven carpets and readymade garments have not yet found a proper place in Japanese market perhaps it is because of the high quality that the Japanese market requires. It indicates that there is lack of incentives to expand local sales in Japan. Nepal's export performance require a full restructuring and here too Japan can help with its superior know-how and experience. Japan can provide technology and skills which are vital elements for improving Nepal's trade profile.

The analysis of direction and composition of Nepalse trade has shown that the major commodities exported to Japn are mostly the same traditional commodities. There is not improvement in quality and quantity. It is due to the instability in trade policy and the lack of improvement in other factors. According to changing scenario of consumer items production and Japan's policy to sale technology rather than the consumer goods Nepal could provide a consumer goods production market where its phased out technological could be utilized. This is because Nepal can supply cheaper manpower and available cheaper raw materials. We can find such examples in our region also.

Foreign investment stimulates economic growth of the country not only by a flow of the capital but also by an inflow of technology, both of which help to create the jobs and employment opportunities. As such, recently government of Nepal has opened the country for foreign investment by creating favorable climat for investors. But Japan's contribution on trade and investment has been almost all negligible and remains the same even at present while its ODA position is very strong. It seems that Nepal is not an attractive investment destination for the Japanese investors perhaps because of her size and small market. Though recently Japanese investor began to invest in Nepal mostly in tourism and construction sectors, the volume is very negligible. Everest Hotel on the highest level of the world, Himalayan Hotel and Hokke Hotel at Lumbini are of the some examples. Trade and investment have been again favorable to Japan. It is important to note here that trade and investment are the backbone of the development in any country. It is necessary to increase balance trade and investment for the economic developement of Nepal. So as the well wisher of Nepal, Japan should focus on correcting the trade and increasing the investment rather than enlarging only the volume of aid. Japan's minor effort and little kindness can be a great help for a country like Nepal. There are plenty of scope for Japanese investor in the sector like hydro-electricity, tourism and agricultural etc. where Japanese technology with skill and capital investment with Nepalese resource and labour might work very well with excellence result favorable to both the countries.

From the close observation of the Nepal-Japan relations, one can thus come to the conclusion that the relations between the two countries has been very close and intimate from Nepalese point of view. Japan's commitment to act as a development partner of Nepal has remained unshaken. Unlike the past decades, coming years will be full with challenges and opportunities. The changing international situation and increasing domestic problems might bring the complicated situation which might require more mutual understanding and cooperation in different aspect between the two countries. For that, besides socio-political economic aspect, focus should be made in cultural aspect too. Despite having many similarities between the two countries, this sector needs more attention. Some of the persisting problems of Nepal-Japan relations are the existing wider gap in the area of income, trade, information, perception and dependency on each other. Information is an important area where a correct approach is needed. Flow of insufficient information in each direction is a major cause of this gap. Infact, the HMG/Nepal has to adopt effective information policy about Japan because whatever information it use to supply is largely constrained by the language. The existing arrangements for the collection and dissemination of information are unsatisfactory. It will be very difficult to overcome these problems if timely necessary steps will not be taken by both the countries as per the necessity of the time and circumstance the changes in the world situation might have caused fundamental shifts in bilateral as well as international relations. Nepal and Japan have to respond to the world by changing the priorities in their foreign policies, while non-alignment is still remains the cornerstones of Nepalese foreign policy and is believed it will remain in future as well. However, Japan's foreign policy is something different then Nepal but still Nepal's nonaligned policy is not considered as obstructing factor in their relationships rather it is proving a helping factor. It will be no exaggeration to say the Nepal-Japan relations will have to face many challenges in the coming twenty first century. Despite these, future of Nepal-Japn relations seems to be bright due to its strong foundation. No doubt, economic relations will play a major role in strengthening the relations between the two countries, but other factors like the institution of monarcy, relgion, the natural beauties of wonderful Himalayas, similarites in cultural and finally the strong direct contact between the people of the two countries will definitely help for bringing the two countries more closer by fostering more understanding and cooperation between each other.

References

1. Kazuaki Arichi, Special speech delivered at Japan-Nepal Society welcome reception, November 29, 1996.
2. Purnendra C. Jain, Japan's Relations with South Asia, Asian Survey, Vol., XXXVII, No. 4, April, 1977, p. 340.
3. S. Hidaka, Nepal and Japan. A survey of Japanese activities 1899-1966, Kodansha, Tokyo. 1967.
4. Ryuzo. Takayama, Autobiography of Rev. Kawaguchi, Bunkuo University, Kodansha Publishing.
5. Harendra B. Baruwa, "*State student from Nepal to Japan*"COSMOS International Exchange of Education. Association of International Education, Japan 1978. p. 11.
6. *Ibid.* 1.
7. Nepal-Japan Economic and Technical Cooperation Exhibition, Nepal-Japan Students and Trainees Club, Embassy of Japan, JICA and JOCV officer in Kathmandu, 1982.
8. The Rising Nepal, May 9, 1978. p. 8.
9. Thapa, Yogendra Bahadur, Nepal's Trade with Japan (1976 / 76-1982/83), Central Department of Economic, Tribhuvan University, Kirtipur. 1984. Unpublished Master Thesis.
10. Sigdel. Bamadev, Discussion on Nepal-Japan Cooperation. Journal of Nepal-Japan Studies, Vol. 1, No. 2000.

16

India's Relations with Nepal during Nehru Era

Iqbal Khanam

Nepal is India's very close neighbour. It is a londlocked country situated in the Sothern slops of Himalaya. It has Tibet in the North and China in the South. It has common border with India and China. Nepal shares with India in socio-cultural and religious tradition. India's policy towards Nepal has largely been governed by its security need and the protection of its national interest. The national frontier is the Himalaya that surrounds Nepal on three sides leaving the only outlet the contineous territory with India. Therefore, India's security from northern border has been intimately associated with Nepal. Before the independence India's northern border was safe because of British control over Tibet. Immediately after the indepencence India did not evolve any defence oriented policy towards Nepal and relied largely on the existing policy. Nehru regarded Nepal as a sovereign state but he regarded it as an essential part of Indian security. Therefore the first step which India took towards Nepal in the interest of the country was the conclusion of Stand Still Agreement. The agreement provided that until a new treaty was concluded the old treaty of 1923 signed between the British Government and Nepal would continue to remain the basis of Indo-Nepalese relationship. Another step taken by India was the agreement regarding the Gorkha recruitment in the Indian Army. The practice had been introduced by the British Government in May 1915. The newly independent India also entered in to tripartite Agreement with the Government of UK and Nepal in November 1947 whereby Nepal agreed to allow Twelve Gorkha battalion to be employed in the Indian army and Eight in the British.[1]

With the emergence of Peoples Republic of China as a powerful state and its occupation of Tibet, the later ceased to serve the role of a buffer and ultimately compel India to take keen interest in Nepal for the defence and security of the country from the side of China. The threat to India's security became real because the Himalaya on the North of Nepal could be penetrated at quite a few places particularly the Nara Pass, Kodari Pass and the Kuti Pass in Nepal.[2] Nepal because of its strategic location become an important buffer state between India and China and occupied an important strategic position in India's northern security system.

Nehru the architect of India's foreign policy adopted a strategy of good neighbourliness towards Nepal for the protection of its northern border. He did recognise Nepal's independence but was opposed to the interference of other powers in the internal affairs of Nepal because this would jeopardise India's security. It was but for the same reason that Nehru evolved a theory of India's "special relationship" with Nepal.

India's policy towards Nepal was governed by the emergence of Peoples Republic of China. The basic idea was that it would not be in India's interest to adopt a policy of confrontation with China because at that time India did not have sufficient military power to fight against Pakistan and China simultaneously. Therefore, in order to prevent any threat to its security and to maintain peace and prosperity in the Himalayan region Nehru pursued the policy of friendship with China.

The maintenance of close or special relations with Nepal became cordinal objective of India's foreign policy from the point of view of its own security. Referring to India's interest in Nepal Nehru said in the Lok Sabha on 6 December, 1950.

"Apart from our sympathetic interest in Nepal we are also interested in the security of ouw own country." He added "much as we appreciate the independence of Nepal, we can not risk our own security by anything going wrong in Nepal which permits either that barrier to be crossed or otherwise weakens our frontier.[3]

These words of Nehru have served as a basis of India's policy towards Nepal is perhaps the most striking example of Indian opposition to Chinese presence. The first step taken by India for the protection of its security from inside of China was the conclusion of the Treaty of peace and friendship with Nepal on 31 July, 1950. The treaty specifically provided that neither Government shall tolerate any threat to the security of the otherby a foreign aggressor and enjoined upon them the responsibilites "to consult each other and deveise effective counter measures in case of any threat." The treaty also provided that Nepal would consult India before importing any war equipment from any country other than India but gave the right to Nepal after such consultation to import from or through the territory of India arms and ammunition of war like material and equipment necessary for the security of the country.[4] The question of arms purchase from China was implicity ruled out.

Thus the treaty of peace and friendship concluded between the two countries recognised each other sovereignty and independence and declared that the two countries agreed to mutual consultation on matters relating to each others national security. The obligation for mutual consultation on matters of defence were further emphasised in letters exchanged between the two countries at the time of conclusion of the treaty. India established 17 check posts to watch the passes between Tibet and Nepal and Bhutan manned jointly by Indian and Nepalese personnel. An Indian military mission was set up on Kathmandu for the organisation and training of Nepalese armed forces. India also supplied arms to Nepal for the defence of the country. It was in pursuance of these provisions of the treaty that India blocked the establishment of diplomatic relations between Nepal and China for the next few years.

The "special relationship" between the two countries was further strengthened by the signing of the separate treaty of trade and commerce on the same day. The treaty acknolwedged Nepal's full and unrestricted right of commercial transit of all goods and manufactures through the territory or ports of India from third countries without the payment of duty. The treaty also provided for fixing the same level of duties by both on imports from third countris.[5] India agreed to make available to Nepal to the maximum extent possible, commodities essentials to its economy also secured their routes and method of transportation which were most convenience and economical. The arrangements were reciprocal but India was keen to help Nepal in the development of its economy. Thus India's economic relations with Nepal were regulated by the treaty of trade of commerce. Nepals main trading partner was India. By 1960 about 95 per cent of Nepal's trade was only with India.

Jawahar Lal Nehru the architect of India's foreign policy was of the view that Nepal being a buffer state between India and China must enjoy its sovereignty and independence. The treaty of Peace and Friendship acknowledged the complete sovereignty and independence of Nepal. But at the same time a sense of insecurity from the side of China, made it imperative for Indoa to take greater interest in the internal development of Nepal. Nehru felt the Nepal could better safeguard the interest of India if there was peace and stability in the country. but peace stability and economic development in Nepal could be ensured only through the political system responsible to the people. Nepalese Congress was always sympathetic to the movement for democracy in Nepal. The treaty of friendship negotiated in 1949 could not be signed as Nepali Rana leaders resisted India's proposal for democratic structure of government in Nepal. India supported the anti-Rana force to establish democratic government in Nepal.[6] The change of Government also brought significant changes in the attitude of Nepal towards India Nepal looked towards India for guidance both in internal and external affairs. India maintained its position in Nepal by reaching a political understanding with China over Nepal and Tibet. It also took steps to further bring Nepal into close relationship with and put the defence and foreign policy of the two centres on a more formal basic. The two countries remained closed to each other and coordinated their foreign and defence policies until there was a change of government in Nepal.

In 1955 some new developments occured in Nepal which had dual impact on Indo-Nepalese relations. One of the most important development was the passing away of Kind Tribhuvan and the accession of King Mahendra to the Nepalese throne. This brought about significant changes in the policy of Nepal towards India and also added certain new dimensions to the politics of Nepal. King Mahendra did not act like Tribhuvan had and instituted the socalled National Panchayat to maintain his power and position in the country.[7] These developments in Nepal caused concern in India. India could not provide any help to the king because panchayat system was a setback to democracy in Nepal. This attitude of India agitated the king and his followers which led to a phase of suspicious relationship between the two countries.

The main problem of India was that it was frightened of Chinese influence in Nepal would be a direct threat to Indian security. To prevent that scenario India tried to face the situation with diplomacy on one hand it tried to cultivate friendly relations with China to maintain peace in the region and on the other it tried to impress upon the king that only a democratic Government could bring political stability and accelerate economic development of the country.

The Sino-Indian agreement on Tibet in 1954 had placed Nepal in precarious position and it could not ignore the neighbourhood of China. Therefore, with Indian assistance negotiations for normalisation of Sino-Nepalese relations started and on 1st August 1955 Nepal and China agreed to open diplomatic relations. Again Nepal under the sponsorship of India was admitted to the United Nations at the end of 1955. Both these events were bound to enhance Nepal's status as an independent of Indian influence. Nepal, friendship with China qualitatively changed the situation for India. China used the opportunity to play the game and encouraged anti-Indian sentiments in Nepal. It also gave concession on a broder treaty while obtaining the right to built the Kathmandu Kodari Road.[8] Nepal gave to China a good chance of implanting its strategic presence in the country and assume the role of the protector of Nepal's territory and independence. The King in a bid to be regarded as a champion of Nepalese nationalism supported anti-India elements in the Kingdom and gave the impression that it was pursuing a prochina policy.[9]

While India was not opposed to Sino-Nepalese steps for the normalisation of their relations, What India feared was that its relations with Nepal might be substituted by China. Nehru hinted this when he visited Nepal in June 1959. He had pointed out that although one should be friendly with all countries. "We must not forget that the basis of all relations is an older relation. It we renounce an old relation to form a new one, then neither of the two is stable for relations to prosper "he added" there had to be mutual trust".[10] Friendship with Nepal for the security of the country was absolutely necessary, therefore India could not allow its relations with Nepal to suffer while its relation with China was steadly deteriorating. Nehru once again asserted India's special position in Nepal by repeating and reminding the clauses of the Treaty of 1950 when he said in the Lok Sabha on 27 November 1959 that "I just say to repeat what we have said previously that any aggression on Nepal would be considered by us as aggression on India.[11]

At a press conference held in New Delhi on 3 December 1959 Nehru revealed a paragraph of the letter exchanged between the two governments when they signed the treaty of peace and friendship in 1950. The inclusion of his paragraph altered the relationship between the two countries at least in terms of security. It said "neither Government shall tolerate a threat to the security of the other by a foreign aggressor. To deal with such threat, the two Governments will consult each other devise effective counter measures.[12]

It was a warning to China to keep their hands of Nepal and a reminder to Nepal of its treaty obligations, B.P. Koirala visited India in January 1960 following his visit a press communique issued on 28 January stated that Nepal and India have vital interest in each others freedom, integrity security and progress and agreed that the two Governments should maintain close consultation in matter of common interest.[13]

In 1960 certain steps were taken by Nepal which caused concern in India regarding its relations with Nepal. For instance Nepal signed a treaty of peace and friendship with China in 1960 without consulting India in violation of Indo-Nepalese Treaty of 1950. When the treaty of trade and transit came up for renewal in 1960 different interpretation of new draft created uncertainity. However, due to the close personal relations that existed between B.P. Koirala and the Prime Minister Nehru differences were sorted out. India was also disturbed by the failure of democracy in Nepal. The King of Nepal by a proclaimation had dismissed the Koirala Government, suspended the provisions relating to fundamental rights of Nepalese citizen and banned political parties in the country. The king assumed full powers of the state. Actually India's support to democratic forces in Nepal and the King fear of India as the potential threat to his authority have been constant source of tension between the two countries. As the King seemed to have very little sympathy with India. India could not maintain the same level of relationship with Nepal. Actually Nepal's desire to strike an independent course of actions in foreign affairs was viewed in India with the suspicion India took all these developments seriously because of its security interest in Nepal. The Sino-Nepalese Boundary Agreement regarding road construction from Lhasa to Kathmandu concluded on 16 October 1961 caused concern to India because it was an expression of open hostility towards India Nepal's new policy seemed to be a calculated move for opening new options, not only in terms of diplomatic relations but also increased economic assistance as well as the process of weaning itself away from the close ties it had established with India. China supported Nepal's policy to disengage itself from the pattern of relations that had originally been established by the Indo-Nepalese treaty of peace and friendship in July 1950. China wanted Nepal to come under its influence by replacing India. Themost significant sign of Chinese interest in the area was China's proposal for establishing a Himalayan Federation of Mangol people residing in the region. This was proposed to Nepal in 1962 under which Himalayan states were to be united together.[14]

The visit of Nepalese King Mahendra to New Delhi in April 1962 provided an opportunity for both the countries to make fresh attempt to improve the deteriorating state of relations. The two countries acknolwedged that mutual interests could not be served by the suspicion against each other. The joint statement issued on 23rd April recognised that both India and Nepal have a vital interest in each others sovereignty, independence and territorial integrity and affirmed their intension to consult together on appropriate measures of mutual assistance at the request of either party.[15]

The Indo-China conflict 1962 made the situation more delicate and difficult for Prime Minister Nehru. Nepal played a neutral role in the conflict and did not condemn chinese aggression on India. The Chinese aggression made India more conscious of the need to maintain cordial relations with its immediate neighbours India felt that an unfriedly neighbour could became a source of majortrouble using China which posed a serious threat to its security at that time. The danger from the side of Nepal caused concern to Indian because of anti-India campaigns launched by the Nepalese people and authorities. Nehru gave a fresh look on the existing situation and adopted a policy of "appeasement" towards Nepal in the light of the policy of isolation it had pursued during the conflict with China. India showed its willingness to improve relations with Nepal and restore the goodwill that had been eroded during 1962. The first move in this direction was the visit of Lal Bahadur Shastri, the then Home Minister of India. He visited Kathmandu on 2 March 1963 with the specific purpose of examining new approaches for the development of better relations. He had a series of talks with King Mahendra. Tulsi Giri and V.B. Thapa the joint declaration issued on 5 March 1963 emphasised that both India and Nepal were sovereign nations and India had no desire other than to have the friendly relation with Nepal. It was deceided by the two countries that "frank consultation on all issues of common interest would continue to settle small differences.[16]

On his return from Nepal Shastri reported to the Parliament that India would act as "big brother" and would play a vital role in the progress of Nepal.[17] In fact the visit of Indian Home Minister Lal Bahadur Shastri to Nepal played an important role in smoothening deteriorated Indo-Nepalese relations. It removed the fear and suspicions that Nepal had so far developed against India. First concrete sign of this new trend was evident on King Mahendra' visit to India when in the joint declaration issued on 30 August 1963 more emphasis was given on "development assistance" and extension of cooperation to "Nepal's trade diversification needs". It was felt that such measures would ensure not only the growth of better relations but would prevent Nepal from seeking kinds and agreements detrimental to Indias interest. Over the decades that followed India had consistently tried to preserves the "special relationship" with Nepal which Nehru had established in 1950.

From the above analysis we can conclude that Nepal because of its strategic location has played an important role in India's northern security system. India need Nepal as dependable neighbour for the defence of its northern border. Therefore, to ensure the security of the country from the side of China a 'treaty' of 'peace and friendship' with Nepal was concluded in 1950.[18] The treaty established special relationship between the two countries in the matter of defence and foreign affairs. The relationship between the two countries was further strengthened by the treaty of trade and commerce. India has been of great help to Nepal in the process of its economic development. It has fully finance and implemented cooperation schemes for the development of Nepal's water resource like Kosi and Gandhak project. The emphasis of India's aid has remained in providing Nepal such technical know how and creating such infrastructure which may make it capable of exploiting indigenous resources in a way to minimise its dependence on foreign assistance. Indi has also supported the establishment of democratic system of government in Nepal. The relation between India and Nepal are historic example of how much can be achieved through mutual cooperation between two sovereign independent neighbours. While it is true that there have been occasional differences of opinion, these have been of no more than passing significance.

References

1. Kessing's Contemporary Archieves, 13 December 1947.
2. See Chakravarti. The evolution of India's Northern border, New York, 1971.
3. Jawaharlal Nehru, India's Foreign Policy : Selected Speeches, September 1949-April 1961, New Delhi, Publication Division 1961, p. 36.
4. For Text of the Treaty See S.D. Muni, Foreign Policy of Nepal, New Delhi, National Publishing House, 1971, pp. 283-85.
5. *Ibid.*, pp. 286-87.
6. Nehru No. 3, p. 436.
7. Statesman, New Delhi, 17 December, 1950.
8. See Leo Rose, Nepal : Strategy for Survival, Oxford University Press, 1971
9. V.P. Dutt, India, India's Foreign Policy, Vikas, New Delhi, 1994, p. 256.
10. Nehru No. 3, p. 436.
11. Lok Sabha Debates, New Delhi 2 Session 3-5, 27 November 1959, p. 22.
12. Statesman (New Delhi) : 30 November 959. See also Asian Recorder (New Delhi), Vol. No. 51, 19-25 December, 1959, p. 3061.
13. *Ibid.*
14. Foreign Affairs Record, New Delhi, vol. VI, January 1960, p. 14.
15. Harish Kapur, India's Foreign Policy 1947-92, Shadows and Substance, Sage, New Delhi, 1992, pp. 103-16.

16. For text see Foreign Affairs Record, New Delhi, Vol. VII, No. 4, April 1962, p. 99.

17. Foreign Policy of India : Text of Documents 1947-64, New Delhi, p. 348.

    See also, T.N. Kaul, Ambassadors Need Not Lie, Vol. 3, India and Asia, New Delhi, Lancer, 1989.

18. Iqbal Khanam, Indian Security perceptions and Nepal, M.D. Dharamdasani (ed.) Nepal in Transition, Varanasi, Shalimar 1997, pp. 24-25.

17

SAARC for Regional Peace

Bishnu Hari Nepal

Immediately after the military take over, Gen. Musharraf was in a great trouble. It was understood, anything could happen to dictatorial Pakistan. The Commonwealth had expelled this country from its membership. India, the strongest SAARC member, together with the other international community, was amongst the vehement critic of the expulsion of the elected government of Pakistan. Hence, she never appreciated a red carpet for Gen. Musharraf at the SAARC Headquarters. As a result, despite Nepal's full preparation, the Eleventh Summit in Kathmandu in November 1999, had to be postponed indefinitely.

Contrary to the strong opposition from the democratic world, Gen. Musharraf was successful to prolong his military power in the name of mitigating corruption and safeguarding the national interest of Pakistan. The sustenance due to capacity building, and his experience of the military tactics, virtually helped his regime, to achieve recognition from the world powers, including P-5s, the PRC, standing on the frontline. India, due to her strained relations with Pakistan, during this period, tried her best to defend her national interest and the cause of democracy very carefully. For both India and Pakistan, the Kargil shock of the immediate past and its aftermath have remained as deep wounds for ever.

In diplomacy, as foreseen, nothing is permanent. Once the strongest opponent India had red carpet for Gen. Musharraf in New Delhi, to hold the historic Agra Summit, between PM Vajpayee and Gen. Musharraf. For maintaining protocol to his India visit, Gen. Musharraf got an opportunity further to tell his people, to get himself promoted from CEO to President of Pakistan. Despite the sincere preparations and attempts of negotiation, up to the last minute of the Summit, Agra left but both the leaders in despire. Even a simple note of the visit or MoU could not be signed. For diplomatic circle, it was crystal clear, how tense the situation was.

In other words, the dark clouds of war over beautiful Kashmir remained still threatening. Last November, Vajpayee flatly rejected to meet President Musharraf in New York during UN General Assembly. Since then, only Kathmandu has remained as a ray of hope for talks between the two SAARC giants, during the Eleventh Summit, 4-6 January, 2002. On this perspective, this Summit has been perceived as the most important one in the history of SAARC, for, India and Pakistan are expected to have separate talks during this occasion. Obviously, this talk is also vital, being the first Summit after Agra and after the rejection of the proposed meeting at New York. In the eyes of Political Scientists, without regional peace and security; so to say, in the present scenario, without improved Indo-Pak relations, SAARC adheres no special significance, This can be learnt from the sixteen years old history of SAARC in retrospect.

It is because, at a juncture, where the two key members of relatively a small regional organisation like SAARC, are always at a state of war, the question ariese, after all, what is the function of SAARC with respect to maintaining peace and security in the region in reals sense ? Since SAARC does not allow bilateral matters to be raised within its constitutional framework, still, the query goes to how the leaders utilise this occasion, to rejoice in their minds and carry on their bi-lateral matters with a better perspective and in a friendlier environment, finding time to engage themselves out of the official SAARC agenda ?

In this regard, the story of two generals, one of them present President of Pakistan and his then counterpart Indian war veteran sitting together in person in a regional function in Colombo, immediately after the Kargil War, had international significance and got wide range of coverage in the print media. Flying back to Pakistan Gen. Musharraf achieved power through military coup, without bloddshed. That time, it was never possible bilaterally, for two generals, meeting together and sitting together, without the regional arrangements.

Emphasis of the theme here is to analyse the role played by SAARC, direct or indirect, having influence upon the psycho-analytical aspecdt of the decions making processes of the regional nuclear powers. Crystal clear that this state of mind of the decision makers deserves the most important component of the process, giving influence in creating and maintaining regional peace and balance of power system.

Any student of diplomacy is aware of the fact that post-colonial South Asia has always remained unstable and insecure. Sino-Indian war of 1962 was between two largest populations of the world. Both People's Republic of China and Republic of India became nuclear powers in 1964 and 1974 respectively. The very year, when Bangladesh was born, in 1971, China entered the UN and attained the prestigious position of the Permanent Member of the Security Council. These developments were aiding South Asia, maintain regional balance of power system, of course, without any integrated regional diplomatic arrangement.

In mid-seventies, for instance, India seemed more engaged in her internal politics, even imposing emergency in that country. But, despite her unrest at home, India was able to merge Sikkim to her in 1975. Understanding such regional scenario, late King Birendra brought two important proposals to the world : Feb 25, 1975 during his Coronation, he proposed that Nepal be declared a Zone of Peace, which, received support from 116 countries of the world, except friendly India. Frankly, the Nepalese pro-multi-partyleaders might be regretting intenally today that why they did not give emphasis to this Nepalese noble notion, during post-1990 period. If done so, perhaps the plight of the country, due to People's War or so, would not worsen like this, what the present witnesses.

Second that late King Birendra in 1976, for the first time among South Asian leaders, called upon for the regional cooperation arrangements in South Asia, during South Asian Consultative Committee Meeting in Nepal. In fact, this farsighted notion soon took official shape, and that too, at the active initiative of the then Bangladeshi President, declaring SAARC by its seven members in Dhaka, on Dec. 8, 1985.

Its headquarters serving from Kathmandu exemplifies Nepal's contribution and active role to establish this regional mechanism for regional peace and cooperation. This also avails encouragement that even smaller countries deserve a say within SAARC and can play a crucial role for the regional peace-making and peace-keeping manoeuvre. Pragmatically, it deserves more urgency, when two, out of seven, most important members and nuclear giants, are, at the stage of war. If we flash back their peace policies in the region, India has outlined her nuclear policy not to be the first country to use nuclear weapons. Similarly, Pakistan has publicly stated that it would not hesitate to defend its people with nuclear weapons, if necessary.

In such situation, it is difficult to omit the bitter fact that they have fought four major wars during post-1947 period. Among them, the 1971 war was costliest for Pakistan, loosing East Pakistan. On the other hand, it was the greatest achievement for late Indira Gandhi in her political life, being able to crate Bangladesh. Thus, signing of Security Pact by India with the then USSR, the same year in 1971, also was a clear counter balance for regional security, with special reference to the entry of China to the Security Council. The Security Pact with USSR also benefitted India during the crucial phase ahead, when US openly offered late Zia-ul-Huq four billion US dollars package in the name of Afghan cause in early 80's.

These strategic factors aided to the regional need assessment in South Asia facilitating the establishment of today's SAARC. Particularly, such diplomatic environment helped follow the Line of Control, sketched out by the Shimla Agreement, between India and Pakistan, bilaterally, in 1972. All the time, Kashmir dominated the Indo-Pak relations, as the core point. Post-1971 period, more than two and a half decade, until Kargil War, 'no major warfare' took place between these countries. This can be considered as the positive side of the SAARC diplomatic environment and international scenario, resulting comparatively better state of tranqulity, diminishing post-war hazards in the entire region.

Today, experts and authorities are talking about the agenda of the Eleventh Summit like poverty alleviation packages, combating terrorism, child trafficking and women rights etc. One should not forget that they are talked about from the inception of SAARC. The SAFTA, SAARC Open University and other socio-economic and ethno-cultural relations also are not new themes. Whatsoever agenda in different fields, if observed sincerely, on grounds of conflict resolution procedures and strategic capability building, India stands on the epicenter of the SAARC map.

Take the case of the Second Pokharan Nuclear Test conducted by India and its immediate test-response from Pakistan under Nawaz Sharif. It sharply picturises the sensitivity and danger of the situation, not only bilaterally, but also regionally. Equally important, one should not forget the fact that nuclear giant China is the next door neighbour of SAARC countries. Such threats and counter threats, due to nuclear armament race in the region, are carried out in the name of self-defence, connoting Art. 51 of the UN Charter.

Not signing CTBT by USA, China, India and Pakistan and total negation of 1972 ABM Treaty from President Bush, both have the direct impact in the SAARC region. This is very crucial in the Indo-Pak border, specially, post-Afghan War period ahead. Therefore, Kathmandu Summit, as a Summit itself, for almost after three years, is a success to some exten, but SAARC members, particularly India and Pakistan, should not forget that SAARC had already passed anti-drug and anti-terrorist conventions in 1987 and 1988 respectively. The SAFTA bears significance only when the members possess homogeneity instead of stratified approaches. History has witnessed, due to clashes of opinions between these two influential members, SAARC has not been able even to define terrorism properly.

18

Party Politics in India and Nepal A Comparative Analysis

M.D. Dhurumdasani

In a liberal democratic system, political parties play a vital role as an instrument of political modernisation. In fact, political parties are the only institutionalised means to mould the political behaviour of citizens, mobilies support for the polity, serve as a linkage between elite and mass, socialise people for democratic culture and stimulate them for the successful working of the system. In the traditional societies the role of political parties was very limited but as a society steps on the path of modernisation, the role of political parties also gains greater importance. This is particularly true to India and Nepalwhich after gaining independence from the British and Rana rule respectively are marching ahead on the path of political modernisation and where the political parties are playing significant role in consolidating the democratic process and representative government. In this context, we should mention that there are three important components which are key to a competitive political democracy, electorate, legistature and the executive. The political parties play decesive roles at all the three levels. They midilise people for political participation in the elections and making bid for the formation of the government. Even if they are out of power, they provide an alternative to the actual government and articulate needs and demands of the people which otherwise might be neglected.

In this study, the political parties have been taken to be the key in understanding the current trasitional state of both Indian and Nepalese politics because they have not only been one of the most instrumental agents in ushering in the multi-party system in the Himalayan Kingdom but also because upon them rests the responsibility for filling in the power vacuum created by the shift from a system of governance based on perempotry commond of the King to one largely depend on party politics. In case of India also, with the decline of one party dominant system which brought about some sort of political stability of the system, a new phase of coalition and minority governments has been ushered and India has also entered in a transitional phase of politics and the questions are being raised whether the current political situation will be condusive to growth of smooth functioning of democratic system or not. In this context the role of political parties as an instrument of stability or destabilising the political system will also be taken into consideration. In order to draw a better understanding of the environment in which parties operate, a brief survey of the evolution of the party system and their status in the polity will be made.

Evolution and Status of Party Politics in India and Nepal

In India which is a largest democracy in the world, till 1988, the Indian National Congress, the oldest and more organised parties, maintained its dominance as a ruling party and one party dominance system as it was called remained as feature of political system. The other opposition parties baring a brief period of Janata rule remained fragmented and disorganised and could not enjoy power at the Centre. It was only in the 1989's elections that for the first time no single political party secured absolute majority in the Parliament. The Indian National Congress which still remained largest single party declined to form the government and therefore the Janata Dal under the leadership of V.P. Singh came forward to form a coalition government with the support of extreme right BJP and the extreme left the CPI, CPM, etc. The country thus entered into phase of coalition politics which is by nature unstable and uncertain. Anti-Congressism became the common element for unity of various political parties which formed the government at the Centre. Gradually, this proved to be ineffective in keeping the political parties together and when the BJP withdres its support in November 1990, the V.P. Singh's government had to resign. After that Chandrashekhar formed the government with the support of the Congress who also had to resign after a period of four months and ultimately the country had to face another election in May-June 1991. This time the Congress formed the government with ADMK and other smaller parties supporting it from outside. Thus, a new phase of minority governments was introduced in the Indian politics.

The political trends that have emerged today clearly reveals that the coalitional politics has become order of the day. As such, the governments are bound to be unstable and weak. Since the fall of Narasimha Rao and one party dominant system three governments have taken the reigns of power and now a new coalition was formed under the leadership of rightist party BJP. Although, it was a welcome sign that BJP as single largest party was supported by small parties, nevertheless, the pressure it faced from its coalition partners, clears shows that the ruling BJP required accommodating qualities in leadership which fortunately, the former Indian Prime Minister seems to have had. Moreover, if the other coalition partners are restraining themselves from precepitating a political crisis for the time being, it is mainly because they are all scared of facing an election. Besides, a new class of leadership has emerged in the political parties whose sole aim is to grab power, having no ideology or norms. In fact, they are more of power seekers than political leaders. To them their political interests are much more important than the national interest. And finally, it is hoped that witn the coming of power of the BJP, a new phase of reconcilliation and accommodation was started which is a welcome sign for a nationa based on plural democracy and secularism. Now, the Congress Party has formed a new coalition Government under the leadership of Man Mohan Singh.

In Nepal, organised political parties are of very recent origin. The Rana political system did not allow any kind of organised poltical activity. In 1921, In India a Gurkha League was formed at Dehra Dun. After 1930, the league assumed a political role. It criticised the Rana government and the British government in India. In fact its role was limited to the upliftment of Nepalese living in India. Inspired by the Praja parishad movement in the Indian feudal states, some young Nepalese formed a political party named as Praja Parishad at Kathmandu in 1937. The Party failed in its mission and its members had to suffer capital punishment for anti-Rana activities. Inspired by the Indian leaders, Nepali National Congress in Line with the Indian National Congress was formed in 1947 at Calcutta and B.P. Koirala became the working President of the Party. The NNC started its programme as overthrow of the Rana regime and the establishment of a democratic system. The party played a crucial role in the revolution of 1950 and ultimately succeede in overthrowing the Rana rule with the active assistance of New Delhi. Thus, for the first time political parties played a significant role in bringing about democratic system in Nepal.

After 1955, with the accession of King Mahendra the situation became more complicated for functioning of the political parties. King Mahendra had special dislike towards the political parties. However, political parties continued their demand for partiamentary democracy which was established in 1959. The Nepali Congress took over the reigns of power but it was short lived.

After the establishment of the Panchayat System, political parties were totally banned. However, political parties continued their demand of liberalisation of the political system. For the first time the prominent left UML and Nepali Congress despite their ideological differences, united themsleves against the Panchayat system and ultimately got success in ending the 30 years Panchayat system and a new era of liberal democratic system was introduced in Nepal.

In the post panchayat era, two major political parties-Nepali Congress and UML which fought for democracy, are competiting with each other to gain political power, in the country. The Nepali Congress claims that it is the only party which is torch bearer of democracy in the coutry due to series of historical role it has played-toppling of the Rana Regime, serving as a major political forces during the panchayat system and in reviving democrating system in the country after 1990. Infact the Nepali Congress has tried to minimise the role of UML in the democratic movement against the Panchayat system and have succeded to some degree in making their party's image synonymous with the notion of democracy in Nepal. However, the Nepali Congress in practice has approached democracy from the point of view of promoting individual interests of rival factions. Notwithstanding the constitutional injuction that all parties must adhere to "the norms of democracy" (Article 113.2), the congress functioned principally on feudal lines based on an informal alliance of the three big chiefs called the troka. With the death of Ganesh Man Singh, the major rivals in the party are Bhattarai and Koirala group and the latter is now dominating the Nepalese political scene and has assumed the post of the Prime Minister. However, the point which we wish to emphasise that each chief has own band of faithful followers who pay him Chakri (Court) on almost similar lines as did the courtiers of former Ranas. The personal rivalries of the leaders did not matter so long as the Congress was in the opposition and was fighting the panchayat establishment. But as soon as the Nepali Congress has taken over reign of power, the lack of organisational coherrence has hampered the working of both government and the party.

Another dangerous development which is against the spirit of democracy is the consolidation of family rules like Indian National Congress. The hereidatory rule or **"Vansha Vad"** promoted by the Nepali Congress is creating dissatisfaction among the workers of the party which will ultimately led to di-stabilisation of the democratic system itself. Unlike the central leadership or what is known as "High Command" of the Indian National Congress, which manages to keep control over warring factions at the Centre, State, District and local levels, the factions of the Nepali Congress sows the seeds of dissension at all level of NC ranks. This is where we should locate the source of Nepal's political instability.

The other major political party working in Nepal is Unite Marxist Leninist Party known as UML. The UML represents a combine of half a dozen left groups which until very recently followed their own goals and objectives. Some UML constituents still adhere to the physical liquidation of the local landlords as class enemies but the central leadership of UML is no more interested in their revolutionary socialist democracy. In fact they have agreed to work within the framework of Parliamentary democracy and now they are even no more against the monarchical system.

The third force in the politics of Nepal is Rastriya Prajatantra Party. The leaders of this party were closely associated with the Panchayat system but now they consider themselves committed to the ideology of democratic liberalism which includes concepts like nationalism and support for constitutional monarchy. This party is playing decisive role in the formation of the governments at the national level.

The other party Sadbhavana Party which is basically a regional party was formed to serve the interests of the Terai region, has also joined the mainstream and playing the role of King maker in the national politics, despite the few members at its disposal.

Conclusions

The current state of party politics both in India and Nepal presents a gloomy picture which is not a healthy sign for democratic set up. This borne out of the fact that the parties which ought to be based on political ideology, policies and programmes to cater the needs of the people are unable to set principles and norms governing the relationship between the party and the government. This has adversely affected the credibility of the party and also functioning of the democratic government. In India as well as in Nepal, the leaders of the political parties undermining the political ideologies and institutions are engaged in consolidation of their personal interests. In both the countries, fall of governments in such a short period was prompted not by any kind of ideological differences among the parties but only due to their personal rivalries. As a result, while established political parties and leaders have lost their credibility, the reactionary forces get their morale boosted from the growing feeling that the new regims is nothing but a new wine in the old bottle. In fact it is only 'marriage of convenience' that is responsible for political instability in both India and Nepal.

Thus, too many weak political parties having no ideological base and the lack of a strong opposition is determental to the functioning of democracy. The democratic system in Britain had survide and flourished because of well developed party system whereas the unstable political conditions for which party policies is largely responsible are encouraging the trends of criminalisation, corruption and personalisation of politics, terrorism and the manifestatio of political discontent. That is why, democracy both in India and Nepal is being called as **"Functional Anarchy"**.

The solution to the above challenges could be find out if leaders of the political parties visualise that excessive emphasis on group identities, albiet in the name of social justice and personal interests will lead to the erosion of national unity and crumbling of edifice of democracy which have been achieved by them after a long struggle and sacrifice. Indeed, the existence of well knit and strong political parties committed to democratic values and norms and revitalising people's faith through good governance can only create environment for sound and stable democratic system in both the countries.

References

1. *Political Parties and the Parliamentary Process in Nepal– A Study of the Transitional Phase,* POLSAN, Kathmandu, 1992.
2. Lok Raj Barl, *South Asia – Democracy and the Road Ahead,* POLSAN, Kathmandu, 1992.
3. S.K. Srivastava & M.D. Dharamdasani : *Modernization in Nepal,* CSN, B.H.U., 1986.
4. M.D. Dharamdasani : *Democratic Nepal,* Shalimar, Varanasi, 1992.

5. M.D. Dharamdasani : *Nepal in Transition,* Rajdhani Publications, Jaipur, 1997.

6. Ramakant & P.L. Bhola (Ed) : *Post Cold War Development in South Asia*, RBSA Publishers, Jaipur, 1995.

7. *Politics in India* : Vol. II, No. 10, April, 1998.

8. *South Asia – Vision & Perspective,* Pakistan, 1994.

9. M.D. Dharamdasani (ed) : *Indian Journal of Nepalese Studies,* Vol. V & VI, 199596, CSN, B.H.U.

19

Japan's Regional Standing and Nepal-Japan Relations

Nishchal Nath Pandey

Current South Asian Scene

South Asia has been called "a region of unending struggle and violence" primarily due to the fact that almost all the countries of the region are currently at odds with one of the other type of a conflict. Because of this preoccupation to stabilize one's polity, resolve differences with warring factions or groups and manage resources for an ever-rising defense expenditure, the countries have not been able to focus on salient issues such as raising the standards of living of their citizens and the overall economic development of their respective societies.

South Asia's seven countries are bound by a common geography, a shared civilization and ethnic, linguistic, religious and social attachments. On the other hand, intra and inter political disputes in these countries is so common that insurgencies, terrorism, repression, state failure, civil-religious clashes and armed confrontation have become a hallmark of our region. As if as a curse coerced upon us, we have been slow in embarking upon the path of economic liberalization and regional integration – an approach long undertaken by other regions notably Europe and East Asia. The basic reasons behind this have been the inability or even more appallingly, the undesirability to change the status quo on the part of our leaders.

Eric S. Margolis in his book "War at the Top of the World" says, "A great game is afoot at the top of the world. The chain of mountain ranges, plateaus and valleys that begins in Afghanistan and Kashmir and then sweeps four thousand km across the Indian sub-continent to Myanmar is fast becoming one of the globe's most volatile and dangerous geopolitical fault zones. Along that line, four nuclear armed powers-China, India, Pakistan and Russia are locked in a long-term rivalry that may erupt into a major international conflict."

In this backdrop, one clear pattern, which emerges, with all the existing conflicts is the tendency of our political leaders to whip up public sentiment, enage in petty selfish game and strive to sustain the conflict for monetary and political gains rather than diffuse it for the betterment of the peoples that vote them to power.

While intra-state conflicts with one outfit or the other have engaged individual nations of the region, problematic dyadic relationships is a yet another distrassing feature. India shares a border with all the six South Asian countries while none are connected by a border with the other. Moreover, India is a hotly contested issue in elections in other South Asian countriess while relations with neighbors seldom become such a crucial election issue in India. Therefore, Indo-Pakistan, Indo-Bangladesh, Indo-Sri Lanka and Indo-Nepal relations are quite customarily like traffic lights. Moreover, Nepal-Bhutan relations too have been capsized by a long-standing dispute of the Bhutanese refugees living in the 7 camps in eastern Nepal and affecting us economically, socially and environmentally.

How Can we Achieve Peace?

Easier said than done, for another twenty years, South Asian countries could suspend all their political problems and concentrate on economic development and once, the region reaches a certain level of economic affluence; it will be stress-free to set aside mistrusts and political misunderstandings. Whereas, a militarist approach to security has been proved as inadequate, our goverments have increasingly relied on the security forces to managing domestic chaos and internal conflicts rather than focusing on human development and providing good governance. There must be more attempts to raising self-awareness for making peace, frame new behaviors and new perspectives for a far more peaceful new millennium in our region.

Unless, problematic relations are resolved through economic, political and cultural confidence building measures, a breaking away from the current mess is simply not feasible. And, unless economic potentials are explored and bilateral economic cooperation is thoroughly worked upon, it is difficult to chill out differences. In fact, it is the chicken or the egg story. Which one do we do first-resolve political differences and wait for economic cooperation or vice versa?

South Asian Association for Regional Cooperation (SAARC) established 17 years ago amidst great hopes and dreams of the poverty stricken South Asian people must be allowed to grow to its full potential. Only through SAARC can we achieve a future that is bright for all of us. Unfortunately, this organisation has not been allowed to grow to its fullest potential owing to the same rivalry existing between India and Pakistan. Therefore, while there is always lip service paid to curtail militarization, there is seldom anything concrete done for the same.

The Role of Japan in the Future

The causes of conflict in South Asia are multiple and complex. Its prevention requires an integrated, comprehensive approach adjoining political, security, economic, financial, environmental, social, educational and development policies, based on the rule of law, democracy, respect for human rights, a free press and good governance. No single country on its own can support and encourage all that to South Asian countries except Japan. In this context, it is worthwhile to note a statement of Prime Minister Koizumi who at his very first policy speech said "in order for Japan to continue enjoying prosperity and peace, it is essential that we steadfastly devote ourselves to international cooperation." It is this profound vision, which will help South Asia to realize that it ought to engage in economic cooperation than political rivalry.

Since Japan joined the United Nations in 1956, cooperation with the United Nations has been a hallmark of its foreign policy. Japan has now become the world's second largest economy and based on this asset, it has the ability to assume ever a greater global responsibility particularly if it becomes a permanent member of the UN Security Council. Although Japan is the world's largest donor of offical development assistance, the world hasn't been able to utilize Japan's full potential for conflict resolution. Japan is at the same time, committed to promoting international disarmament and non-proliferation while firmly maintaining its three Non-Nuclear Principles of not possessing, not producing and not permitting the introduction of nuclear weapons into its territory. Moreover, it has been playing a leading role in disarmament of conventional arms, including small arms and landmines.

One naturally expects Japan to continue this thoughtful, pro-peace and pragmatic policy especially in the context of South Asia being nuclearized. Japan's initial reactions to the tit for tat nuclear tests conducted by India and Pakistan were strongly negative. Japan suspended aid, imposed sanctions, called on the G8 to respond, and briefly recalled its ambassadors from Islamabad and Delhi. Being the only country, which has experienced the horror of nuclear weapons, this decision was seen as pragmatic and sensible. Both in the short and long run, Japan could contribute positive in international politics through development assistance, participation in peacekeeping operations of the UN and helping developing countries of South Asia to help themselves. The International Peace Cooperation Law, enacted in June 1992 in the wake of the Gulf War, enabled Japan for the first time to engage more fully in UN peacekeeping operations and international humanitarian relief operations, including the dispatch of SDF units. After the enforcement of the International Peace Cooperation Law the Japanese government dispatched personnel and provided contributions in kind in connection with international election monitoring activities in Angola, Cambodia, Mozambique, and EI Salvador. Furthermore, in May 1999, a bill was passed enabling Japan to help ensure security in emergencies in areas surrounding Japan.

The whole world has changed in the last half a century and Japan has emerged as an economic superpower. The Soviet Union disintegrated and the years of the Cold War ended. There are more conflicts centering around ethnicity, religion and economics. Terrorism has spread its tentacles and must be met through our combined efforts. The efforts of the UN as an international body and the US as the world's only superpower are noteworthy in this regard.

With its emphasis on peace building and its generous assistance to ailing economies including warring countries, Japan can definitely play a constructive role in mediating long-standing conflicts, as it is not viewed as being hegemonistic or biased. It is destined to contribute certainly to the peace and amity of the world and therefore Japan's more active role in international relations is without doubt desirability.

Nepal-Japan Relations

In this background, let us analyze the history, nature and prospect of Nepal-Japan relations. The cultural ties between Nepal and Japan dates back in fact to much earlier days before direct people to people contact started in 1899, when Reverend Ekai Kawaguchi, a Japanese Zen Buddhist pundit and ascetic, visited Nepal.

It goes without saying that Japan and Nepal share a lot of similarities in terms of culture, religion, and even in terms of sentiment. The traditional culture of Nepal and Japan are closely linked together through the underground stream of history, which permeates both our cultures. The Newari language spoken widely by Newars in Nepal is very similar to Japanese. Besides, Nepal has always been a favorite destination for Japanese tourists. Diplomatic relations were established on September 1, 1956, ensued by the opening of the Royal Nepalese Embassy in Tokyo in 1956, and the Japanese Embassy in Kathmandu in 1968.

The warm and cordial relations between the two monarchies have been an important element of the bilateral relations. Their Late Majesties King Mahendra and Queen Ratna visited Japan in 1960. In the same year, Crown Prince Akihito and Princess Michiko (present Emperor and Empress) Nepal. The Imperial couple visited twice. His Late Majesty King Birendra studied in Japan. Japanese Prime Minister Mr. Yoshiro Mori's visit to Nepal in 1999 was another milestone in the history of friendly relations between our two countries.

Japan has been Nepal's largest ODA provider and assists mainly in Human Resources Development, Social Sector (Health and Education),

Agriculture Development, Economic Infrastructure, Environmental Conservation, etc. Nepal-Japan relations while embodying the essential tenets of friendly bilateral relationship also share the common desire for peace in South Asia and around the world.

20

Japan's Engagement Policy towards Burma

Mikio Oishi

1. Introduction

Although the question of Japan's role in the post-Cold War Asia has been repeatedly asked since the early 1990s, no convincing answer has been given yet. This is mostly due to the fact that for the past decade the country has been deeply engaged with its economic, political and social woes, which are still deteriorating. Such a current state of introversion is not conductive to the nation actively defining its positive role in the international community. However, Japan is still the leading economic power house in Asia and its action can exert tremendous impact on the people in the region. For this reason, it is still a profitable enterprise to examine the ways in which Japan can use its power for constructive purposes in Asia.

There are at least two roles that Japan may legitimately play in this region. One is that of an advocate of certain values that are considered to improve human condition such as democracy and human rights. As a member of the G7 group of advanced nations, Japan is expected to contribute to a peaceful world order by endorsing such values.[1] Especially, since Japan adopted the ODA Charter in 1992, it has been supposed to administer its ODA with a view to promoting democracy and human rights in recipient countries.

Another role, which has been less highlighted than the first role, is related to a range of activities to create peace in the region, particularly the role of peacemaking, which is an endeavour to bring about an agreement between the parties to conflict. Compared with Western countries, Japan has clear advantages in this option. More than anything else, Japan has never been involved in armed conflicts in the post-World War II period as a primary party. Its Constitution prohibits it from using military power to settle international disputes. Thus, it has always been in a good position to approach conflicts as a neutral third party. Particularly, for the past few years, it has been increasingly linking its ODA to peacemaking and peace-building within countries that are plagued with conflicts.

This paper will explore the prospects of these roles for Japan by examining Japan's ODA policy towards Burma as a case study. Burma provides an interesting case, as it is possible for a third party to involve itself in the Burma problem either as an advocate of democracy and human rights or as a (neutral) mediator who intend to reconcile the conflicting parties. Japan has been by far the largest aid donor to Burma since the 1950s, and Burma is considered as the most pro-Japanese nation in Asia, stemming from special ties between Japanese and Burmese leaders dating back to the period of World War 11. Japan is therefore in the best position to influence the country in either of the two optional roles. To investigate the first option, the paper will look at the decision-making structure of Japan's aid policy. On the other hand, the paper will adopt William Zartman's "ripeness theory" in order to examine the second option.

2. The Decision-Making Structure of Japanese ODA

There are three main characteristics of the decision-making structure of Japanese ODA that can be identified.

Firstly, there is no single, organisation that oversees its ODA policy.[2] Grants and technical assistance are administered by the Ministry of Foreign Affairs (MOFA) and its subsidiary, the Japan International Cooperation Agency (JICA). On the other hand, "yen loan", which occupies a large part of Japanese ODA is decided through a consensus among the Ministry of Foreign Affairs (MOFA), Ministry of Finance (MOF), Ministry of International Trade and Industry (MITI) and Economic Planning Agency

(EPA).[3] As each of these ministries has a veto power, the final decision on yen loans is usually a product of compromise among them, which deprives the administration of yen loan of overall coherence. Furthermore, each ministry has its own constituencies and needs to be sensitive to their interests: the MOFA has to take heed of what the international community has to say about Japan's ODA administration; the MOF's main concern is the effective implementation of the national budget and repayment of debts by recipient countries; and the MITI tends to promote the interests of the business sector in Japan.

Secondly, there is what is called "the iron triangle" which is the backbone of *Japan Incorporated.* The triangle consists of government bureaucrats, politicians from ruling parties and business interests. It dominates Japan's policy-making, of which the ODA administration is only a small part. In this structure, the business interests exerts decisive influence on what the bureaucrats decide about aid through the intervention of powerful politicians.

Thirdly, related to the second reason, the opposition and grassroots movements are excluded from the ODA decision-making process.[4] As a result, the values existing among the people can hardly be reflected in Japanese ODA. This is unfortunate, as citizens' movements in Japan have produced the ideas and values which may be able to effectively "humanise" Japanese ODA. It is true that the MOFA is more eager than other ministries to promote democracy and human rights in the recipient countries of Japanese aid. However, this is hardly because the MOFA officials are personally committed to these values. It rather indicates the ministry's vulnerability to the external pressure, especially that of the US, which since the end of the Cold War has been spreading its own "global standard", consisting of democracy, human rights and market economy. Thus, with no established mechanism to reflect humanistic ideas in foreign policy decision-making, Japan has yet to articulate these home-grown values in the international arena.

This paper will see how these characteristics have been reflected in Japan's ODA administration towards Burma, particularly in its intervention into domestic problems in Burma.

3. A Ripe Moment

To evaluate the performance of Japan's aid policy towards Burma in terms of peacemaking, this paper adopts Zartman's "ripe moment" theory. A ripe moment refers to a situation in which the parties feel inclined to opt for a negotiated settlement of a conflict rather than continue it. It consists of three elements: a Mutually Hurting Stalemate (MHS), a Formula for a Way Out (FWO) and Valid Spokespersons (VSPs).[5]

An MHS exists when "both sides are locked in a situation from which they cannot escalate the conflict with available means and at an acceptable cost".[6] In this situation, the parties perceive that they cannot achieve their goals by unilateral means and that the status quo (i.e., continuing the conflict) is increasingly unsustainable. An MHS often sets in after a crisis, and exerts a powerful impact on the parties if accompanied by a sense of an imminent catastrophe. It is based primarily on the parties' perception and is therefore subject to manipulation. That is, it can be created artificially.

Secondly, an FWO refers to a realistic and viable alternative to the continuation of the conflict. It need not be a solution to the conflict. However, it should at least appear to open a better future for both parties than the current stalemate.[7] It may encourage compromise on smaller tradable issues, but should more or less address the vital needs of the parties.

Lastly, VSPs are the persons who engage in negotiation as the legitimate representatives of each party. There are three requirements for them to be effective: First, they should command a substantial following of mainstream opinion within their respective groups. Second, they should be moderate enough to carve out a problem-solving coalition in the middle.[8] It is often difficult for the spokespersons to meet both requirements. If they are too moderate, they cannot represent their constituency's interests and are often discredited, while there are obviously extremely limited prospects for extremists to conduct successful negotiations with their opponents. Third, their legitimacy should be recognised by their opponents.

Thus, when the parties perceive the high costs of continuing the conflict while at the same time foreseeing positive outcomes through negotiation by legitimate representatives, they are likely to begin considering negotiation as an option.

As each of these elements depends largely on the parties' perceptions, which can be subject to influence, there is a good potential for a third party mediator to play an important role in creating a ripe moment. They can perform three functions, two of which are: creating or enhancing the MHS and providing or helping to create a FWO. In performing these functions, mediators can "sharpen the stalemate and sweeten the proposed outcome",[9] usually by exercising the political or economic leverage available to them. The third function is to make VSPs from both parties mutually acceptable as partners to a negotiation.

However, perhaps, the greatest challenge for a would-be mediator is gaining entry into the conflict. The government in particular may regard the offer by a mediator as an interference in internal affairs.[10] Particularly, mediator's effort to create the MHS may negatively affect the perception of the primary parties towards the mediator. Thus, it is a challenge of the mediator to create and maintain the MHS without undermining its position as a neutral party.

An aid donor like Japan is in a good position to act as a mediator in a conflict within or between the recipient countries. It can perform these functions by using its ODA in two different ways, called "positive linkage" (*sekkyokuteki-kanyo*) and "negative linkage" (*shookyokuteki-kanyo*).[11] In the former, an aid donor provides or increases ODA in response to developments in recipient countries which are deemed desirable from the standpoint of peace in order to encourage the new tendency. In negative linkage, on the other hand, the donor stops or reduces ODA in response to undesirable developments.

Before discussing Japan's intervention in the political turmoil in Burma that has been ongoing since 1988, it is proper to first provide a short review of Japan's ODA policy towards Burma during the period of 1954-1988.

4. Japan's ODA Policy Towards Burma 1955-1988

Japan's ODA towards Burma goes back to "war reparations",[12] which began in 1955. Burma as the first recipient of Japan's reparations received funds for the construction of the Baluchaung Dam and the "Four Major Industrialisation Projects", planned to manufacture light vehicles, heavy vehicles, agricultural machinery and electrical appliances. Under these schemes, US$250 million was provided in goods and services between 1955 and 1965. It was followed by "semi-reparations" worth US$131.5 million from 1965 to 1972. The ODA proper started in 1969 as "yen loans", which were to be provided to Burma for 19 times until 1988 with a total amount of 403 billion yen (US$3.4 billion, 1 US$=120 yen). A large part of them was "commodity loans". This means that Burma purchased from Japanese companies necessary goods for the projects that had been initiated under war reparations. In 1977, Japan started to provide the country with grants, which by 1988 had an accumulated value of 98 billion yen (US$817 million). In this year, Japanese ODA had grown to occupy some 80 per cent of the bilateral aid that Burma received from overseas.)[13]

Compared with other Southeast Asian countries, Burma has received disproportionately large amount of ODA from Japan.[14] This reflects the special ties between the political elites of both countries and the existence of a powerful Burma lobby that has developed in the history of the ODA administration. There is a Burma "iron triangle" comprising bureaucrats involved in administering ODA, politicians with special connections with the Burmese elite and a business group of consultant companies, developers, manufacturers and general trading houses (sogo-shosha) operating in the country.[15]

The most significant feature of Japanese ODA towards Burma in this period was that except for ODA-related trade, no significant Japanese private investment in Burma or bilateral trade between the two countries accompanied ODA. Since the 1962 military *coup d etat*, the government had adopted the "Burmese Way to Socialism", a kind of autarky economy based on a mixture of socialism and Buddhist teachings. Thus, Japanese ODA was, as it were, put into an economic vacuum. Without no local supporting structure, the ODA projects were never able to sustain themselves, but needed constant input of the yen loans, resulting in huge cumulative debts. Overall, Japan's aid did not help Burma's economic development, but presided over its economic downturn. The main beneficiaries of Japanese ODA were business interests in Japan and the small number of the Burmese elite. The ordinary Burmese suffered from the economic mismanagement and political oppression by the military regime.

The next section will look at how Japan has used its ODA in order to bring about positive change in Burma since 1988 from the standpoint of the three elements of a ripe moment and the acceptance of mediator by the parties.

5. Japan's ODA Policy Towards Burma Since 1988

In the wake of the 1988 massacres, Japan suspended its ODA towards Burma in collaboration with other donor countries.[16] For a while, it did not recognise the State Law and Order Restoration Council (SLORC), which took power in the September 1988 coup. However, Japan was increasingly put under pressure from its own Burma lobby, which demanded an early resumption of ODA. The structure of ODA administration as discussed above made the Japanese officials extremely vulnerable to such pressure. Japan also possessed pressing concerns, such as the need to maintain the good relationship with the ruling elite in Burma and its desire to invite Burmese representatives to the funeral of the Showa Emperor.[17] Thus, after five months of the coup, Japan recognised the SLORC and partially resumed its aid to Burma. Soon, a new concern added to the existing ones. China approached Burma in its international isolation in the aftermath of the Tiananmen Square Incident in June 1989. As China's influence over Burma increased with its military and economic aid, Japan felt additional pressure to be more friendly with the leaders of the military government. It needed to do something favourable towards the Burmese elite on a regular basis.

Thus, two factors have influenced Japan's ODA policy towards Burma since 1988: pressure from Japanese business sector and Japan's own desire to maintain its friendly relations with the Burmese in order to counter the increasing influence of China on Burma. The gradual reopening of Japanese ODA to Burma since 1989 can be seen in this context.

Every year since 1991, Japan has provided Burma with debt relief, which had been administered 19 times totalling 57.2 billion yen (US$476.7 million) by the end of 1998. It has been provided on a regular basis (twice or three times a year) irrespective of the human rights situation in the country. Japan has also given grants for such projects as food production improvement (1994, 1998), food aid (1995), nurse college expansion (1995), emergency grant after floods (1997), maternal and child service improvement (1998) and grassroots grants (every year since 1993). Finally, it resumed yen loan of 2.5 billion in 1997 for the extension of an airport.

Advancing Human Rights and Democracy in Burma

Since the adoption of the ODA Charter in 1992, the Japanese government has been required to pay full attention to "efforts for promoting democratisation ... and the situation regarding the securing of basic human rights and freedoms in the recipient country"[18] in ODA provision. However, Japan has largely failed in acting as an advocate of democracy and human rights towards Burma. This has been because of the two influencing factors to ODA, which were briefly pointed out above.

Firstly, the pressure from the business sector prevented Japan from single mindedly pursuing the role of the advocate of human rights and democracy. The best example is the 2.5 billion yen loan which was reopened in 1997 for the expansion of the Rangoon International Airport. The project, having been contracted out to Japanese construction companies before, was one of the projects which had been suspended since 1988. The project was resumed when the tension was high between the pro-democracy movement and the military government. In terms of promoting democracy and human rights, it did not make sense to provide aid to Burma at that time. However, rather than paying attention to Burma's internal situation, Japan more easily responded to the voice of Japan's Burma lobby, including the contractors of the suspended project, calling for the re-opening of the yen loan.

Secondly, Japan's own desire to maintain good relations with the Burmese elite has generated a certain pattern in its aid administration, which may be called a "carrot and carrot" policy. Following its positive linkage approach, Japan has provided aid to Burma at the smallest or even superficial signs of improvement in its political situation to encourage desirable changes. When such changes actually took place, Japan provided even more aid for reward. For example, it provided Burma with 1 billion yen (US$ 8.3 million) agricultural grant in March 1995 when the SLORC's two strongmen, Gen. Tan Shwe and Lieut. Gen. Khin Nyunt met Aung San Suu Kyi, who was put under house arrest. Soon after Aung San Suu Kyi was released from house arrest in July of the same year, another grant of 1.625 billion yen (US$ 13.5 million) was given for the Rangoon Nurses College. However, after all, these measures did not advance human rights and democracy in Burma. The relationship between the SPDC and the NLD soon deteriorated after the NLD boycotted a National Convention session in November 1995 and the SPDC expelled the NLD from the convention in retaliation.

Mutually Hurting Stalemate (MHS)

Japan's action did not contribute to the creation of a mutually hurting stalemate (MHS), either. Its suspension of aid to Burma in 1988 was a negative linkage policy. If Japan had stuck to this policy in collaboration with other aid donors, it might have exerted strong impact on the SLORC, thus contributing to an MHS. However, Japan began to neutralise the effect of the aid suspension by the positive linkage policy as demonstrated by the provision of grant projects and the resumption of the suspended yen loan project.

Although Japan acted to mitigate the plight of the military junta, the MHS seems to have set in around 1999, due mostly to the real prospects of the collapse of country's economy, stemming from the economic sanctions by Western countries, international movements to boycott the products of the companies investing in Burma and the East Asian financial crisis in 1997. The leaders of SPDC started to realise that the more oppression they were engaged in, the more economic repercussions there were.

For the SPDC, the downfall of President Suharto in Indonesia in 1998, the 1999 ILO suspension of Burma for its practice of forced labour and the 1999 World Bank report on the country's economy may have converged to mark a turning point in its perception of the situation. The first event meant the demise of any viable model of a military-led government, as Indonesia used to be the major inspiration for the junta generals who have been constructing a new constitution.[19] The second marked the first case in which the ILO banned any government in its 80 year history.[20] The last identified mismanagement by the military as the main cause of Burma's current economic woes, and recommended major political and human rights reforms in order to achieve economic prosperity.[21] This report was compiled with the extensive cooperation of the SPDC, and seems to have made a strong impact on it.

Formula for a Way Out (FWO)

Japan's ODA did not contribute to the formula for a way out (FWO) at least until 2002. Unlike the Cambodian Crisis 1997-98 in which it played a major part in restoring peace to the country by its "Japan Formula", Japan has not been able to come up with a formula or scenario for the reconciliation of the opposing camps in Burma. Although Japan has taken every opportunity to call on the military junta and the NLD to start a dialogue, it has not given any suggestion as to how such a dialogue is made possible. It has not even clearly made the provisions of ODA to Burma conditional on the commencement and progress of the dialogue. Without any FWO at hand, Japan's ODA policy towards the post-1988 Burma lacks coherence and a strategy. In other word, Japan was not successful in strategically incorporate its ODA into an FWO.

Such an FWO has been provided by ASEAN. In May 2002, Aung San Suu Kyi was released from her second house arrest. Before her release, a series of secret dialogues had been held between her and representatives of the ruling State Peace and Development Council (SPDC). These dialogues have been mediated by a Malaysian career diplomat and former Chairman of UN General Assembly, Razali Ismail, whom the UN has appointed as Special Envoy to Burma. The dialogues have also been supported and encouraged by Malaysian Prime Minister Mahathir Mohammad, who has maintained close contact with the leaders of the military government, particularly with SPDC Chairman, General Tan Shwe.[22]

What is special of ASEAN's current involvement in Burma is that an "ASEAN Formula" has been taking shape since April 2000 when Razali Ismail was appointed to as a UN mediator. ASEAN has suggested that in exchange for the junta's agreement to start the talks with Aung San Suu Kyi, ASEAN will collectively defend the junta from international criticisms and seek to end its economic sanctions by Western countries. Such an approach indicates a major departure from ASEAN's traditional principle of non-interference in the internal affairs of a member state.

The formula's greatest attraction to the parties would be the fact that ASEAN would act as a guarantor of the process. Thus, its role would include looking into the vital needs of the parties. This may be achieved, for example, by promising the NLD that there will eventually be democracy in the country and by granting SPDC a sense of legitimacy, which it desperately needs before it can function properly in negotiations. Related to the legitimacy problem, it is important for both parties to settle the human rights issue. Mahathir points out its importance for the peace process:

> "The Myanmar military is unlikely to hand power to a civilian government unless there is a guarantee that there would not be reprisals in the future."[25]

Fortunately, the NLD has on many occasions made it clear that the junta generals would not be punished for their past wrong-doings.[24] Thus, ASEAN can act as a guarantor of the NLD's promise.

On a more practical note, an ASEAN proposal to form an interim "national government" seems to be a powerful ingredient of the formula.[25] The proposed government would comprise the SPDC, the NLD and probably the representatives of ethnic minorities, and would formulate a new constitution under which a new general election would be held.[26] It is unrealistic to expect the military to immediately renounce power after almost 40 years in government. For this reason, it might be important for the NLD to drop its call for the SPDC to respect the results of the 1990 election.

During this interim period, the NLD and SPDC would be given the time to sort out their differences through daily contacts.[27] It is unlikely that ASEAN would countenance the military's intention to stay in power indefinitely, as there is no longer a model of a military-led government within ASEAN. In this respect, Mahathir indicates ASEAN's intention to educate the Burmese government and people about the value of democracy with an aim to eventually create a civilian government. As he puts it,

> "...we feel that the benefits of the kind of liberal democracy that we have in ASEAN countries should be exposed and made known to the people and Government of Myanmar so they will not reject the system."[28]

It seems that by linking up to the ASEAN Formula, Japanese ODA has finally acquired a direction and become meaningful, while enriching and sweetening the formula. Japan is now more explicitly indicating that the provision of ODA is conditional on the progress of the political dialogue in Burma. In May 2002, Japan decided to provide an 628 million yen (US$5.2 million) emergency grant for the repair of the Baluchaung Hydropower Plant in response to the release of Aung San Suu Kyi. This project may play a significant role as part of the ASEAN formula. Apparently, the circumstances surrounding Japanese ODA is changing for the better, as Aung San Suu Kyi recently softened her long time opposition against ODA and investment from Japan. She is now prepared to endorse Japanese projects under the strict control of accountability, transparency and monitoring.[29] Thus the Japanese government is required to help enhance these qualities for its own ODA projects and, indirectly, for investment from Japan. Depending on how these issues are handled by the stakeholders, that is, the NLD, the people near the project site[30], SPDC, Japanese government and Japanese companies, these projects may create favourable condition for the cooperation between the NLD and the SPDC, thus enhancing the FWO.

Valid Spokespersons (VSPs)

Perhaps, one of the more successful outcomes of Japan's ODA policy since 1988 is related to valid spokespersons (VSPs). It is not necessary to say that Aung San Suu Kyi enjoys an unassailable position as the spokesperson for the pro-democracy movement in the country.[31] However, for a long time the junta leaders did not officially recognise Aung San Suu Kyi as a valid spokesperson for the movement. According to the generals, she is a "housewife" who should remain home and should not interfere with politics. However, when they realised Aung San Suu Kyi's political calibre, they first put her under house arrest. When they knew that she was able to exert influence on Burmese people despite confinement, the authorities unsuccessfully requested that she go into exile. After her release from house arrest in July 1995, the junta tried to undermine her position by obstructing her political activities (e.g., her personal secretary was jailed) and isolating her. Following several confrontations, the pressure mounted on the SPDC and it was forced to recognise her officially as a valid spokesperson.[32]

Japan has taken every opportunity to urge the SLORC/SPDC to recognise Aung San Suu Kyi as junta's dialogue partner. It has been in a good position to do the job because of Japanese officials' easy access to the military leaders. Coupled with ASEAN's increasing recognition of her as a political force in Burma, Japan has contributed to the generals' acceptance of Aung San Suu Kyi as the valid spokesperson for pro-democracy camp. It seems that as long as Japan and ASEAN uphold the position of Aung San Suu Kyi, the junta cannot any longer marginalize or neglect her in the domestic politics. Now the SPDC has to find a way to accommodate her. This situation is quite new, unthinkable a few years ago. It seems that the political development in Burma has reached a point of no return because of the establishment of Aung San Suu Kyi as a political figure of a regional and international standing.

Maintaining the Role of Mediator

Another positive result of Japanese ODA is that Japan has managed to maintain its close ties with the Burmese elite, as was discussed before. These ties will be an asset for Japan when it plays a role of mediator between the NLD and SPDC more effectively than before. In this sense, its ODA policy to Burma since 1988 seems to be poised at last to reap benefits, although the policy has been an impediment to the creation of the MHS for a long time. Japan is currently in a good position to support and guarantee the peace process in Burma in collaboration with ASEAN. This is possible because of its standing towards both the SPDC and the NLD. Huge economic resources that Japanese ODA brings about provide Japan with leverage on the political parties.

6. Conclusion

This paper has investigated two options in the way in which Japan can contribute to the peace in Asia by using its ODA. From the investigation, it seems obvious that Japan cannot act as an advocate of humanistic values such as democracy and human rights in Asia, although its ODA Charter commits Japan to these values in its ODA administration. The most fundamental reason for the inability is the decision-making structure of its ODA, which is more sensitive to the business interests than the domestic situation in the recipient countries. If Japan is to take a leadership in this role, it needs a fundamental revamp of the ODA decision-making structure. Particularly, it needs to create a decision-making structure in which NGOs can participate in the formulation of ODA policy.

No less important, Japan will probably have to come up with its own humanistic values, which may not be equal to the kind of democracy and human rights that the US has vigorously promoted since the end of the Cold War. According to the American scheme, these two values and the market economy form the "global standard" to be spread over the world. A number of NGOs, including Japanese ones, are opposed to the global dominance of market economy, and becoming increasingly ambivalent of the US version of democracy and human rights. In this sense, Japan may be able to tap the humanistic values that exists among Japan's grassroots movements.[33] These endogenous values would add consistency and vigour to Japan's advocacy work.

Despite great potentials in Japan's role in advancing humanistic values in Asia, a more realistic role for Japan, at least for a short term, should be the that of a mediator in conflict. The case study has shown several points to take note.

Firstly, a human rights situation need to be reformulated by Japan as a conflict. For this, there needs to be an established party or valid spokespersons representing the victims of human rights violation or oppressed people. It is not enough that there are human rights violations or that democracy is suppressed. The situation needs to be polarised enough so that there are two established conflicting parties which Japan can mediate.

Secondly, there should be coordination among third parties involved in the conflict and that perhaps one party cannot perform all of the functions required to create mutually hurting stalemate (MHS), to provide a formula for a way out (FWO) and to help establish valid spokespersons (VSPs) on both sides and to mediate them. Particularly, the tasks related to an MHS may often contradict those related to an FWO, and to a lesser degree, those related to VSPs. Creating a MHS may also undermine the position of a would-be mediator towards the primary parties. For this reason, it seems, there should be a division of labour among the third parties, and yet a coherence among the different activities needs to be maintained.

References

1. There is an intriguing question as to whether or not the kind of democracy and human rights that the US and its Western allies are promoting together with the market economy can truly benefit the people in Asia. This is a large question and not the main focus of this paper.

2. ODA can be divided into two large categories: bilateral assistance and multilateral assistance. In the former, aid goes directly from a donor country to recipient countries and consists of loans, grants and technical assistance. In the latter, aid goes to recipient countries through multilateral institutions such as the World Bank, the Asian Development Bank and UN agencies.

3. Kazuo Sumi, *ODA Enio no Genjitsu (ODA, the Reality of Aid)*, Tokyo: Iwanami-shoten Publishers, 1989, pp. 38-39.

4. David Arase (1993), "Japanese Policy toward Democracy and Human Rights in Asia", *Asian Survey*, Vol. 33, No. 10, pp. 948-52.

5. I. William Zartman, "Dynamics and Constraints in Negotiations in Internal Conflicts", in I. William Zartman (ed.), Elusive Peace: Negotiating an End to Civil War, Washington , D. C.: The Brookings Institution, 1995, p. 8.

6. *Ibid.*

7. *Ibid.*, p. 18.

8. *Ibid.*, p. 22.

9. Zartman, "Dynamics and Constraints...", p. 21.

10. *Ibid.*, p. 20.

11. Ministry of Foreign Affairs of Japan, *Japan's ODA 1995*, Tokyo: Association for Promotion of International Cooperation, pp. 47-48.

12. War reparations were not part of ODA, but played an important role as a harbinger of Japanese ODA.

13. Donald Sekins, "Japan's Aid Relations with Military Regimes in Burma, 1962-1991: The Kokunaika Process", *Asian Survey*, Vol. 32, No. 3,1992, p. 249; Mekong Watch Japan, "Development, Environment and Human Rights in Burma/ Myanmar: Examining the Impacts of ODA and Investment", Public Symposium Report, 15 December 2001, Tokyo, pp. 8-9; Sumi, *ODA Enjo no Genjitsu*, pp. 20-22,

14. Teruko Saito, "Japan's Inconsistent Approach to Burma", *Japan Quarterly*, January-March 1992, p. 24.

15. *Ibid.*

16. *Ibid.*, p. 23. Six grant projects worth 9.1 billion yen and 19 loan projects worth 125 billion yen were suspended. However, 65 per cent of the grant projects and 20 per cent of the loan projects had already been completed. The remaining uncompleted projects were to be resumed gradually after February 1989.

17. Saito, "Japan's Inconsistent Approach, p. 18.

18. Ministry of Foreign Affairs of Japan, *Japan's ODA 1992*, Tokyo: Association for Promotion of International Cooperation, pp. 44-67.

19. Martin Smith, *Burma: Insurgency and the Politics of Ethnicity*, London: Zed Books, 1999, p. 429

20. Sarah Stewart, "ILO Mission to Verify Junta's promises on Forced Labour in Myanmar", *Agence France Presse*, 16 Sept. 2001.

21. Thomas Crampton, "No Reforms, No Progress, World Bank Tells Burma', *International Herald Tribune*, 13 Nov 1999.

22. "Myanmar problem cannot be solved by confrontation" [Mahathir interview], *New Straits Times* (Malaysia), 29 January 2001.

23. "Myanmar junta unlikely to go without guarantee: Mahahir', *Kyodo*, 06 August 2001.

24. Alan Clements and Aung San Suu Kyi, *The Voice of Hope*, London: Penguin Books, 1997, p. 86, pp. 200-20 1, p. 233; Alternative ASEAN Network on Burma, "The Burma Junta Grits its Teeth", Bangkok: Alternative ASEAN Network on Burma, 1999, p. 3.

25. "Things are moving fast in Myanmar", Asiaweek: July 20, 2001, p. 14.

26. "Myanmar problem cannot be solved...".

27. This period would also include national reconciliation in which the perpetrators and victims of human rights abuses would be reconciled by finding and sharing the truth of what had happened in the past, and thus a national healing would be made possible. See, Alan Clements and Aung San Suu Kyi, *The Voice of Hope*, pp. 86-87.

28. "Myanmar problem cannot be solved...".

29. "Democracy still elusive", *The Daily Yomiuri*, 21 July 2002; "Japan ready to up Myanmar aid if junta strikes deal with Aung San Suu Kyi", *Agence France Presse*, 6 August 2002.

30. There is a high possibility of human rights abuses arising from a larger presence of the military in the project area unless an effective monitoring system is established. See Mekong Watch Japan, "Development, Environment and Human Rights in Burma/Myanmar, pp. 19-21.

31. Aung San Suu Kyi possesses a genuine charisma, emanating from her character and from the fact that she is the daughter of

General Aung San, the hero of the country's struggle for independence. No one else in the pro-democracy camp has such standing. She has also proved her leadership qualities through more than 10 years of nonviolent struggle, including the 6 years of solitary confinement in her house.

32. Bertil Lintner, "A Ray of Hope", *Far Eastern Economic Review*, 25 Jan. 2001, pp. 22-23.

33. There are signs that such a reform is imminent. The Japanese people are more aware of the incompetence of the iron-triangle based politics. On the other hand, civil society is gaining strength mostly through successful local initiatives.

21

Japanese State and Welfare : An Assessment of Development and Challenges

Dr. H. S. Prabhakar

I

Japan was undoubtedly an unblemished example of a successful capitalist economy until early 1990s. Achievement of extraordinary growth in 1950s and 1960s and Japan's emergence as the first industrialised democracy brought all round laurels. Its economic performance was characterised by stable growth, low rates of unemployment and inflation. Despite high yen, Japan continued to register fairly high trade surpluses against the U.S. and Europe through out the 1980s, albeit this caused frequent friction. Usually, the economic success is attributed to distinct Japanese political and economic institutions.

Nevertheless, since 1993 Japan has witnessed unusual political and economic changes/difficulties seen ever before. In the political front, Japan witnessed the ending of one-party dominance of the conservative Liberal Democratic Party and was succeeded by a series of coalition governments. The recession caused by the burst of the bubble economy still continues leading to a reexamination of historical and institutional analysis of Japanese political economy.

II

There is very little written material on Japanese social welfare policy in English. Japanese scholars who work in this area seldom write in English. The term welfare society rather than welfare state has been used and promoted by conservative Japanese politicians and bureaucrats in the last two decades. Some even call it Japanese-style welfare society. The term welfare socicty usually refers to Japan's unique welfare mix in which the family and individual effort play a central role. The term welfare state nevertheless refers to some kind of social contract between the state and the people in regard to social welfare.

However, some writers[1] have attempted to trace the development of Japanese welfare society at least since *Meiji* period by scrutinising the social, cultural and political discourses on social welfare in general. Despite apparent policy changes, one can notice continuity in the trajectory of welfare state development. To cite an instance: the basic policy discourse on social welfare before the Occupation reforms, continues during the postwar period too. While postwar Japanese society was rebuilt along more democratic lines, the Occupation reforms rendered the social welfare the state's constitutional responsibility. This is why the debate is usually on the nature of social welfare. No wonder the outcome is a set of welfare policies which may not have coherence but no doubt display internal contradictions.

It makes an interesting attempt to examine the social and political discourse on the welfare policy evolution in Japan. Addressing questions such as the following becomes important : why the conservative, growth-oriented Japanese state has adopted progressive social policy with a visible focus on welfare? How a relationship exists between employment and welfare? How Japanese state was able to achieve its policy aims of economic growth through promotion of equality?

Japan primarily followed a labour-oriented welfare policy with a focus on labour-market management principles, investment in education and universal social insurance with a variety of protectionist measures for small businesses and farmers. All these emerged certainly from a wide debate and incorporating the idea of social protection with an economic management framework. In facilitating such an environment the state utilised the expert knowledge and experience of those (social bureaucrats, academicians, politicians, social and political interest groups) who provided perspectives on issues that were politically and normatively acceptable during policy formulation and implementation.

Japanese social policy is particularly progressive as it does particularly emphasise equality. Also that Japanese social policy is if anything is quite residual and there is emphasis on the idea of sameness[2]. Japan like many other industrialised countries also offers universal education but the equality of public education is considerably undermined by social and educational structures that favour private education system. Income distribution in Japan does appear to be more equal than in most other industrialised countries. Even so, it appears to be heading reverse since 1980s albeit very marginally[3].

It is possible to argue that the achievement of this relative income equality since the end of the World War II as not so much a result of social policy focus on equality *per se,* instead rather a result of general economic growth that facilitated an overall income rise. The income-doubling plan of the 1960s practiced by the Liberal Democratic Party certainly helped reduce income gaps between rural and urban families/workers that existed earlier.

The economic aim of the Japanese state has been to foster industrial activity and promote business. Different objectives have permitted different means. The Japanese regulatory process has become more cooperative and consensual. The case of Japanese welfare policy making process displays remarkable continuity and resistance to change and yet is subjected to continuous change through reforms. Also as a process it is less opaque than commonly assumed, more pervasive, more intrusive, more arbitrary and more accepted by public. Whatever be its results, it is in fact more structured and therefore predictable. Composed of socio-economic alliances, the Japanese political-economic institutions created highly successful industrial and public policies.

The change in economic policy that is : the opening and deregulation of the market during economic globalisation also brought about changes in welfare and labour-management relations. In fact, these changes constitute Japanese modest welfare state representing a better consensual capital-labour relationship. Due to interest coordination between capital and labour in private enterpirses, there occurred a decreasing distinctiveness of ideological difference. Changes in Japan became more visible and observable only in the 1990s. The magnitude of political and economic challenges that Japan is still facing has been responded to by insufficient and ineffective policy reforms.

III

The past appreciation and the present criticism of the East Asian miracle have brought the question of role of government to the forefront. East Asian governments have played a far more active role in which they put market at the center of the development strategy. East Asian states set out to create and regulate institutions that promoted savings and helped allocate resources. They promoted investment in infrastructure, human capital and the new technologies. Learning from the East Asian model becomes necessary not only for lessons on remarkable growth but also about recent crisis and how to avoid the same. Often the state is forced to intervene in society because of anti-social effects of capitalism. Since the economic system itself contains no means to combat its own socially destructive workings, there exists a high degree of statism. State intervention also occurs as a form of protection against the workings of the market.

In the case of Japan, state intervention is the key to development and success in the 'free market'. The state intervention is neither capitalist nor socialist, instead it is just functional and necessary. The need is for an interactive partnership between state and society.

The case of Japan could be described as 'a victim of its own success'. Japan's problems are deep seated and structured which are impervious to fiscal stimulus and low interest rates[4]. They can only be solved by restructuring-a process that is moving at an excruciatingly slow pace.

IV

Japan's social security systems now provide public relief from risks that are beyond the scope of an individual's resources. In so doing, they contribute to the stability and development of the society and economy. However, it has not been such a long time since this system of public relief was established in a unified manner. It is only since 1874, that after a centralised government had been established in Japan, that the Social Relief Regulations was enacted which provided rice to extremely poor people without family who could not engage in productive activities because they were too old, too young, sick or disabled. However, this was a system which assumed a spirit of mutual aid among the relatives and neighbors, offering limited relief to the needy people. Later, a large number people turned needy during the prolonged depression which followed World War I, and in 1929, the Relief Law was enacted which clearly defined public relief obligations and expanded the range of beneficiaries.

Japan's modern public health administration grew out of the introduction of the Western medicine and the measures against epidemics of acute communicable diseases, followed by measures against tuberculosis and high infant mortality. The main emphasis was placed on the concept of 'social defense' for upholding the overreaching national goals of increasing industrial production, national wealth and military power. For example, the Tuberculosis Prevention Law, which was established in 1919, was enacted out of a recognition that the prevalence of tuberculosis patients was sapping national strength. The establishment of the Ministry of Health and Welfare in 1938 was grounded on the decline in the physical strength of the Japanese people due to increased tuberculosis patients, and the consequent need for the establishment of an administrative system to deal with these problems.

As the capitalist society developed in Japan in the 20th century, labour movement intensified and the time was appropriate for the introduction of a social insurance system. The essential programs of the social insurance system were established during this period, with the Health Insurance, a scheme of medical care insurance for employed people being established in 1922, a National Health Insurance system for the self-employed and farmers in 1938, and a pension program for workers in 1941. By 1945, the medical insurance system actually covered about 60 per cent of the whole nation. The system received a devastating shock in the World War II, placing it on the verge of collapse. However, after the war, the recovering economy redirected the system towards universal medical care insurance and pension systems.

Thus, this period saw the tentative establishment of a system of assistance to the needy, public health administration and social insurance. The system, however, was characterised by 'charity' and 'benevolence' to contribute to increased production, national wealth and military power.

Even so, it lacked the modern concept of 'social security' which was introduced only after the war.

V

Academic interest in role of employers/corporations in welfare state development has marginally increased of late. There are many different ideas about why firms should have and actually do have interest in social protection schemes, and why employers have historically not always taken a hostile stance in the social policy debates. Japan's firm-based welfare schemes resemble in many respects the US-model of large employer welfare capitalism[5]. Business coordination and wage compensation are so prominent in Japanese political economy that Japan is often treated as a counter-model to the market liberalism of the Anglo-Saxon variant[6].

The major Japanese industrial conglomerates, *KEIRETSU*, organised both export-oriented and domestically oriented firms-horizontal *Keirestu*, and the large employers and SMEs were often linked to each other through supplier relations-vertical *Keiretsu*[7]. This prevented sharp intra-industrial conflicts even from arising. The Japanese state with protectionist and regulative measures insulated the home market, encouraged cartel formation, enabled SMEs to modernise[8]. Cartels and protectionism remained legitimate instruments of economy in postwar Japan.

SHUNTO, the annual spring offensive, came in to being in the late 1950s[9] and unions used *Shunto* as an instrument to achieve labour movement unity[10]. Large corporations used *Shunto* to construct wage policy through bargaining tactics both within and across the industry[11].

Japanese corporations changed their attitudes towards state and policy once wage coordination became entrenched. Most of the large corporations practiced what is popularly known as life-time employment system. The state played the role of a direct structurer and overseer of occupationally-linked pensions[12]. The common assumption is that the private provision of social benefits is proof of the liberal character of welfare state regime[13]. A careful examination of Japanese 'welfare production regime' reveals that the Japanese welfare state came to underpin business coordination much more than purely voluntary schemes would have been able to[14].

After the collapse of Soviet-style communism, the 'Japan Inc' economic model stood as the world's only real alternative to Western free-market capitalism. American revisionist writers[15] argued in the late 1980s and early 1990s that the U S could not compete with Japanese unique form of state-directed insider capitalism and even said that 'US would become an economic colony of Japan'. They even warned that 'US must either compete with Japan or go the way of the USSR'[16]. Today, the reality is, Japan has not attained world-wide dominance, on the contrary, it has suffered a 'lost decade' of economic stagnation. 'Japan Inc' model has not eclipsed Western-style capitalism, instead there is an emerging consensus on both sides of the pacific that the Japan model has failed. Japan's problems appear obvious and to revive its fortunes, it needs to restructure and revise policies and institutional relationshp.

The state-directed insider capitalism that Japan followed, established a close relationship between business executives, banks and government officials who strongly influence the economic outcome. By strategically allocating capital through a tightly controlled banking system, Japan drove foreign competitors leading to high market share and increased profits.

Japans's current economic problems contrast sharply with the vision of Japan that US had feared in 1980s and 1990s. James Fallows wrote, 'Japan and its acolytes like Taiwan and Korea have demonstrated that in head-on industrial competition between free-market societies and capitalist developmental states, the free-traders will eventually lose'[17]. Chalmers Johnson was more succinct when he said,'Cold war is over and Japan won'[18].

Prestowitz described MITI – now renamed as METI – ideology as follows : "key objectives of any economy .... is to create an industry that produces technologically sophisticated products with high income elasticity and a rapid growth ....that objective can not be achieved without government intervention"[19].

VI

The high economic growth of the 1950s and 1960s led to talk of the 'Japanese miracle'. During the 1970s and the 1980s, the Japanese economy won further praise for its skillful adjustment to the oil shock and rising yen. From 1990 to 1997, growth crawled along at an average rate of 1.4 per cent. Besides low rate of growth other systemic weaknesses noticed were : insufficient funds in the national pension system, increasing levels of long-term government debt; a rising rate of unemployment, surplus labour lingering within enterprises, huge non-performing loans and assets with banks and financial institutions.

Before 1970s, the Japanese government had measures in place to restrict competition in the agriculture, retail transportation, coal mining and other areas. These were also subjected to large-scale injection of public investment. From the second half of the 1970s, promotion of the infant industries gradually gave way to protection of ineffective service-sector industries as transportation, whole sale and retail trade[20]. Policy management increasingly stressed compensating such losing industries dominated by low productivity. Because of very high cost, big exporters moved their domestic manufacturing bases overseas. This 'industrial hollowing out'.

Continued through 1990s and the potential for improving productivity in Japan was lost and low growth became endemic.

VII

Since 1993 reformers have focused more and more on redistributing power from the highly centralised national government to regional and municipal administration in terms local autonomy block grants and decentralisation. Still it is not clear if the local entities are ready for the new responsibilities. Through out the postwar era, Japanese local governments have exercised certain power than understood. For instance, in the areas of housing subsidies, land use regulation, and the development of welfare state, Muramatsu offers a fascinating reinterpretation of the meaning of local autonomy in the contemporary context[21].

The Japanese welfare state since a decade is facing a growing population of old people, falling birth rates and a pattern of increased in-migration of persons of other nationalities. These challenges are posed at a time of economic stagnation and demand for downsizing the government. While responding to these problems, how will Japan restore economic dynamism besides providing social support for special needs equitably is watched with great attention.

Japan is number one in health outcomes as measured in terms of life expectancy at birth and infant mortality rates. This is important because governments around the world are struggling to find the right formula for health policy[22]. It is striking that the infant mortality rate in Japan is 4.2 per thousand[23] while health expenditure is 7 per cent as a share of GDP[24]. All the Japanese are obliged to belong to a health insurance fund, either at work or their location of residence.

There are cross-subsidies between the pools as well as general revenue transfers from the government to the pools for the elderly and non-employees, a system which improves equity. Cost control is built in by strict use of a government-mandated fee Schedule both for medical procedures and for drugs. Japan has achieved remarkable success in two of the main indicators for assessing health–system performance: access and cost. Besides access, cost and quality another indicator is health outcomes where too Japan has done well. A few basic organisational structure can make all the difference in performance[25]. The entire Japanese approach is based on 'egalitarian values' which include mandatory health insurance and freedom of choice for patients in the selection of a physician and facility[26].

Some of the disadvantages of the system as complained by people are : long waiting times for short consultation with physicians, lack of accountability by the health system, run down and understaffed hospitals, low quality and quality of medical research, and poor quality of medical judgement.

VIII

Japanese economy is under the process of aging with an unprecedented pace. Families, fertility, social security system, saving habits are strongly affected or restricted by the process of rapid aging. Japan is a large open economy. Aging problems can be partly resolved by immigration or by capital outflow to the world[27]. Allowing immigration causes social resistance. This is a structural choice facing an open economy with an aging population. Besides, there is an effect of government deficit and public pension policies on the tax burden, capital accumulation and economic welfare in the transition to aging Japan[28]. The balance of government debt as of the end of the year 2000 totaled a record of 522.1 trillion yen, up 9.3 per cent from previous year[29]. The central and the local debt in 2001-2002 will likely touch 666 trillion yen, that is more than 130 per cent of GDP.

Japan's 135 banks which wrote off a combined 2.2 trillion yen ($ 18 billion) in bad loans in the first half off FY 2000-2001 saw an additional 3.6 trillion yen loans go sour during the same period. This suggests that banks are amassing more bad loans than are disposing of them. The banks had total outstanding bad loans of 31.8 trillion yen as of 30 September 2000. Bad loans increased partly because of a decline in land price which has reduced the value of collateral. The number of corporate bankruptcies also increased during the period[30]. The Japanese government said that it is considering measures to facilitate a clean up of the non-performing loans weighing on banks. The move would likely trigger more business failure and unemployment[31].

Japan's leading private think tanks forecast a slow down in the domestic economy in the next financial year due to curbs on capital investment and consumer spending. The 2001-2002 economic forecast by 16 leading research institutes averaged 0.8 per cent, down from 1.3 per cent for the financial year ended 0n 31 march 2001[32]. The budget of 2001-2002 prioritises economic revival while also focusing on fiscal situation. This is the fourth largest budget since World War II, after 1995, 1999 and 2000.

The government and the ruling parties have been just as wrong in their analysis of the economic situation. They have continued the stopgap spending policy that has inflated the government debt to catastrophic proportions. The government and ruling parties as well as government-dependent banks and heavily indebted corporations have to bear greater responsibility. The BOJ is quite right in urging banks to clear their bad debts, structural reforms and strong leadership on the part of the government. As things stand, now banks have no choice than to speed up debt write off.

IX

"With in the 20th century growth paradigm, effective and stable economic growth and an improvement in the citizens` standard of living had been achieved by maintaining a universal pattern of social role-sharing such as men dedicating themselves to their work (corporation) and women maintaining home and the aged were protected by the society"[33]. However, in light of the dorp in to a period of low economic growth, the 20th century growth paradigm is no longer convincing. There is a need to carry out reforms which are characterised by congruity among policies and identification of new target.

Japan currently faces several serious problems. One of them relates to social security. A part of the firms do not contribute to the social security system nor want to join the system. The aging of Japanese population will have significant macroeconomic effect. Naturally as one becomes aged, will display unavoidable decline in physical abilities, and gap in physical strength between the elderly will increase. It is therefore important to provide the elderly with diverse employment systems and opportunities, flexible work style and job style according to the physical abilities. Following factors become important : the arrangement of a social infrastructure, assistance by technology and establishment of social system[34].

Japan's domestic statistics show that one in five Japanese is over the age of 65 and the fertility rate 1. 34 per couple. Japan enjoyed extremely low unemployment for most of the post-war years. Between 1953 – when the government started to collect relevant statistics – and 1995, the jobless rate never exceeded 3 per cent. When Japan plunged in to post-bubble funk, the jobless rate hit 4 per cent in mid-1990s, reaching a high of 4.9 per cent in February 1999 and March 2001 with more than 3 million people out of work[35]. Jobless at 4.9 per cent means that there are 3.7 million people out of work.

There was a long held understanding that major Japanese corporations – which maintained a paternalistic view of the employer-employee relationship – would rarely lay off or fire workers because they put the interest of workers ahead of share holders. Now it looks just a myth[36].

The post-war jobless rate was kept low because Japan enjoyed steady economic growth. Such practices of life-time employment covered only a limited portion of the entire work force and only applied to male full-time workers at large corporations which account only for 20 per cent of Japan's entire fork force. Companies are now seeking workers with specialised knowledge and skills as they shift from mass production to knowledge-intensive service and production system.

Middle aged and elderly people formerly in the white-collar jobs who were forced to accept early retirement are the main force among the job seekers today[37]. Many firms introduced a new salary system in the late 1990s under which management salaries will not change with age but with the capabilities and achievements of the employees. Jobless are unable to respond to employment demands in newly emerging business fields, due to advanced age and lack of proper skills, according to the Labour Ministry.

The annual spring labour negotiations – *Shunto* – have grown increasingly irrelevant to most working people due in part to concerted effort to chip away at the seniority-based wage system to the fact that salaries have hit a ceiling in the recent years[38]. Unfortunately labour unions continue to focus their bargaining efforts on extracting pay hikes from the largest employers while ignoring other issues confronting today's workforce. But if they choose to ignore the needs of the employees of SMEs, part-timers and other irregular employees, they risk turning Shunto in to only an annual ritual. Ten years ago, part-timers made 72 per cent of what full-timers earned. But today they earn only 67 per cent of what their full-time counterparts make. Part-timers whose number exceeds 10 million work less than 35 hours a week. Now for the first time Japanese trade union confederation –*RENGO* – is pressing employers for a hike in the hourly wage of 10 yen per hour[39].

X

The economic portents begin to look menacing as the world's two most powerful economies face stagnation if not recession. If these two dominant countries – the US and Japan – fail to find remedies, they risk bringing others down with them[40]. The deflationary spiral in Japan's domestic economy leaves monetary policy ineffective. The banking system is in a mess which the local equity market‘s drift to a 20 year low has now exposed[41]. The declaration of deflation last month has accompanied by a new definition of the term as 'a state in which prices keep falling', deviating from the previous official description as 'a state in which prices are falling while economy is receding'. It is an admission of dearth of economic policy option left at the administration's disposal. The looming economic crisis is a national outcome of the choices that Japan has made[42]. Japan is facing a shortage of skilled workers and only foreign workers are generally willing to fill the difficult dangerous and dirty jobs that many Japanese refuse to engage in. But the public has remained suspicious of outsiders particularly the Chinese. The Japanese Justice Ministry, a conservative institution that often reflects nationalist sentiments has stymied the entry of foreigners[43]. The Justice Ministry suggested that travel agents should post a $ 6000 bond each for Chinese tourist, a bond forfeited if the tourist remains in Japan. Immigration authorities want similar commitments from the employers of foreign workers. And the Health Ministry officials say they do not want to pay the medical bills of foreigners[44].

Finance Ministry predicts that Japan's national burden rate will rise to 36.9% in 2001. Still very unfamiliar to general public, the term 'national burden rate' refers to the ratio of taxes and social welfare contributions to national income. This increase will occur because employment insurance premiums are set to rise, and collection of the full amount of premiums under the government-run nursing care insurance system is due to begin from fiscal 2001. In fiscal 2001, the fiscal deficit will be equivalent to 8.4 per cent of national income. Adding this to the national burden rate gives a potential burden of 45.3 per cent. The potential burden rate has remained above 40 per cent since 1992[45].

XI

Secrecy, or restricted information, is often used by the government officials to restrict outsiders participation in decision-making. The resulting exclusivity of the decision-making process increases both influence and benefits to be had for the government officials. Limitation on information restricts competition in the decision-making process. Increasing openness can be a powerful tool in reducing the influence of the special interests and improving government performance. Secrecy makes it more difficult to correct errors and to evaluate officials. Government officials have always sought to find rationale for the secrecy. Secrecy creates an aura of authority that is essential for the effective exercise of power.

In Japan, public works projects have long been seen as jobs for the government. Therefore it is difficult to say that information about these undertakings is shared with the public. Since Japanese public finance is in crisis, it is time to create an open system that allows residents choose the kind of infrastructure they really need. The freedom-of-information law is to take effect from April 2001 will be a major step in that direction[46]

Even so, "MOFA destroyed highly confidential diplomatic documents ahead of introduction of Information Disclosure Law"[47]. Resident participation is a public exercise that allows residents acquire a sense of involvement as taxpayers.

XII

Japan should be Asian shock absorber but it has problems of its own. As Finance Minister, Kiichi Miyazawa acknowledged, "the government`s finances are in a catastrophic situation. The economy is deflating as prices continue to fall. The banking system is saddled with too many big non-performing loans. The political uncertainty sorounding Prime Minister Mori prevents the government from taking action"[48].

The view that Japan lacks leadership is widely shared not only about political but about government bureaucracy, business, academia, journalism-indeed most segments of Japanese society[49]. Expectations are low that any hard hitting reforms emerging under anew LDP leader after Mori too.

The ambivalent status of the middle class is Japan's latent strength. Though 10 per cent of the middle class has been affected in the 1990s, it has cautiously been reducing consumption to save money just in case things got really bad. There is a great pent up demand for a variety of consumer goods. The key to harnessing the potential economic energy of the Japanese middle class is to clean up the financial system so that the middle class has faith in the stability of the economic system. As of now, the government policy is to continue loans to many moribund corporations to pump them up. As a result, now banks are at loggerheads with government a time when they face a harsh commercial climate. Japan has resources to address its problems[50]. The way out for Japan's economic problems is not through exports but through strong domestic growth brought about by deep structural reforms"[51].

Conclusion

Interpretation of the role of Japanese state range from the 'developmental state' model to that which portray government intervention in the form of industry-specific policies. Nevertheless, all agree on the state's role in crafting macroeconomic policies during 1950s and 1960s and its difficulties in getting such policies work in the 1990s. The role of the state at the apex of the high growth era differed visibly from the role it played subsequently in the period of slowed growth.

The debate over the economic role of the Japanese state gained currency because many developing countries attempted to emulate Japan and advanced countries expected to learn Japan's mechanism for miraculous growth. Today, still countries look to Japan to discern obstacles to sustained development and growth, seeking to learn from Japan's mistakes.

Japanese state influenced the industrial structure and the pattern of socio-economic development and did not control it. Most prolonged period of economic stagnation and the resulting crisis suggest a different role for Japanese state than that being fulfilled at present. Japanese domestic forces push for further deregulation and shifting role of government while foreign governments call for more intervention where as consensus on the exact role of the state is yet to be found.

Notes and References

1. Mitsuko Takahashi, The Emergence of Welfare Society in Japan, Avbury, Aldershot, Hants., U.K. 1997.

2. Deborah J. Milly, Poverty, Equality and Growth : The Politics of Eonomic Need in Postwar Japan, Harvard University Asia Centre, Cambridge, Mass., 1999.

3. Toshiki Tachibanaki and Tadashi Yagi, "Distribution of Economic Equality in Japan : Towards a More Unequal Society", in Peter Gottschalk, Bjorn Gustufsson and Edward Palmer, eds. Changing Patterns in the Distribution of Economic Welfare : An International Perspective, Cambridge University Press, Cambridge, 1997.

4. Jonathan Watts, "Identity Crisis has Japan in Turmoil", *The Guardian*, March 14, 2001.

5. Esping-Anderson,G. 'Hybrid or Unique? The Japanese Welfare State between Europe and America'. *Journal of European Social Policy,* 7, 1977, pp. 177-197.

6. Streeck W. and Yamamura K. (eds). The Political and Social Origins of Nationally Organised Capitalism : Japan and Germany in Comparison, 2000.

7. Westney D.E. The Japanese Business System : Key features and prospects for Change, in Peter Drysdale and L. Gower (eds). The Japanese Economy Part I, Vol. IV : The Nature of the Japanese Firm, Routledge,London, 1998, pp. 151-175. And Nakatani I. "The Economic Role of Financial Corporate Grouping, in P. Drysdale and L. Gower (eds). The Japanese Economy Part I. Vol. IV : The Nature of Japanese Firm, Routledge, London, pp. 176-209.

8. Pampel T.J. Regime Shift : Comparative Dynamics of Japanese Political Economy, Ithaca, Cornell University Press, New York, 1998, p. 61.

9. Hamada K. and Kasuya. The Reconstruction an Stabilisation of the postwar Japanese Economy : Possible Lessons for Eastern Europe ? in R. Dornbusck, W. Nolling, R. Layard (eds) Postwar Economic Reconstruction and Lessons for the East Today, MIT press, Cambridge, 1993, p. 170 (155-187).

10. Koshiro K. "Development of Collective Bargaining in postwar Japan" in Taishiro S. (ed). Between Power and Plenty. Foreign Economic Policies of Advanced Industrial States, University of Wisconsin, Madison, 1978, p. 212. (191-224).

11. Brown C., Nakata Y., Reich M., and Ulman L. Work and Pay in the U.S. and Japan, Oxford University press, New York, 1997, p. 161.

12. Shinkawa T., and Pampel T.J. "Occupational Welfare and the Japanese Experience", in M. Shalev (ed). The Privatisation of Social Policy ? Occupational Welfare State in America, Scandinavia and Japan. Macmillan, London, 1996, p. 170.

13. Esping-Anderson G. n. 5, p. 183.

14. Estevez-Abe M. The Welfare Growth Nexus in the Japanese Political Economy, 1996 (a Conference paper).

15. Chalmers Jhonson, Clyde Prestiwitz, James Fallows, Karel Van Wolferen.
16. Chalmers Johnson. Japan: Who Governs ? W.W. Norton Co., New York, 1995. p. 9.
17. James Fallows. "Containing Japan", *Atlantic Monthly*, May 1989, p. 40.
18. Johnson. Japan, p.
19. Clyde Prestowitz. Trading Places, Basic Books, New York, 1993, p. 256.
20. Richard Katz. Japan : The System that Soured : The Rise and Fall of the Japanese Economic Miracle, M.E. Sharpe, New York, 1998
21. Michio Muramatsu. Local Power in the Japanese State (trnsl: Betsey Scheiner and James White), University of California Press, California, 1997.
22. *Journal of Japanese Studies*, Vol. 26, No. 2, 2000. p. 270-274.
23. John Creigton Campbell and Naoki Ikegami. The Art of Balance in Health Policy : Maintaining Japan's Low Cost, Egalitarian System, Cambridge University press, New York, 1998, p. 90
24. *Ibid.*, p. 3
25. *Ibid.*, p. 20.
26. *Ibid.*, p. 115.
27. Koichi Hamada. Structural Choices in a Rapidly Aging Society (abstract), 2000.
28. See: Ryuta Ray Kato. Deficits in an Aging Japan, Economic Research Institute, Economic Planning Agency, Tokyo, September 2000.
29. *Mainichi Daily News*, 24 March 2001, p. 1.

30. Lindsay Whipp. Japanese Bank's Bad loans Grow faster than Disposal, Bloomberg News, 25 March 2001. (Bloomberg.com).

31. Report from Tokyo. Miki Anzai and Mari Murayama. 26 March 20001. Bloomberg.com

32. Quoted from *Nihon Keizai Shimbun*, 25 March 2001.

32. Yukio Suzuki. "Too Little, Too Late Reforms". *The Japan Times* (Editorial) 26 March 2001.

33. Kenji Yamada. Reconstruction of the Social System in a low Birth Rate. Project Abstract, Nomura Research Institute, Tokyo. 2000.

34. Hitoshi Shirai. Future Prospects of the Aging Society in terms of Corporate Management and Technology, Project Abstract, Hitachi Research Institute, Tokyo. 2000.

35. Reiji Yoshida. "Life Time Employment Myth Fades", *The Japan Times*, 9 March, 2001.

36. *Ibid.*

37. Yutaka Nishimura. The Industrial Employment Stabilisation Centre of Japan, Tokyo, in *The Japan Times*. 9 March 2001.

38. Part-timers Pay, *Mainichi Daily News*, 15 March 200

39. *Ibid.*

40. Leader. "Economies Under Threat : Apprehensions Grow in the US and Japan", *The Guardian*, 14 March 2001.

41. John Aldersley. "Peddling the demise of Japan's miracle cycle" *Sydney Morning Herald*, 18 March 2001.

42. "Positive Side of Deflation", editorial, *Mainichi Daily News*. 17 March 2001.

43. Uli Schmetzer, "Japan Seeks Foreign Labour on Own terms" *Tribune*, 16 March 2001.

44. *Ibid.*

45. Shinji Kayano. "Japan at Turning Point over the Balance of Burden" *The Yomiuri Daily*, 21 February 2001.

46. Editorial in *Asahi News*, 25 march 2001.

47. *Mainichi Daily News*, 31 March 2001.

48. "Making Sense of the Slide". *The Japan Times*, 15 March 2001.

49. Glenn Fukushima. "Understanding Leadership in Japan", *The Japan Times*, 28 March 2001.

50. Robert J. Fouser. "Enduring Strength of Japan`s Middle Class", *The Korea Herald*, 21 March 2001.

51. Jim Mann. "Exports Not the Answer, Bush Tells Japan", *Los Angeles Times*, 20 March 2001.

References

Allison, Gary D. and Yasunori Sone (eds). Political Dynamics in Contemporary Japan, Cornell University Press, Ithaca, New York, 1993.

Callon, Scott. Divided Sun : MITI and the Break down of Japanese High-Tech Industrial Policy 1925-1993, Stanford University Press, Stanford, 1995.

Frank Gibney, Unlocking the Bureaucrat's Kingdom : Deregulation and the Japanese Economy, Brookings Institution Press, 1998.

Gerald L. Curtis, The Logic of Japanese Politics : Leaders, Institutions and the Limits of Change, Columbia University Press, 2000.

McKean Margaret. "State Strength and Public Interest" in Allison and Sone, 1993.

Nakano Koichi. "The Politics of Administration Reform in Japan-1993-1998 : Toward A More Accountable Government", *Asian Survey*, March 1998.

Pampell T. J, Comparative Dynamics of Japanese Political Economy, Cornell University Press, Ithaca, 1998.

Rafael James and Thomas Rohlen. "How Many Models of Japanese Growth do we Want or Need"? in Henry Rowen (ed) Behind East Asian Growth : The Political and Social Foundations of Prosperity, Routledge, London & New York, 1998.

Vestal James. Planning For Change : Industrial Policy and Japanese Economic Development-1945-1990, Oxford University Press, Clarendon press, Oxford & New York, 1993.

Wodall Brian. Japan Under Construction : Corruption, Politics and Public Works, University of California Press, Berkeley, LA, 1996.

Zysman John. Governments, Markets and Growth, Cornell University Press, Ithaca, New York, 1983.

22

Indo-Japan Relations: Understanding of South Asian Context

Arun Chaturvedi

India and Japan occupy important place in international relations. Japan being economic power in the present day international relations and India being leading state among developing states have shared commonalities in past. Both have serious concerns in the economic and peace issues concerning world affairs in general and South Asian affairs in particular. Understanding of these issues in wider context of South Asia is essential for the scholars of Indo-Japanese relations. The present paper deals with

(a) Understanding of South Asian Trends in Indian perspective.

(b) Understanding broad Foreign Policy objectives of Japan and various trends in Japanese Foreign Policy concerning South Asia.

(c) Suggesting areas where more cooperation between two important countries i.e. Japan and India could effectively shape international relations.

(d) To understand the themes of economic proximity and intellectual dialogue.

On Understanding Japan's Foreign Policy Issues

Japan has been recognised as major economic power in international relations and its foreign policy objectives can broadly be noted as:

1. Peaceful solutions to regional conflicts.
2. Further promotion of arms reduction and non-proliferation.
3. Ensuring a prosperous world economy.
4. Co-operation with developing countries and countries in transition in their nation building, Japan is for long years the top donor of the Official Development Assistance (ODA) in the World.
5. Contributing to the solution and alleviation of global issues-it is making all efforts in solving the problems concerning environment, population and diseases.

Japan's foreign policy concerns remained mainly on peace issues which have allowed Japan to develop after World War II, when Japan was smashed because of nuclear attack in 1945. This event has put Japan among the countries who know the meaning of nuclear attack. This has developed peculiar attitude on Nuclear issue on which Japan is most sensitive.

The understanding of Japan's security needs have to be developed with the understanding of their own security needs. The theme of Japan's security is based on:

1. Firmly maintaining Japan-US security arrangements. The Japanese Diet on 24th May 1999 passed new bills which will allow the Japanese self defense forces to take part in operations by the U.S. Armed forces not only in self defense but also in areas around Japan in the event of emergencies;
2. Securing Japan's own appropriate defence capability. In Nov. 1995, the Government decided on a New National Defense Programme out line that maps out defense arrangements for the post cold war era indicating required level of defense capability for the future and
3. Making active diplomatic efforts to ensure international peace and security. Japan has been actively engaged in security dialogues and cooperation within the Asia Pacific region and has participated in ASEAN Regional Forum (ARF) conference since its creation.

Japan has been aware of its defence needs and its location near Russia and China, with whom Japan shared tense relations. The defence expenditure of these three states i.e. Russia, Japan and China constitute high defence expenditure. Japan has restricted its expenditure to one per cent of GDP. The defence expenditure of Japan in 1997 was 46.8 billion dollors. The armed forces were in 1996, 235.5 thousand and 47.9 thousand has reserves. (Asian Strategic Review, 1996-97). The cold war tensions in the region between Japan, Soviet Union and China have affected the defence needs. The post cold War developments have its own impact on security thinking in Japan.

Japan's foreign policy conduct's main area remained economic and in various writings on international relations, Japan has been identified in terms of economic power. In international relations thrust as has been pointed out shifted from geo-politics to geo-economics, Robert Harkavy underlined that "Central to the geo-economics imagery is the belief that the World is evolving into three competitive economic blocks including (1) a Japan led Pacific Rim region including Korea, South east Asia and presumably China; (2) a U.S. led Western Hemisphere bloc centered on the North American free trade Agreement (NAFTA) and potentially encompassing Latin America and (3) a German-Centered European bloc, assumed to include Russia and other ex-Soviet states and perhaps also North Africa. (Robert E. Harkavy "Images of the coming international system". Orbis, Fall, 1997, p. 572.)

Japan's Strength has been its banking as World's largest net creditor, its world record trade surplus, and its propensity to invest in plant and equipment (per employee) at a rate triple that of the U.S. and twice that of Europe. Japan's educational levels, particularly its ability to educate the bottom half of its high school classes. Japan's cohesion and homogeneity provides focus its economic might that few others can rival. Thurow concluded that "no nation can organise better to march toward well thought out common goals (Lester Thurow, "Head:The Coming Economic battle among Japan, Europe and America" Cited by Harkvey, *op.cit.*, p. 572.)

It has been suggested that Japan has larger role in Asian affairs in general and South Asian affairs in particular. The issues which can alter it the Japan's understanding of South Asia have to be underlined and it is this context which can provide the proper understanding of Japan's role.'

III

On Understanding South Asia

The region of South Asia prior to the establishment of South Asian Association of Regional Co-operation (SAARC) was considered as one which included Burma and Afghanistan alongwith the present SAARC members, i.e., India, Nepal, Pakistan, Bhutan, Sri Lanka, Maldives and Bangladesh. The two states, i.e., Burma and Afghanistan have been excluded for more complete regional identify.

South Asian States essentially belong to the group of developing countries which may be addressed as Third World for better understanding of this group. These states have shared economic, technological and industrial backwardness alongwith historical colonical past which resulted into continued backwardness even in present times. The South Asian States economy is based on Agriculture and skill cultures from poor growth and technological advancements.

In present context of Globalisation, South Asian States have opened their economies for world market and placed themselves into a very critical phase. The understanding of South Asian States as a group from various economic point of views will be interesting and suggests that the Sough Asian States shares in world economy is essentially weak. The sharing of world population in terms of percentage is group 7 in 1994 was 11.94 per cent and in 1995 was 11.87 per cent where as the sharing of South Asian States during 1994 was 21.36 per cent and 1995 was 21.48 per cent. The sharing of world out in terms of percentage during the period of 1994 by G7 was 68.17 per cent of the GDP and in 1995 it was 67.39 where as the SAARC was in 1994 was 1.51 per cent and in 1995 it was 1.53. The share of in world exports during 1994 of G-7 was 49.39 per cent and in 1995 was 48.67. The share of SAARC countries was in 1994 0.99 per cent in 1995 was 0.88 per cent.

The large sharing of population by South Asian States suggest that they are big and potential market and globalisation in terms of extended markets will create new pressure for South Asian economies where they still future in terms of Technological developments. Their share in terms of export will still remain poor and their economies will continue be dominated by large share of their markets by developed countries.

South Asian States like India and Pakistan have become nuclear after 1998 which has changed the power equation in the South Asia. With nuclear parity, the balance of power in South Asia which had been irrationally remained in favour of India has now partly changed. The relaxation in international situations after the post cold war phase has not changed the South Asian position. Tensions in the area have continued resulting into increased defence expenditure in South Asian States. The defence expenditure of South Asian States of 1990, i.e., Indian expenditure of 8.79 billion dollor increased to 9.81 in 1998, the Pakistan expenditure are in 1990 of 2.95 billion dollor increased to 3.20 dollors in 1995. The Sri Lanka's expenditure of 0.439 billion in 1990 rose to 0.898 in 1997, Bangladesh expenditure of 0.303 billion dollor in 1990 became 0.593 billion dollor in 1997, and Nepals expenditure of 0.036 billion dollor in 1990 increased to 0.041 in 1998.

The increases in manpower of defence forces is yet another indicator showing the growing tensions in South Asia. The armed forces of India in 1990 were 1,200 Thousand they rose to 1,445 thousand in 1998, the Pakistan armed forces which were 550 thousand in 1990 touched 1100 number in 1998, the Bangladesh forces which were 102 Thousand in 1990 became 114.2 in 1997. The increase in number were due to continued internal troubles in South Asian States as well as the increased external threats in South Asia as well. The post cold war phase in South Asian States remained equally tense and the internal conflicts in Sri Lanka and continued tensions between India and Pakistan make South Asia tense and conflictual. The rise in terrorist activities in South Asia makes it more tense.

The 1990 phase in South Asian relations marked with continued external intervention by states out side the South Asian region. The Chinese interests in South Asia continued to grow and during these years Chinese forces and defence expenditure increased. The Chinese defence expenditure of 20.02 billion dollor in 1990 rose to 39.80 dollor in 1998. The Chinese armed forces were 3,500 thousand in 1998. The deeline in numbers of Chinese forces were compensated in terms of modernisation of Chinese forces were compensated in terms of modernisation of Chinese forces. Chinese help in nuclearisation of Pakistan and its continued support to various activities indicate the Chinese interests in South Asian affairs.

American interests have continued in South Asia, though their late realisation of India's growing importance in South Asian States have changed their perspectives in South Asia. America's insistence on various peace process in South Asia particularly between India and Pakistan on Kashmir seems important providing sufficient indications for their growing interests in South Asia. The Russian involvement in south Asia appears to be deeline due to their own internal situations. But their defence interests in South Asia continues. The interests of states out side the South Asia will largely depend on the mutual relations between the South Asian States. The normal relations between South Asian states reduces the chances of external intervention.

South Asia may be called as Indo Centric. All South Asian States share borders with India and therefore more chances for having tense relations with India. The disputes may on issues of border, trade, water, river etc. The balance of power in South Asia is uneven. It is in favour of India. Size and resources of India are vast and have affected the attitude of South Asian States they fear India's intervention and also seek India's favour. This uneven balance in South Asia allowed South Asian States to seek at times out side intervention to balance the Indian power. The early U.S. relations with Pakistan in 1950's marked the phase where India's regional role in South Asia has been reconised and India has been able to play effective role in the South Asian region.

The South Asian economies have been expanding and their are sufficient indications for the need of mutual co-operation. This need has been expressed in 1985 when SAARC was established keeping in view the wider needs of South co-operation. SAARC has been able to develop this concept that bilateral contentions issue may not be allowed to raise in the SAARC. However, the bilateral tensions between India and Pakistan have limited the usefulness of SAARC. The exports by SAARC states have been on the rise, though it may appear that by world standards they are very small yet they constitute an important part of SAARC economy. The plea for South. South co-operation may suffer in terms of poor resources and technologies, but they have significant regional sense where mutual co-operation allows these states to grow and effectively play their role. it is in this content, that South Asian States and their interests in Indian ocean may be critically viewed with basis for South Asian Co-operation and understanding.

IV

The political and security environment in South Asia has become very tense when we discuss the present day South Asia in the Walce of attack on Indian Parliament by Terrorist group on 13th Dec. 2001. Yet the scholars of South Asia can underline the phase where South Asia could become less tense and normal understanding of South Asian issues can be highlighted. South Asia has remained tense primarily due to bilateral tensions among the South Asian States. These tensions can be reduced if the primacy of economic relations can be underlined. It is in this context that we can view the economic relations which we develop between states out side the South Asian Region. Japan is one such state with which India enjoyed long history of economic relations.

The phase after 1990's marked a new change when India started new policy changes in the wake of economic reforms and liberalisation. Indian economy has for basic features that it has large market and immense human resources alongwith rich natural resources.

The trade relations in the phase of 90's have grown in 1998 when bilateral trade between the two big Asian states was to the tune of Rs. 169.8 billion. We import to Japan marine products, gems, jewellery and iron ore. We are exporting general machinery, steel, electric goods professional equipment and transport equipment.

Japan has viewed India as a main area where it can increased its investment, which can for longer basis of relationship between the two. The investment during 1991-98 were to the tune of Rs. 75.1 billion and in 1998 alone it was Rs. 12.8 billion. The Exim Bank of Japan in 1998 regarded in its survey as 3rd most attractive investment destination from long term perspective i.e. 10 years. 5th most attractive destination form medium term perspective i.e. 3 years. There are 90 Japanese ventures in operation in and around Delhi, followed by Mumbai having 44, Chennai 41 and Calcutta with 13 in 1998.

Indo-Japan Trade relations have continued to develop. Japan ranked 5th in foreign direct investment in India and have more than 1000 ventures in 1999 in India. These are small investments, which explained cautious attitude and continuous review of Indian situation. Japan has been India's 3rd largest trading partner. India's export to Japan in April 1999-Jan. 2000 was 1348.59 million USS dollors and import from India during the same period was 1816.25 million U.S. dollors. The closeness between the two Asian states has been underlined during India's PM visit to Japan in 2001 when areas of new developments in economic and other fields have been identified.

Relations between India and Japan have certain areas where difference on nuclear and peace issues is visable and particularly after 1998. Japan's concerns for peace remained priority and tensions in South Asia have increased its worries as this area provide vital oil to Japan. Japan's own experiences with Nuclear destruction has guided its policy considerations.

We may underline few more areas where Indo-Japan interaction can be increased. This area constitute mainly the academic domain, where India and Japan can identify mutual interesting in the field of research and collaboration. These fields can be:

(1) Economic area where studies related to Trade, investment, information. Technology can be explored.

(2) The problems of Human development and Human Security are vital for the people of South Asia. Japan with its vast recources can help south Asian situation to improve.

(3) Collaboration with Indian Universities in various fields particularly in developing proper training facilities in various Universities. Involving the students who want to develop their skills in technology and management.

(4) The common concerns on issue of peace is important for India and Japan. Traditionally both share peace perspectives and their use in modern international context has to be underlined.

(5) Developing Japan studies Centres and Programmes is needed as both states are important for the conduct of international relations. Issues where both enjoy commonalities must be identifies and such themes have to be used more creatively.

23

Creating Competitive Market Advantages in Global Economy: Some Lessons from Japan to South Asia

Vijay Kumar

The global market economy and the developing multilateral trade system has directly or indirectly brought Darwin's theory of "survival of the fittest" to the fore. The open market competition promises every nation an equal opportunity of making a place in the growing consumer world market. But the fitness to this fast and fluctuating market is a matter of inner capacity, scientific ad technical inputs, overall work culture and resources, besides, information network and innovative temper.

Japan, located off the coast of Asia, despite being a part of Asia, is considered a highly industrialised society and a part of the "developed" world—a part of the developed "north" in contrast to less developed "South" in economic terms. So much so that Japan is a member of the Organisation for Economic and Co-operative Development (OECD) which is centred around the Atlantic. Having an extraordinary narrow base of raw materials generally believed to be an absolute prerequisite for industrialisation and its relatively late (post war in contrast to western nations) modernisation, it became, in late 1960's, the third largest nation-state, as measured in terms of gross national product (GNP)[2] In late 1980's and early 1990's there were talks of "Restructuring in the Global Economy: From Pax Americana to Pax Nipponica." The fact that this feat was accomplished not only in the face of paucity of nature's bounty; but also in spite of ravages of world war II, is generally attributed to the Japanese people, who by their plain hard work and genius have brought this transformation.

Several possibilities are hidden in the Japanese economic miracle and the vitality of this nation which could transfuse the South Asian States, rich in natural resources and scientific and technical manpower. This paper aims to draw some lessons from Japan for the countries of South Asia, especially India and Pakistan, in building competitive market advantages in the global economy.

The Global Challenge

Globalisation is one of today's buzz words used by the media, business, policy makers and academic, alike. Many emphasise the benefits of world economic unification while others stress the growing inequalities resulting from liberalisation of economic relations. International organisations and multinationals have been fiercely attacked for supporting globalisation. Yet World Trade Organisation regime is flourishing and new members are seeking entry. "Globalise or perish" seems to be the new mantra of the international economy. Questions about the evolving structure of world order are back on the agenda of contemporary international studies with a shift in focus from political to economic realities. The question of world order today has primarily been taken up by the ascendant political economists of international relations whose analyses are driven, in large measure, on the volume of trade and resultant profit in the global economy and the competition for net volume of trade.

The present scenario well illustrates the transformation of the technological attitude of nations to exploring human potential, building of synergetic enterprise and enabling people and domestic firms to respond to business needs of tomorrow by accepting global market competition.

Japanese Economy

Japan has emerged as a powerful player in the global economy. Having begun to rebuild in the post-second World War period, Japan began to challenge European and American markets by its heavy presence since 1960s. In Japan rapid home market growth stimulated aggressive investment in a number of industries. In steel, tyres, lift trucks, and many other industries, Japan experienced rapid home market growth, which spurred Japanese firms to invest aggressively in automated facilities of the latest vintage. Western producers, facing more mature home markets did not modernise and stuck with older facilities, were unwilling to automate, giving a clear advantage to Japan. Likewise, in consumer electronics, the Japanese home market demanded rapid innovation making product life cycles extremely short. The demand for better quality combined with sophistication and status consciousness of the home buyers made Japanese consumer electronic firms scramble to the next product when foreign consumers were just beginning to buy the generation that was already passe in Japan.

Then the presence in a nation of competitive industries that are related often leads to new competitive industries. Sharing of activities in technology development, manufacturing, distribution, marketing, or services are made easy. For example, copiers and facsimile machines employ many of the same technologies and components and can be distributed and serviced through the same channels. Japan has not only taken advantage of this strategy in turning its leadership in camera industry into copier and facsimile industries, it has also turned its long tradition of success in silk in building its strength in long filament synthetic textile fibers, carbon fibers, water jet weaving machines etc. Prior to the emergence of the facsimile industry, Japan had a leading position in copiers, other office machines, photographic equipment and telecommunication equipment. It was easy for it to gain success in facimile industry because it had competitive advantage in a number of related industries.

Japan Today-The Giant Player in Global Economy

Japan, today, has made a remarkable transition from the factor-driven economy to innovation driven stage since the post-war period. Its companies have evolved from competing on prices to competing on advanced products and processes. It is an example of the state which has focussed on upgrading industry as no other nation including United States has done.

Japan's GNP multiplied by 152 in the four decades from 1950, as compared with 39 times for the other post-war economic 'miracle', West Germany. Its proportion of the World's GNP rose from one per cent in 1950 (when the US share was 39 per cent) to 12.8 per cent in 1990. Its regional predominance is such that its GNP came to make up 66 per cent of that of the whole of Asia (including China, India, Australia and New Zealand). In the significant high tech area of semi-conductors, long dominated by United States (with 83 per cent of World production coming from five US companies in 1965) Japanese output surpassed 50 per cent in 1988 while the US share fell from 51.6 per cent in 1984 to 36.5 per cent in 1988. In the boom years of the late 1980's, Japan expanded by a 'Korea'-sised economy every year and by 'a France' over five years. In late 1980's Japan rose to the position of the world's major creditor nation and capital exporter. Japanese foreign investment, which was traditionally restrained rose from US 4.6 billion in 1980 to US 10.1 billion in 1984-at which point Japan was the third largest holder of foreign assets. By 1986 the annual figure for capital exports had more that doubled again to US 22.3 billion. Japan is already established as a major disburser of foreign aid to the developing countries. More importantly, to our purpose, is the fact that the United States internal deficits have been financed in large measure by Japanese purchases of short term US Treasury bonds-called "junk bonds" by Japanese pejoratively.

Japan's Robotic Industry: A Case Study

How Japan has been able to "walk-tall" in the world economy would be clear if we examine its robotic industry. It is a world's leading producer and exporter of industrial robots. Japanese companies produced over 50 per cent of the world's industrial robots in mid-1980's and its share has kept growing making it a world leader in this area.

Robots were first conceived of in the United States in the 1950s. George C. Devol of the United States was credited with the first robot-related patent in 1954. It was, however, in late 1960s that commercial production of industrial robots began in the US. The first robots used in Japan were imported from the US in 1967. The Japanese robotics industry had its beginning in 1968, when Kawasaki Heavy Industries signed a licensed agreement with Unimation of US. Kawasaki was both a major potential used as well as a producer of related products and services. In 1969 Kawasaki began to sell Unimate robots, the first robots produced in Japan. These early versions were often called "expensive fools" and relegated to the corners of factories to collect dust. But soon Kawasaki redesigned some of the parts of the Unimation machine and upgraded its quality. In the late 1960s, the mean time between failures (MTBF) of an imported robot was less than 300 hours. By 1974 Kawasaki achieved an MTBF of 800 hours and by 1975 it was over 1000 hours, over 100 hours better than the best results achieved by Unimation. By 1984, Japan's installed base of industrial capacity of robots accounted for over 66 per cent of the World's total compared to 14.9 per cent of North America.

Through high levels of automation, reorganisation of work flow, and extreme attention to quality, Japanese companies redefined manufacturing practices in robotics and emerged as world leaders.

This example illustrates how through sheer dedication, hard work, technological innovation and constant search for quality improvement and customer satisfaction, the Japanese industries have challenged similar industries in the world.

Lessons for South Asian Countries

The developing countries in the South Asian region could learn a lot from Japanese success story. Similar cultural milleu, similar anti-imperial attitudes and similar sentiments in building space for themselves in the global market economy could bear strong lessons for India and other South Asian nations in building and sustaining competitive advantages in the economy for their people. If Japan plays an input role in the economies of South Asian countries, it would also gain immensely from the growth of their economies. Japan's success in the economic field were due to many factors:

*Japanese have a unique economic psychological and national ambitions. When at the end of the Second World War, American and other economists advised the Japanese to rebuild their war-torn economy on the theory of immediate comparative advantage based on labour intensive products, the Japanese bureaucratic elite set their sight on making the new Japan into the economic and technological equal, if not actually the superior, of the west. This objective continues to be the driving force of Japanese society.

The Asian nations, on the other hand, including India took their economic lessons from the west and its concepts kept changing decade after decade.

*Japan's post-war economic policy can best be characterised as neo-mercantilism which involves the practice of state assistance, regulation and protection of specific industrial sectors to enhance their international competitiveness and ultimately to achieve national pre-eminence over the 'commanding heights' of the world economy.

On the other hand, Indian economy stressed the need for public sectors overburdened with bureaucratic controls which could not flourish as competitive ventures even within a highly controlled and deeply regulated internal market.

*Japan has a high rate of savings which has been a major factor in Japan's export success and equally high rate of business investment. Japanese industrialisation has mainly been emphasised on catching up with the west and their overwhelming concern with economic vulnerability and political independence. The Asian countries, especially India, Pakistan, Sri Lanka, took a complacent attitude after the departure of the foreign powers and the new elites followed socialist politics at the risk of being relegated on the fringes of the world economy.

* Other than these, three common and constant elements have defined Japanese policy:

(1) a Steady and relentless movement up the technological ladder;

(2) the subordination of all other considerations to the promotion of export markets; and

(3) a remarkable capacity to adapt to changing conditions.

- Japan's often underrated regional, socio-economic and intellectual diversity with a strong sense of nationalism has proved a constant source of vitality to its economy. These have imparted its people artistic and technological innovativeness, capacity for managerial leadership, scientific temper and a strong ability to learn.

These have proved divisive and fractious in most of the South Asian states working as negative forces in the development of the country.

Building Comparative Advantage

Bearing cultural similarity to Asian nations, Japan holds out an example for its Asian neighbours, large and small, for building competitive market strategies. They can learn from Japanese experiences. Today, a nation's standard of living in the long term depends on its ability to attain a high and rising level of productivity in the industries in which its firms compete. "This rests on the capacity of its firms to achieve improving quality or greater efficiency". The comparative advantage-theory of Heckscher and Ohlin propound that all nations may have equivalent technology, but they differ in their endowments of so called factors of production such as land, labour, natural resources, and capital. Factors are nothing more than the basic inputs necessary for production. Nations gain factor-based comparative advantage in industries that make intensive use of the factors they possess in abundance.

They export these goods, and import those for which they have a comparative factor disadvantage. Nations with abundant natural resources and population, like India and Pakistan can export labour-intensive goods like apparel, handicraft, electronic assemblies and products based on their rich endowment of raw materials. However, the concept of factor endowment has radically changed from its early days and has come to include the followings:

- ***Human resources:*** The quality, skills, and cost of personnel (including management), taking into account standard working hours and work ethics. Human resources can be divided into a large number of categories, such as toolmakers, electrical engineers, Planners, designers, application programmers.

- ***Physical resources:*** The abundance, quality, accessibility, and cost of the nation's land, water, mineral, oil deposits, hydro-electric power sources, fishing grounds etc. Climatic conditions are also a part of the nation's Physical resources because it affects exports and imports to its market.

- ***Knowledge resources:*** The nation's stock of scientific, technical and market knowledge has a strong bearing on its goods and services. Knowledge resources are based in universities, government research institutes, private research facilities, government statistical agencies, business and scientific literature, market research reports and databases, trade associations etc.

- ***Capital resources:*** The amount and cost of capital available to finance industry which includes the total stock of capital resources-unsecured debt, secured debt, bonds, equity venture capital etc. The globalisation of capital markets, and the capital flow among nations, is gradually making national conditions more similar worldwide.

- ***Infrastructure:*** The type, quality and user cost of infrastructure including the transportation system, the communication system, mail and parcel delivery, payments and fund transfers, health care, cultural and educational institutions etc. which effect the quality of life and the attractiveness of a nation as a place to live and work.

Another important factor influencing competitive advantage is the character of home buyer needs. The composition of home demand shape how firms perceive, interpret and respond to buyer needs. Nations gain competitive advantage in industries or industry segments where the home demand gives local firms a clearer or earlier picture of buyer needs than foreign rivals can have. Local demands pressurise home firms to innovate faster and achieve more sophisticated competitive advantages compared to foreign rivals. On the contrary 'protectionism' damages the growth of home firms, keeping the prices of their goods unnaturally high and giving rise to various kinds of corruption and manipulation.

Summing up

A strong sense of nationalism coupled with a desire to rebuild the economy has been the major driving force of the Japanese economy. The sense of urgency to rebuild in their own image, the nation and the economy has been lacking in the South Asian nations. After independence the leaders and the people became complacent as the objective to rebuild was lacking. They neither concentrated on building the nation nor focussed on making a place for themselves in the world economy. The causes and consequences of this lack of focus is out of the preview of this paper.

No doubt, each nation has unique set of issues as well as opportunities and constraints in dealing with them. Yet there are clear themes that emerge from analysis of Japanese economy. Building and preserving competition in a challenging global economy is vital for survival of the developing nations of Asia. There is a need to create and maintain appropriate goals for firms and employees and an equal need to inspire the people to face the challenge as one united people.

References

1. J.S. Mill, On Liberty, quoted in J.M. and M.J.Cohen, The Penguin Dictionary of Quotations, Aylesbuiry; Hazell Watson and Viney Ltd: ELBS, 1964 p. 251 no. 9.

2. Hans H. Baerwald, "Japan", in wayne wilcox, Leo E. Rose and Gavin Boyd (eds.), Asia and the International System. Cambridge, Mass: Winthrop Publishers, 1972, p. 34.

3. Richard Leaver, "Restructuring in the Global Economy: From Pax Americana to Pax Nippomica?" Alternatives, XIV (1989), pp. 429-462.

4. Robert Gilpin, The Japanese Problem: Economic Challenge or Strategic Threat?". In Armand Clesse, et.al. (eds.) The Vitality of Japan: Sources of National Strength and Weakness. Oxford: St. Antony's College, 1997, pp. 58-88.

5. Figures quoted in Gavan Mc. Cormack, "The Emptiness of Affluence: Vivality Embolism and Symbiosis in the Japanese Body Politics". In Clesse et. Al, (eds) *Ibid.*: p. 112.

24

Japan's Aid for Participatory Development and Good Governance

J. Balakomaraiah

There is a tendency for local people and communities, whom development is intended to benefit, to be put in a passive position in the process of policy formulation and implementation when the top-down development approach is adopted in situations where local people's and communities' participatory capacity is inadequate. For this reason, there is a tendency for vested interests to rigidity, keeping certain social classes and geographical regions in a position of advantage. Not only has this approach not resolved the deeply rooted problems of the gaps between social classe, economic gaps, inequalities between men and women, regional disparities, and urban-rural gaps, but these gaps and disparities are even widening. Planners now realise to their regret that this has harmed the effectiveness and sustainability of development projects.

The participatory development approach is not intended to replace the tope-down government-led style of development by a local-community-led model. On the contrary, the merits of and the need for the government-led approach must be acknowledged. This approach is necessary for the management of the economy of the nation as a whole and for the coordination of development planning. But at the same time, it must be fully recognised that this approach, as stated above, has demerits in terms of widening disparities and failing to ameliorate poverty. Thus, in order to deal with these problems, the bottom-up approach of participatory development improvement in the quality of participation by local communities should be introduced. Another important point is that the developing country itself is the development agent that is or should be most aware of both the advantages and the disadvantages of government-led development and that decides how to introduce and then applies participatory development in a form that suits its circumstances.

The world is now moving in the direction of political democratisation and economic freedom based on competitive principles, and new roles for government in response to these trends are being sought; development strategies, too, are moving away from the previous economic growth orientation toward greater emphasis on sustainable development. Many countries, though to differing degrees, now realise the need for broad participatory capacity-building to supplement government-led development methods. Yet considering the present status of developing countries where disparities between rich and poor are widening. Can we say that Japan's aid has yielded positive results in terms of promoting participation by local societies and local people?

Japan's aid projects have been carried out in response to developing countries' requests. They have been successful thus far in fostering development policy leaders and central implementation figures in developing countries, in improving social services, and in building infrastructure. It is a fact that Japan has implemented a variety a successful ODA programs in areas that have recently become recognised as especially important alongwith the concept of sustainable development, such as protection of the environment, narrowing regional disparities, and providing such basic human needs. Yet while the spread of development successes to the poor and to local societies and the ultimate impacts of improvement of their access to development are among ODA's aims, they have not been clearly identified as aid evaluation criteria. Often the developing country side has been left with the responsibility for disseminating devlopment's benefits and for consolidating aid's secondary and tertiary impact among people; promoting the people's social capabilities in local societies and developing nation governments in parallel has not always been taken into consideration. In order to make Japan's ODA even more effective and to lend support to sustainable, self-reliant development, it is therefore extremely important to more clearly answer this question. How have development's effects contributed to fostering and enhancing people's economic and social capabilities? To answer that question, we must more precisely asses the intended ultimate beneficiaries' economic and social circumstances and needs and reflect them in aid planning and implementation as well as study the need for and implement assistance in the formation of community organisations and institutions in and through which more people can benefit from aid and participate in development. This is why it is necessary to incorportate the concept of participatory development in to aid.

Finally, it is important to lend assistance to developing country governments to help them create organisations and institutions that can promote policies emphasising participatory development. Aid to strengthen the public sector must not impede the wider enhancement of the capabilities and welfare of the people who form the state's foundation; aid must instead be designed and implemented to enable developing country governments to assume, effectively and efficiently, their roles of soliciting and respecting the voice of the people and lending structure to their overall capabilities. This is why aid for good governance is necessary as the basis for participatory development.

Japan's Aid Perceptions on Participatory Development and Good Governance

Awareness of the issues described above is not necessarily expressed directly by Japanese aid staff in the field using the terms "participatory development" and "good governance," but awareness of these issues is becoming more profound. Many efforts are being made in this direction : for example, by taking into account the environment and women in development (WID) at the preliminary survey stage in prepraration for individual projects, by attempting to survey the population in cooperation projects that involve social forestry, by organising user groups and training farmers to disseminate related skills at the project implementation stage in the building and improvement of rural irrigation facilities, etc. The government's ODA Charter states that Japan's basic aid philosophy is "to help ensure the efficient and fair distribution of resources and 'good governance' in the developing countries through developing a wide range of human resources and socio-economic infrastructure, including domestic systems, and through meeting the Basic Human Needs (BHN), thereby promoting the sound economic development of the recipient countries." In order to put together upon the above-mentioned efforts and orientations and use them as guidelines for future aid, the study committee outlines the following basic perceptions designed to incorporate the concepts of participatory development and good governance into Japanese aid in the future. Japan's ODA must seek an approach to improve people's economic and social capabilities as agents of development through broad-based people's participation in aid implementation in developing nations. Aid is aiming at social justice and at ensuring the sustainability and self-reliance of development.

As stated clearly in the ODA Charter, aid must respect developing countries' ownership of development by assisting their own self-help efforts. That is why it is extremely important for development to be conducted under the aid recipient's initiatives. Yet in order to make possible the kind of development that will enhance aid's effects and build people's comprehensive capabilities, it is important to predict and evaluate how will aid's effects are reaching the people and confirm whether government functions in such a way to guarantee people's access to development benefits. Japan must strive whenever the need arises to improve grassroots organisation and awareness of people and focus on providing support to enable governments themselves to offer and upgrade services needed in order to promote participatory development. At the same time, planners must constantly be examining each project as to what degree people and community groups are taking part in development.

In the light of developing countries' historical, social, and cultural diversity, the ideal form of democracy will not be the same for each developing nation. To promote democratisation, it is therefore necessary to be aware of the difference in initial conditions, pace, and methods of development. It must also be realised that the pace and manner of a country's democratisation should be decided and its democratisation should be carred out by people of individual developing countries. For this reason, Japan's aid must focus on building the foundations of democratisation in developing countries through aid to promote participatory development and encourage good governance.

In order to incorporate participatory development and good governance into ODA, Japan must fully understand the individual diversity of cultures, traditions, and social structure of communities in developing countries and respect beneficiaries' initiatives. It must be understood that the effects of enhancement of people's sustainable participatory capabilities and of government services do not become visible in the short run. In order not to impede development sustainability and self-reliance, simply to achieve short-term aid efficiency, aid schemes and systems must incorporate a long-term perspectives.

Aid for Promotion of Democratisation Human Rights and Reduction of Military Expenditures

Japan's ODA Charter clearly states the basic philosophy and principles of Japanese aid. Its four aid principles include attention to elements related to good governance as a national system directed toward democratisation : attention to military expenditures by the aid recipient, attention to its attempts to devlop and manufacture weapons of mass destruction and missiles, attention to its impot and export of arms, etc., and attention to the securing of basic human rights and freedoms. The Charter advocates that careful attention be apid to these aspects in the granting of aid. This section summarizes the basic approach to responding, from the viewpoint of participatory development and good governance, to the issues cited in the ODA Charter: democratisation, securing of human rights, trends in military expenditures, etc.

In recent years, the major aid donors have adopted an approach that takes into account in their decisions on the distribution and amounts of aid the government policies and stances of developing countries toward democratisation, human rights, and military expenditures factors that donors had not previously linked directly to ODA. Generally tying aid allotement to a recipient country's policies and political trends is called positive or negative linkage, depending on whether the donor response is to increase or to decrease aid. Positive linkage means for a donor to initiate or increase aid when the recipient's behavior relative to democratisation, human rights, and military expenditures clearly undergoes a desirable change; negative linkage means to postpone, reduce, or discontinue aid when the recipient apparently regresse on the question of democratisation, infringes human rights.

This is based on donor's belief that by making known their assessment of the systems and policies of aid recipients via this approach, they can encourage the formulation and implementation of policies that steer developing countries toward greater democracy and encourage the effective use of aid resources. The existing approaches in promoting democratisation, respect for human rights, and reduction of military expenditures, the following difficulties are experienced by donor countries.

There is a need for comprehensive evaluation in aid linkage; it is necessary both to fully reflect public opinion (since ODA funds come ultimately from taxpayers' pockets) and to take into account political and economic ties with the nation and international relations with it and its neighbors. It is also necessary to judge comprehensively both trends affecting democratisation, respect for human rights, and military expenditures by the aid recipient in question and the stance and policies of its government regarding those trends. A simplistic response that ties aid allocations mechanically to democratisation trends based on some sort of uniform criterion democracy is inappropriate.

Then the need for implementation based on international consesus Concern for democracy and human rights is growing in developing countries, as elsewhere, but the process, pace, and method of democratisation and securing of human rights in a country is closely tied to its culture and values, and Western democracy and human rights should not be imposed as universal criteria for judgment. It is important that there be full discussion internationally, including with recipient nations, about whether to apply aid linkage, lest this mover be rejected as a unilateral imposition of donor's values on the recipient. As much as possible, appeals to reciepients should be coordinated internationally. The reduction of excessive military expenditures in particular will be difficult to put into practice until real security can be established and disarmament promoted; this calls for the building of an international consensus.

Impact on lives of ordinary people, especially women and children, are most likely to suffer the direct effects of a postponement, reduction, or discontinuation of aid through negative linkage. In some cases, this can damage the public image of the donors in that country and may not have the intended result of encouraging that recipient country to reform its policies. It must be borne in mind that in addition to causing difficulties for that country's people, curtailment or discontinuation of aid may contribute to isolating them from the international community, a move which risks a further degeneration of the situation in terms of democratisation and human rights. In order to avoid placing people in an even more difficult situation, it is normal practice to continue humanitarian aid.

Promotional Aid for Democratisation

Judging from the relationship between participatory development and good governance, it is extremely important to create a foundation for promoting real democratisation, respect for human rights, and reductions in excessive military expenditures in developing countries. In accordance with the ODA Charter, Japan should continue to monitor democratisation and other trends in the nation as a whole and operate conventional positive and negative linkage. Furthermore, Japan should carry out promotional aid for democratisation at the same time to assist countries to build the foundation for democratisation, as a response that will more effectively promote democratisation by the developing country itself.

Promotional aid for democratisation means ensuring Japan's constant support for developing countries' efforts to build the necessary foundation to promote democratisation, human rights guarantees, and reductions in military expenditures in accordance with the participatory development and good governance approaches.

Amidst the wave of democratisation seen internationally in recent years, many developing countries are again facing the task of harmonising development with the universal values of democratisation and human rights. They also face the need to effectively use their development budget amid tight finances, to construct mechanisms for settling disputes at a time when regional conflicts are erupting all over the world, and to reduce excessive military expenditures through civilian control. Japan not only must bear in mind democratisation, respect for human rights, and military expenditure trends as criteria for an overall judgment of recipients' behavior, but must go a step further and also support the construction of a foundation for democratisation to facilitate a recipient government's switch from mechanisms of domination to mechanisms of service and coordination with the goal of participatory development and good governance.

Laying this foundation is closely tied to participatory development and good governance aid as the foundation for participatory development; and the building of this foundation is promoted by this aid. Specifically, it will become possible in practice for people to express their opinions to the government when the capabilities of community members and groups are improved, their opportunities for political, economic, and social participation are expanded, and improvements in the quality of their participation are promoted by aid.

Furthermore, more information and public disclosure as a result of good governane aid serving as the basis for participatory development will influence promotion of democratisation and reductions in excessive military expenditures. White papers not only release information about arms and the arms trade, but also clarify the stances and policies of developing countries with regard to military expenditures, the R&D and manufacture of weapons of mass destruction and missiles, and trade in weapons.

Improved administration will lead to better planning and implementation of budget and fiscal policy, and stronger checks and balances will lead to the creation of resources needed for participatory development. Progress in the training of police, attorneys, leading to better guarantees of basic human rights and then to democratisation. Improved functioning of the police and judicial systems will facilitate a transition from national security forces to civilian police forces. Promotion aid creates a foundation enabling any recipient nation, no matter what its circumstances, to promote democracy, secure human rights, and reduce excessive military expenditures in ways appropriate to that country. As mentioned previously, the process of democratisation and securing of human rights takes a variety of forms in accordance with the historical conditions of individual developing nations; hence the importance of building a basis for democratisation suited to the individual circumstances of developing countries.

Important Considerations in Aid Implementation

The entity that chooses suitable forms of participatory development, good governanceand pursues them is naturally the government and people of the deveoloping countries, and aid helps in self-help efforts. Participatory development requires changes in the planning, implementation, and evaluation framework of developmental projects so that they promote community participation in project schemes. Both participatory development and good governance require a long-term commitment and a transition from the pursuit of short-term economic efficiency to long-term sustainable development. This requires the Japanese side to actively seek dialog with the appeal to governments of developing countries, related agencies, and organisations at every stage. Policy dialog, aid planning, project formulation, and project implementation to encourage developing countries voluntarily to reinformce the participatory components of development project and promote good governance. Policy dialog requires first and foremost that Japan strongly promote the formulation of aid projects for participatory development and good governance in a form that respect developing countries' initiatives. At the same, it is increasingly important for JICA in specific aid program planning and implementation to support capacity building of developing countries through close dialog and support activities. It is important to have in-depth discussion with counterpart governments over necessary amendments in government institutions and to encourage greater commitment to improvements on the developing country's part by providing technical support. In order to make Japanese appeals more effective, it will be necessary for the Japanese side to have adequate investigative capabilities to conduct preliminary studies and to take the necessary budgeting measures and train suffient staff.

Dialog with Other Donors and International Organisations

Systems have been established for some time that stress international coordination and multilateral agreements in implementing assistance for good governance. For Japan to conduct aid for good governance and democratisation effectively in the future, it must make its basic approach to promotional aid for democratisation. Japan must deepen its dialog based on its own experiences with the international community to enable it to send a clear message about what kinds of aid can be granted to developing countries in the future.

Time with Local NGOs

In order to promote participatory development, it is important for Japan to promote ties with local NGOs in the course of aid implementation. However, Japan must establish guidelines, and compile manuals for their application, concerning the measures to identify appropriate areas and stages of aid for tie-ups with effective NGOs, for economic development.

This necessitates research and studies first of all to identify and classify existing NGOs according to their experience and capabilities. Information about many local NGOs' activities can be collected from Ministry of Foreign Affairs' files containing data about small-scale grant aid projects. It is also possible to collect information about case projects involving local NGO-donor ties through JICA's overseas office network. Based on this information, a functional classification of NGOs should set up to identify at various phases of development which NGOs have what know-how and take part in what activities at which stages of assistance.

Japan must also examine the drafting of guidelines as a way to indicate the areas of aid in which tie-ups with NGOs should be introduced. For example, Japan should seek to increase the opportunities for NGO participation in individual aid project implementation and to promote local NGO participation in planning, namely support for the formulation of regional development plans and the drafting of aid implementation plans. Project formulation might also call upon the services of local NGOs in aid planning surveys conducted by overseas offices. Guidelines and a manual should be drawn up to structure ties with NGOs based on a functional classification of NGOs and a menu of specific tie-up patterns.

Japan's Experience in Good Governance

In order to promote assistance, it is important for Japan to study information on how Japan's experience of nonwestern modernisation can help developing countries. For example, many of the areas included in good governance as the basis for participatory development, such as streamlining of administrative services and functions and creation and improvement of the market environment, are areas where Japan has ample experience in the field to offer through aid. Certainly Japan's laws, systems, and administrative mechanisms should not be transferred without modification to developing countries through aid. Rather, it is know-how adapted to developing countries' individual circumstances that must be transferred. This is the reason why Japan must compile lessons from its own experiences. Japan should fully discuss these proposals with developing countries and the international community. In order to investigate how Japan can make its experiences work for developing countries, JICA and other aid agencies should strengthen research capabilities to compile summaries of the Japanese experiences to build up a stock of know-how.

Methods to Evaluate Assistance

Participatory development has qualitative and multidimensional aims, namely the enhancement of people's participation in development through a change in their awareness, reinforcement of organisations, upgrading of capabilities, and the creation of an environment for participation in regional society. Specifically, it is desirable to continue efforts to establish methods that can be used to evaluate results at the macro level in people-centered, sustainable, self-reliant development, in social justice, and in well-being, while applying such indicators as the human development index (HDI) from the U.N. Development Programme (UNDP)'s Human Development Report. At the micro level, we must study frameworks for monitoring and evaluation by local NGOs of the results of participatory development while strengthening ties with local NGOs in aid planning and implementation, dividing projects into as many smaller subprojects as possible. This calls for putting the above-mentioned guidelines on NGO ties into effect. And through further improvements in project planning and management methods such as project cycle managment (PCM), which is being introduced by JICA, Japan must attempt to state clearly the anticipated outputs and effects of aid and be able to evaluate the specific results of participation by target groups. For this, more effort must be put into research to develop objective evaluation criteria and methods to measure the quality of participation.

Monitoring and Information Collection on Democratisation Trends

Promotional aid for democratisation in developing countries must combine a variety of types of aid, including the implementation of promotional aid for democratisation (support to democratisation as foundation building). In order to consider specific responses, it is necessary to procure information about political trends, human rights, and military expenditures in developing countries, and in developing countries, and in order to procure that information, methods of monitoring and data analysis must be established. Information on human rights guarantees (or on human rights violations) is available through Amnesty International, Human Rights Watch, and other international NGOs, which perform regular monitoring and release reports on the human rights situation in every country. The office of High Commissioner for Human Rights was established by U.N. in 1993. Information on military expenditures is available from the annual UNDP Human Development Report as well as from Sweden's Stockholm International Peace Research Institute (SIPRI) and Great Britain's Institute for International Strategic Studies (IISS), which publish statistical data on arms exports and military expenditures throughout the world. Yet there are difficulties in this field in terms of interpretation because the bases for evaluating military expenditures differ from one organisation to the next. In the future, Japan must take advantage of these outside sources of information, in addition to information gathered by Japan's diplomatic and consular offices in foreign countries to develop various methods to interpret the data.

Professional Personnel for Participatory Development and Good Governance

Japan has already carried out in the past many aid programs with the object of upgrading the capabilities of government organisation and officials in developing countries. Japan's recruiting system of experts from the public sector is quite well organised and has sent national and local public officials to foreign countries as long-term experts. It cannot necessarily be said, however, that Japan has sufficient aid know-how and aid personnel involved in participatory development, good governance laying the foundation for participatory development, and good governance for democratisation. It must be noted in particular that very few specialists and consultants in Japan can conduct the types of social analyses of participation as described below. Aid for promotion of democracy is an ara where almost no experience has been accumulated. It is necessary to collect data about aid know-how and activities of third country experts and local NGOs who are well acquainted with local conditions and use these data in the planning and implementation of Japanese aid. Japan should investigate the most flexible methods of mobilisation to involve highly experienced local NGOs and third-country experts in Japanese projects.

It is also necessary to improve the training of Japanese aid personnel. Aid staff must in particular become more aware of a wider range of issues and improve their capabilities. It is crucial to give better training using the training textbooks and manuals to experts scheduled to be dispatched overseas, to JOCV volunteers, and to consultants and overseas representative office staff. In the long run, it is becoming increasingly important to train Japanese personnel and specialised consultants to take charge of social analyses and education and training programs. Japan must both train speicialists of this kind through JICA training programs etc., and improves aid management systems.

Promotion of More Open Japanese ODA Structures

Participatory development and good governance should not be applied only to developing countries. Japan should also strive to improve their own participation in aid implementation, accountability, and transparancy, realising that these priciples should be reflected in the aid process by donors themselves. It is important for Japan's aid program to have open systems and structures and broaden the base of participation in international cooperation activities by ordinary Japanese citisens (people-participatory development) and attempt to increase the Japanese people's understanding and support for international cooperation (good governance). In order to do this, it is necessary first to reinforce support for the development aid activities of Japanese citizen groups, private organisation, universities, research institutes, local government, and NGOs which together constitute the basis for people-participatory aid. A variety of official schemes assist NGO activities, including, for example, subsidies for NGO projects, Voluntary Deposits for International Aid, and small-scale grant assistance. If JICA, which has been conducting aid projects in developing countries, were to create opportunities for participation by Japanese NGOs and other groups in its aid planning and implementation, this would lead both to wider use of their know-how and, in turn, to accumulation of field experience by Japanese NGOs and citizen groups as well as to strengthening of their organisational capabilities. The promotion of public relations, disclosure, and hearings on aid can be expected to promote further understanding and participation by the Japanese people, hence good governance in the implementation of Japanese aid itself.

Japanese Aid Implementation Methods and Local People's Self-Help Efforts

Japan needs to make its emphasis on community participation clear to recipient governments and actively promote participatory project formulation. Insightful assessment of community needs and receptivity, the promotion of community participation at the planning and design stage, and the incorporation of technical cooperation to generate the community's maintenance and management capability needs to be reinforced through the compilation of participatory development manuals designed for aid project survey members and by exercising better guidance toward consultants and general construction companes undertaking aid work under contract. In cooperation projects that are designed to promote literacy and and generate income for women, it is important to meet recurrent costs until local people have acquired sufficient self-reliant maintenance and management capability through their self-help efforts. JICA should simultaneously examine the transfer to overseas offices close to the site as well as to aid project managers with the power to make decisions and carry out budget arrangements.

Social Analyses of Aid Project Cycle to Promote Participatory Development

In order to provide assistance for participatory development and for good governance, Japan must first understand the circumstances under which the people of a specific country participate in development. It must then consider what aid is neede based on an adequate understanding of community-level political, economic, and social structures, as well as the conventionalmutual aid organisations and systems that exist in the society, which either promote or constrain this participation. Accordingly efforts must be made to alleviate negative effects and consideration must be given to training programs for greater awareness to organise communities and upgrade capabilities by using informal systems. It is important to establish methods for social analyses for planning so that the analyses can be incorporated into implementation plans. Measures have been taken by JICA and the OECF at the preliminary survey stage to address both the needs of women in development (WID) and environmental concerns in aid projects. Specific members have been assigned to survey missions to study possible actions on women in development issues and to conduct Environmental Impact Assessment (EIA), established according to environmental guidelines. Social analysis for participatory development is not something that exists separately from these measures, but is an integral part of the social impact assessments included in environmental impact assessments and the attention paid to issues of women in development.

Promoting Community Participation

Infra-structure facilities that are closely tied to the lives of local community people in developing countries, such as elementary schools, public health centers, shallow wells, and small-scale bridges and other infrastructure, are traditionally built and maintained by local people themseleves through self-help efforts. Aid from developing country governments is usually limited to the supply of construction materials.

The participatory approach may not be applicable to all parts of a general project grant aid scheme, but methods should be devised to promote participation by local people themselves in planning and construction depending on the content of the project. For example, in community development projects using aid form Japan, it is possible to utilise the village' traditional organisation as a de facto subcontractor and, while ensuring this organisation's responsibility for construction and management of the facilities, thereby offer aid for facility construction that respects the community's self-help efforts to the maximum feasible extent. As currently being attempted in rural water supply projects, aid in this field requires that at the basic design survey stage, local people's opinions be studied and in-depth discussions about specifications and implementation plans include local people in order to make facilities easy for them to maintain and manage. It is also possible for Japan to suggest to recipient governments and other implementing agencies (including village-level administrators) that some part of project construction duties falling within the scope of the recipient nations' responsibility is carried out by members of local communities.

Support for Community Organisation Activities

In general grant aid schemes and other kinds of cooperation, aid funds are allocated solely to pay for services and to procure materials and supplies required by the project, the recipient government holds nothng in reserve. Yet in a project that will build vocational training facilities for women. It is important to build the facilities and to procure funds to support women's post training productive activities. The first step is to request that the developing country's government retain funds in the budget, another approach is to use counterpart funds from aid for increased food production (food aid) or non-project grant aid (non-project grant aid for structural ajdustment support), which are only given to countries carrying out structural adjustment programs, to provide finanancial support for recurrent costs involved in participatory-type projects. If non-project grant aid is provided to support purchases of Japanese machinery related to basic human needs and education, counterpart funds for this can be allocated for promoting community participation projects in the recipient country.

References

1. A report on Participatory development and good governance report of the Aid Study Committee, Government of Japan, Japan.

2. Cawkell A.E., (1996) : Evolving an information Society, *Journal of Information Science,* Vol. 22, No. 2.

3. Damodar Siva Kumar, "Social Intermentions for e-governance, decentralised Democracy, Panchayati Raj and Sustainable development : Challenges and Opportunities, http: // www.inomy.com

4. George Mathew (2001) : E-Governance and Panchayati Raj : Kurukshetra, Annual issue, October.

5. Iqbal Narain, The Idea of Democratic Decentralisation, Indian Journal of Political Science, Vol. XXI, No. 2.

6. Sanjeev Chopra, (2001) : Panchayats in Scheduled Areas, *Kurukshetra,* Vol. 49, No. 8, May.
7. Sarah Joseph, (2001) : "Good Governance Agenda" The Hindu, July, 31.
8. Siva Subrahmanyam K, (2000) : Reforms in Panchayati Raj, Mending the Amendments, Kurukshetra, Vol. 49 No. 2, November.
9. Sundaram K. V. (1997) : Decentralised Multi Level Planning : Principles and Practice (Asian and African Experiences) Concept Publishing Company, New Delhi.
10. Thorpe Peter, (1984) : The Impact of New Information Technology in the Developing Countries, Journal of Information Science, Vol. 8.
11. UNDP (2001) : Making New Technologies Work for Human Development, Human Development Reforms, Oxford University Press, New York.
12. World Bank (2002) : Building Institutions for Markets, World Development Report, Oxford University Press, New York.

Index

O

P

T